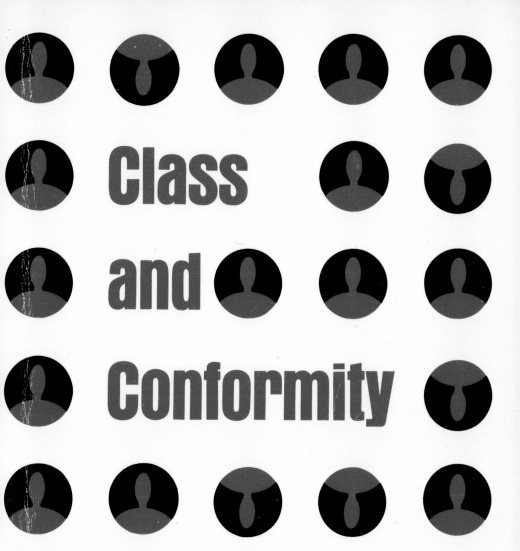

Class and Conformity

A Study in Values

Second Edition

With a Reassessment, 1977

Melvin L. Kohn

Class and Conformity

Class and Conformity
A STUDY IN VALUES
Second Edition

MELVIN L. KOHN
With a Reassessment, 1977

The University of Chicago Press
Chicago and London

MELVIN L. KOHN is chief, Laboratory of Socio-Environmental
Studies, National Institute of Mental Health.

The University of Chicago Press, Chicago 60637
The University of Chicago Press, Ltd., London

First Edition published by The Dorsey Press, 1969
Second Edition, with "Reassessment, 1977," published
by The University of Chicago Press, 1977

Printed in the United States of America

81 80 79 78 77   5 4 3 2 1

International Standard Book Number: 0-226-45030-9
Library of Congress Catalog Card Number: 77-85194

To McAl

Table of Contents

PART I. CLASS, VALUES, AND ORIENTATION

Stability and Change
A Reformulation
Plan of the Book
The Studies
Social Class
Indices of Class
Adequacy of the Hollingshead Index

Defining and Indexing Parental Values
Class and Values
An Appraisal of the Index of Values
Class, Its Components and Its Correlates
Conclusion

Nation, Class, and Values
The Relationship of Self-Control to Obedience
Conclusion

Revised Index of Parental Values
Class and Values
The Age and Sex of the Child
Dimensions of Valuation

BIBLIOGRAPHY

INDEX

List of Figures

List of Tables

Preface

This book had its beginning in a riddle. The puzzle was first confronted in research that John Clausen and I were doing, in 1954, on social factors in the development of schizophrenia. We had confirmed what many earlier, clinical studies had affirmed, that schizophrenic patients are likely to have had family relationships quite different from those of presumably normal people of comparable social background. But the differences seemed to be present only for middle-class, not for working-class schizophrenics. And this finding was not, as one might have supposed, because middle-class schizophrenics had had different experiences from those of working-class schizophrenics. On the contrary, it seemed from our limited data that social class mattered considerably for the family experiences of the "normal" comparison group but not for the schizophrenics. In effect, schizophrenics of whatever social class had experienced family relationships characteristic of working-class families but different from those of normal middle-class families.

These results made us immensely curious about the effects of social class on family relationships, both for what further investigation might suggest about the etiology of schizophrenia and, even more, for what it might suggest about the effects of social structure on personality and behavior in general. Our data, while intriguing, were limited, both in the range of questions asked, and in being based on a sample of non-schizophrenics selected to have social characteristics comparable to those of the schizophrenics rather than representative of the population at large.

Other studies of class and family, of which there were by then a fair number, did not satisfy our curiosity. In part this was because the studies seemed inconsistent in their findings, and most were so deficient in their methods that we could not be at all confident of extracting dependable generalizations from them. Later, in what must be counted a brilliant synthesis, Urie Bronfenbrenner succeeded in resolving the inconsistencies and thereby demonstrating that despite weaknesses one could come to some fairly firm conclusions from these studies.

But not even such critical mastery of the extant data could produce conclusions about issues that had not been studied. Research on social class and parent-child relationships had been largely a by-product of research on infant-training practices, inspired by a narrow interpretation of psychoanalytic theory and not at all informed by an interest in social structure. Few research workers seemed interested in parents' values or goals for their children, or in characterizing the major dimensions of parent-child relationships. To learn much about parents' values and about parent-child relationships more broadly conceived would require stepping out of the confines of past research.

So, with Clausen's encouragement, I designed a new study of social class and parent-child relationships. This study was to be carried out in Washington, D.C. Although Washington had some disadvantages as a research site, there seemed reasonable justification to hope that appropriate sampling could compensate for the inherent limitation of Washington being "atypical." It seemed, too, that Washington's atypicality could serve only to diminish social class effects, not to exaggerate them.

An important strategic decision was to exclude from the study people at the very bottom and very top of the social class hierarchy. (This decision was based in part on the racial composition of Washington, for the lowest socioeconomic strata of this city were almost entirely black, and it would not make much sense to compare a black lower class to predominantly white working and middle classes.) In retrospect, this decision appears to have been unwise. It would have been valuable to secure data about the family relationships of the people at the bottom of the socioeconomic scale—both because that is where the most schizophrenia seems to occur, and because knowledge about the life conditions of the poor might be valuable for social planning.

Another strategic decision was to focus on parental values. From my perspective as a sociologist, I thought that the predominant effects of social structure on behavior would be through the medium of values: that social class would affect parents' values, and that their values would importantly affect their behavior toward their children. So the thrust of the inquiry would be to learn about parents' values and then to trace the consequences of their values for their relationships with their children.

This proved to be a productive approach. First, there was the discovery that social class has a decided connection with parental values—that middle-class parents are more likely to emphasize children's self-direction, working-class parents their conformity to external standards. Then came the search to find whether or not this difference in parental values could provide a key for understanding class differences in parents' disciplinary practices. The finding was that middle-class parents tend to respond to misbehavior in terms of their interpretation of the children's intent in acting as they do; working-class parents, in terms of the direct and immediate consequences of the misbehavior. Moreover, the difference in parental values has ramifications far beyond disciplinary practices—it affects major dimensions of parent-child relationships.

The analyses that led to these three sets of discoveries were published as they were completed. With those reports, the study seemed to be at an end. But the most fundamental question of all still remained: *Why* does social class affect parental values? My own early answer to this question was that the characteristics emphasized by middle-class parents are somehow appropriate to the actual circumstances of middle-class life, while those emphasized by working-class parents are more appropriate to the circumstances of working-class life. As a general formulation, this is probably true, but it was unsatisfying because it was too unspecific. The more important the difference in values became as an intellectual tool for understanding the effects of social class on parental practices, the more important it became to understand precisely why class position matters for parental values.

The Washington study provided no directly pertinent data. In speculating about possible reasons why class *might* matter for parental values, I became more and more impressed with the remarkable parallel between the occupational conditions characteristic of each social class and the values espoused for their children by parents of that social class. Middle-class occupations characteristically deal more with the manipulation of interpersonal relations, ideas, and symbols, while working-class occupations deal more with things. Middle-class occupations are likely to be free of close supervision, while working-class occupations are more subject to standardization and direct supervision. In short, middle-class occupations demand a greater degree of self-direction; working-class occupations require that the individual conform to rules and procedures established by authority.

It did not seem likely that these occupational differences could completely explain the class differences in parental values. On the contrary, social class probably exerts so powerful an effect on human behavior because it represents the combined effects of occupation, education, and other potent variables. But the parallel between occupational circumstances and parental values seemed in this case to be centrally at issue. In this instance, the other variables constitutive of social class appeared to be secondary and reinforcing. Increasingly, the really critical variable seemed to be the degree of self-direction characteristic of occupations in the two social classes.

There was an opportunity to test these speculations in research that my colleague, Leonard Pearlin, then carried out in Turin, Italy. Pearlin proposed a comparative study, designed to see whether or not social class had the same effect on parental values in this very different cultural context as it had in Washington, and to provide a test of my speculations about the importance of occupation for explaining the effect of class on values.

The Turin study posed difficult problems of execution, which Pearlin solved with great imagination. To be able to repeat the comparison of middle- to working-class parental values, it was essential that the study be closely comparable to the Washington study. But for the study to be meaningful in Italy, to have an integrity of its own, it had to be more than an American import—it had to make sense to Italians. The solution was an intricate blend of close comparability where comparability was essential, together with the pursuit of the locally germane wherever possible. It was a solution that was possible because the phenomena studied in Washington and the general methodological approach used there proved to be relevant in Italy. It also required the aid of some highly talented women who, in the course of conducting the pretest interviews, sensitized us to the nuances of meaning that make for true comparability.

Pearlin and I analyzed together that portion of the Turin study that deals with class and values. The results were very much in keeping with the earlier speculations. Although Italian and American parents emphasize different values for their children (nationality, in fact, matters more than social class), the essential class differences found in Washington exist in Turin, too. In both countries, the crux of the matter is that middle-class parents emphasize self-direction, working-class parents conformity. Furthermore, *occupational* self-direction seems to account for a very substantial portion of the class difference in fathers' valuation of self-direction or conformity for children. It even accounts for an appreciable part of the class difference in their wives' values.

At about the time that Pearlin did his study in Italy, Carmi Schooler and I began planning the National study, a comprehensive investigation of the relationship of occupation to values and orientation. This study was to be limited to men, since questions of career and occupational commitment may be more problematic for women. Thus, insofar as the study deals with parental values and practices, it is limited to those of fathers. The loss is not as great as one would at first suppose, since the Washington and Turin studies show that the relationship of class to parental values and practices is much the same for fathers as for mothers. The gain is in the opportunity for systematic analysis of the relationship of occupational conditions to values and orientation.

The National study made it possible not only to test the interpretation of social class and parental values that had been developed from the Washington study and tentatively confirmed in Turin, but also to extend the power of that interpretation. Because this study is based on a large sample, representative of all men employed in civilian occupations throughout the United States, it enabled us to assess the generality of the relationship of social class to parental values. Moreover, in providing refined indices—particularly of the occupational conditions thought to be determinative of the exercise of self-direction in work, but also of many other class-correlated conditions of life—this study afforded a far more thorough test of the relevance of occupational self-direction to the class-values relationship than had been possible in Turin. Most important of all, the National study provided the materials with which to develop and to evaluate two important extensions of the interpretation.

One extension is the demonstration that the distinction between self-direction and conformity, which we had found to underlie class differences in parental values, is also basic to class differences in men's values for themselves and their orientations to work, to society, and to self—and thereby affects every facet of behavior. The other extension is the demonstration that *occupational* self-direction is importantly implicated in all these class relationships. The experience of occupational self-direction provides an interpretive key to understanding not only the difference in middle- and working-class parental values for children, but the broad sweep of class differences in men's conceptions of reality.

The organization of this book emphasizes the logical development of these ideas rather than the chronological sequence in which the studies were carried out. There is some loss in this, principally in the burden it puts on the reader of having to go back and forth among complex studies, each with its own distinct methods. The gain is in logical coherence. The substance of social science knowledge comes from the process of speculation, testing, new speculation, new testing—the continuing process of using data to test ideas, developing new ideas from the data, doing new studies to test those ideas. I have tried to organize this book to illustrate that process.

Washington, D.C.   Melvin L. Kohn
July, 1969

Acknowledgments

The studies on which this book is based were conducted in collaboration with colleagues in the Laboratory of Socio-environmental Studies of the National Institute of Mental Health. John Clausen encouraged my undertaking the Washington study and aided in its planning; Eleanor Carroll played a major part in executing that study. Leonard Pearlin originated and conducted the Turin study, with only little help from me, and was full partner in the analyses of the Turin data reported in this book. Carmi Schooler and Morris Rosenberg joined in formulating the National study; Schooler shared fully in developing the interview schedule, constructing and refining indices, planning the strategy of data-analysis, and carrying out the initial analyses. Lindsley Williams perfected the strategy of data-analysis and carried out the many complex programming and statistical tasks of this research. The ideas and the efforts of these, my friends and collaborators, are deeply appreciated.

Seldom has an author been blessed with such imaginative (yet careful), enthusiastic (yet critical) research and editorial assistance as I have consistently enjoyed from Elizabeth Howell, Margaret Renfors, Carrie Schoenbach, and Mimi Silberman. To see every opportunity for occupational self-direction exploited to its fullest, one has only to observe them at work. This book has become as much theirs as mine, a matter of pride to me and, I believe, to them.

For their generous advice on statistics and research design, I am indebted to Samuel Greenhouse, Elliot Cramer, and Jacob Cohen.

So many people have played a part in carrying out the surveys and in preparing and analyzing the data, that I have resorted to the device of acknowledging their contributions at appropriate places in the Appendixes. It would be an injustice, though, to fail to make special note of those who played critical roles in the field operations of the three surveys: Eleanor Carroll, Mary Freeman, Paul Hanlon, and Eleanor Wolff (the Washington study); Pier Brunetti, Leonard Pearlin, and Ina Cabutti Velline (the Turin study); Marilyn Haskell, Paul Sheatsley, Eve Weinberg and the staff of the National Opinion Research Center (the National study).

I have learned much from penetrating critiques of an earlier version of the manuscript. For the acumen and honesty of their critiques, I wish to express my profound thanks to John Campbell, William Caudill, Yngvar Løchen, Leonard Pearlin, Morris Rosenberg, Carmi Schooler, Roberta Simmons, Marian Yarrow, Lindsley Williams, Robin Williams, and my wife, Janet.

Finally, I acknowledge with pleasure two very special debts: to my mentor and long-standing friend, Robin Williams, for setting a scholarly example that I have tried to emulate; to my superiors and good friends, Robert Cohen and John Eberhart, for creating and maintaining enviable conditions of freedom for unfettered inquiry in the Intramural Program of the National Institute of Mental Health.

Credits

The Figures in Chapters 4 and 5 were prepared by David Hausmann of the Medical Arts and Photography Branch of the National Institutes of Health.

The American Sociological Association has granted permission to make use of my articles previously published in the *American Sociological Review* (24, 1959: 352-366; 31, 1966: 466-479), and in *Sociometry* (23, 1960: 372-392). The University of Chicago Press has similarly permitted use of my articles published in the *American Journal of Sociology* (64, 1959: 337-351; 68, 1963: 471-480).

The following copyright holders have given permission to quote from the indicated authors: Alfred A. Knopf, Inc. (Williams, in Chapter 1); Crowell Collier and Macmillan, Inc. (Barber, in Chapter 1, and Williams, in Chapter 2); Holt, Rinehart & Winston, Inc. (Bronfenbrenner, in Chapters 2 and 7); The Free Press, a Corporation (Merton, in Chapter 10); John Wiley & Sons, Inc. (Waller, in Chapter 11); and the American Sociological Association (Lipset, in Chapter 11).

Reassessment, 1977

Class and Conformity marshals the evidence of three studies to attempt a thoroughgoing interpretation of the relationship of social class to values and behavior. The argument, essentially, is that there is a consistent and meaningful relationship between people's social-class positions and their values and orientation; that the class-values relationship has important implications for behavior; and that the class-values relationship, in turn, can be interpreted as resulting from systematic differences in conditions of life, occupational life in particular, associated with social-class position. The many thoughtful reviews of the book (especially those by Di Palma, 1971; Martinussen, 1971; Miller, 1971; Porter, 1970; and Silverman, 1971), while posing important questions for further research, all attest to the validity of this thesis. But, as with any interpretive scheme that is used and extended, experience demonstrates that many modifications should be made.

In the eight years since the book was first published, my colleague, Carmi Schooler, and I have reconceptualized important parts of the interpretive chain, refined many of the principal indices on which our earlier analyses had been based, opened up new interpretive problems, and, most important of all, turned speculative discussions about the direction of causal effects into rigorous data-analyses from which much firmer conclusions can be drawn. Our efforts have been joined by those of many other scholars: initially, in the use made of the book by other authors to buttress or extend interpretations of their own data, thereby showing the consistency of their data analyses with our interpretations; subsequently, in the growing number of replications, derivative studies, and extensions of the thesis into areas sometimes far removed from those with which we had dealt. In this essay, I reassess the book's argument in light of subsequent research and thinking; then I summarize the more important extensions of the thesis and discuss some open questions for further research.

THE RELATIONSHIP BETWEEN
SOCIAL CLASS AND VALUES AND ORIENTATION

The first element of the thesis is that social class is consistently related to values and orientation: The higher a person's social class position, the greater is the likelihood that he will value self-direction, both for his children and for himself, and that his orientational system will be predicated on the belief that self-direction is both possible and efficacious. The lower a person's social class position, the greater the likelihood that he will value conformity to external authority and that he will believe in following the dictates of authority as the wisest, perhaps the only feasible, course of action. How valid does this element of the thesis now seem? We begin with a re-evaluation of the concepts "social class," "conformity," and "self-direction."

Social Class and Social Stratification

I followed the usual American practice of making no differentiation between social class and social stratification. Now, after an immersion in the Polish sociological literature, I think it would have been useful to distinguish between social stratification generally and the specifically Marxian usage of the term "class," meaning a group defined in terms of its relation to ownership of the means of production (see Wesolowski, 1969). The phenomena with which I deal—the hierarchical distribution of power, privilege, and prestige—define a system of social stratification; wherever I speak of class position, it would be more precise to say position in the stratificational order.

Nothing has happened since the publication of the book, though, to make me doubt that, in terms of their impact on values and orientation, the two most important dimensions of stratification are occupational position and education. (Income is less important, and subjective class identification is virtually irrelevant.) Were I to do the analyses anew, I would probably employ one of the newer measures of occupational position—for example, the Duncan measure or the Hodge-Siegel index used by the National Opinion Research Center—not because Hollingshead's classification is in any way inferior, but because there is some advantage for comparative analysis in using indices employed in other investigations. In any case, I no longer see an advantage in creating a single composite index of social class; I'd simply use separate indices of occupational position and education and measure their additive impact (see Otto, 1975; Kohn, 1976a).

On one pertinent issue I feel less certain today than when the book was written. Then I felt relatively safe in concluding that occupational position and education each contribute independently to the effects of social class on values and orientation. Now I am less confident that one can precisely assess the independent contributions of two highly correlated variables (see Blalock, 1963; Farrar and Glauber, 1967; Gordon, 1968). Still, several analyses of more recent data confirm the original conclusion (e.g., Stephen Olsen, 1971; Kohn, 1976a; St. Peter, 1975; and my unpublished analysis of the 1975 NORC General Social Survey data). So, cautiously, I still believe that education and occupational position have additive, independent effects on values and orientation; but I am no longer as confident that the findings, even though repeatedly confirmed, are altogether reliable on this point.

Self-direction and Conformity to External Authority

I had feared that the term "conformity to external authority" would be misinterpreted, that people would read into it Riesman's well-known concept other-directedness, or else the conformity to peers that has been the subject of so much research in experimental psychology. Therefore, I emphasized that conformity to authority is a very different phenomenon indeed. Apparently, that distinction was clear to readers, for there seems to have been no confusion in the subsequent literature. But my usage of "self-direction" may not have been as clear, for some think that I have given it too positive a cast—imbuing it with connotations of moral autonomy and even of altruism. Bowles and Gintis (1976) suggest that I am really describing internalization of social norms and that, hence, "oversocialization" might be a more appropriate term. But this would make an unwarranted judgment. What I meant by self-direction is thinking for oneself—the opposite of following the dictates of authority. People who value self-direction are not necessarily more (or less) altruistic than are those who value conformity to authority. (On this, see Schooler, 1972.) And, certainly, people who value self-direction are just as much products of their life-conditions as are those who value conformity. But whatever the processes that brought them to hold the values they do, and however noble or selfish their goals, people who value self-direction think it desirable to try to act on the basis, not of authority, but of one's own judgment and standards.

Social Class and Parental Values

There have been several studies testing our finding that social class is correlated with parental valuation of self-direction or conformity to external authority. None of the studies is a precise replication of ours: in some, the sample is small or not truly representative of the population to which the investigator generalizes; in some, the characterisitics that parents were asked to judge are not quite the same as those about which we inquired. But these studies do test our conclusion that the higher parents' social class positions are, the more likely they are to value self-direction for their children, and that the lower their social class positions are, the more likely they are to value conformity to external authority. The finding has been confirmed in Taiwan by Stephen Olsen (1971); in France by Perron (1971); in Great Britain by Platt (n.d.); in Ireland by Hynes (1977); in West Germany by Hoff and Grueneisen (1977a, b) and independently by Bertram (1977); and in the United States by Franklin and Scott (1970), by Clausen (1974), and by Campbell (1977). There have also been several intensive studies of working-class life, using methods quite different from the formal, structured techniques we used, that confirm the picture of working-class parental values (and practices) that I drew (see, in particular, Sennett and Cobb, 1973, and Le Masters, 1975).

The most extensive test of the relationship between social class and parental values was provided by the National Opinion Research Center in its General Social Survey of 1973, addressed to a representative national sample of 1500 people. The survey included a modified version of the parental values questions used in our national study, along with a standard battery of questions about social background. The Wrights (1976), in their analysis of these data, and I (Kohn, 1976a), in a separate analysis of the same data, found the relationship between social class and fathers' valuation of self-direction/conformity to be essentially the same as that reported in this book. These data confirm also that social class continues to be nearly as strongly correlated with fathers' valuation of self-direction when all other major lines of social demarcation are statistically controlled. And, in an extension that goes beyond the analyses of this book, these data show class to be substantially correlated with mothers' valuation of self-direction—both when women's own educational and occupational positions and when their husbands' are used as the index of class position. These correlations, too, remain substantial with all other major lines of social demarcation statistically controlled.

In 1975, in another of its annual General Social Surveys, the National Opinion Research Center again included the parental values questions. I have repeated the analyses, with essentially the same results. In these data, once again, the correlation between social class and parental valuation of self-direction remains strong even when all other major lines of social demarcation are statistically controlled.

I think it fair to conclude that the relationship between social class and parental valuation of self-direction or conformity to external authority has been convincingly confirmed, both in the United States and abroad.

There are three issues bearing on the correlation between social class and parental valuation of self-direction that deserve attention: factorial invariance, changes in values, and the magnitude of correlation.

Factorial Invariance

Every factor-analyzable body of data on parental values I have examined contains a strong self-direction/conformity factor. This includes the data of the Washington study, the Turin study, the national study, Stephen Olsen's Taiwanese study, Hynes's Irish study, Bertram's German study, Campbell's U.S. study, and the 1973 and 1975 NORC General Social Surveys. Of course, other factors may or may not be the same as those found in the national study, depending in part on whether the questions on parental values refer to children of specified age and, if so, whether there is sufficient variation in the ages of the children for a "maturity" (age) factor to emerge. In any case, self-direction/conformity is an important dimension of parental values in all these bodies of data.

Changes in Values

Although it has no necessary bearing on the relationship between social class and parental values, it is pertinent to ask whether there have been changes in parental values, especially in parental valuation of self-direction or conformity to external authority, over the few years for which data are available. The evidence, unfortunately, is equivocal (see Kohn 1976a): there is no substantial evidence that there have been changes, but also no conclusive evidence that there have not. Whether or not there have been changes in values, though, the magnitude of the correlation between social class and parental valuation of self-direction is as strong in the latest available data, the NORC General Social Survey data of 1975, as in earlier studies.

The Magnitude of the Correlation

The correlation between social class and fathers' valuation of self-direction, in the national study data, is 0.34, and it is of roughly similar magnitude in subsequent studies. To me, this correlation seems substantial. True, it is not nearly so large as we have come to expect from analyses of the interrelationship among various components of social structure or from analyses of the interrelationship among various facets of orientation; but correlations between any single dimension of social structure and psychological phenomena never are very large. After all, there are many other determinants of values and orientation—idiosyncratic personal experience, situational constraints, cultural and institutional imperatives, and facets of social structure other than class itself.

It should also be noted that this and many of the other correlations reported in the book—several of them a good deal smaller than 0.34—may be understated. We deliberately used orthogonal factor analyses to create indices, because this procedure ensures that the relationships we find between social class and the various facets of values and orientation are independent relationships. Furthermore, we refrained from adjusting correlations to compensate for unreliability of measurement. Thus, all the correlations should be read as minimum estimates, probably underestimates, of the true magnitude of correlation. If our purpose is, as I believe it should be, to interpret the relationships between social structure and psychological functioning, rather than to engage in the atheoretical exercise of trying to account for as much of the variance in psychological phenomena as possible, then these conservative procedures are warranted. The absolute magnitude of relationships is unimportant (see Blalock,

1964), until one deals with complex causal models, when assessments of magnitude should be shorn of measurement error.

Values for Self

The correlation between social class and men's values for themselves (0.17) is only half as large as that between social class and fathers' valuation of self-direction or conformity for their children. But if values for self and values for children are part of a single general orientation, these correlations should be of roughly similar magnitude. In Chapter 5 I argued that the index of values for self is at fault, that in modifying the questions about parental values to be appropriate to adults, we had provided the respondents too few characteristics indicative of conformity to external authority. There has been an opportunity to test this explanation in a follow-up survey that Schooler and I have conducted with a representative subsample of the original respondents ten years later. In this study we ask a new set of values-for-self questions, containing more characteristics indicative of conformity, such as "law-abiding," "respectable," and "able to keep out of trouble." An index of valuation of self-direction vs. conformity, derived from this new set of questions, correlates 0.25 with social class. Although this is still not as large as the class–parental values correlation, it is large enough to conclude that we are now dealing with correlations of roughly similar magnitude. A weak link in the interpretive chain has thereby been strengthened.

Orientation to Self and Others

There has been so much further research on the relationships between social class and such aspects of social orientation and self-conception as authoritarian conservatism and self-esteem that it is impossible to cite it here. There is an even larger body of research dealing with the relationships between social class and aspects of orientation not directly studied in this book but obviously very close in meaning to those we did study, an important example being Rotter's (1966) concept of internality or externality of locus of control, on which there is an immense literature. Certainly, if any of these inquiries had produced findings inconsistent with ours, there might be cause to doubt my interpretation. But, with the possible exception of

Simpson's (1972) finding that the relationship between education and authoritarianism may not obtain in all countries, none of the studies of which I know presents findings that are in any important way inconsistent with ours. Thus, we have supportive, even if not definitive, evidence that the structure of this part of the argument is solid.

In addition to much new evidence further confirming the long-recognized relationship between social class and authoritarianism, there has also been new conceptualization of authoritarianism. Even before the publication of *Class and Conformity*, Kelman and Barclay (1963) had argued that authoritarianism can best be interpreted as measuring breadth of perspective. Their argument is certainly consistent with my treatment of authoritarian conservatism as implying a lack of open-mindedness and with my discussion of the relationship between intolerance of deviant political beliefs and a conformist orientation. But although I said that tolerance of nonconformity requires breadth of perspective, I did not develop the implications of this idea. Picking up where I left off, Gabennesch (1972) has suggested that what is centrally at issue is a process of reification: "We may infer from Kohn's findings that individuals with narrow perspectives seem more likely to view the social world in fixed, absolute terms. Such people appear to conceive of social reality as encompassing a superordinate normative dimension, an external locus where events are determined, where moral authority resides, and to which men must adapt themselves" (pp. 862–63; see also Roof, 1974). Gabennesch draws a parallel between this conception of authoritarianism and Piaget's conception of moral realism (see my discussion of Piaget in Chapter 2). An equally important connection to which Gabennesch's analysis draws attention is that between authoritarian conservatism—seen as reflecting narrowness of perspective and reification—and intellectual flexibility. There are intimate interrelationships among intellectual flexibility, breadth of perspective, and self-directed values and orientation.

VALUES AND BEHAVIOR

The second major element in the thesis of *Class and Conformity* is that class differences in values and orientation have important implications for behavior. The evidence presented in Chapters 6 and 7 clearly indicates that middle-class parents' higher valuation of self-direction, and working class parents' higher valuation of conformity to external authority, influence their disciplinary practices and also the allocation, between mother and father, of responsiblity for providing support to, and imposing constraints on, their children. The major limitation of this evidence is that, although it comes from parents' and children's independent reports about parental behavior, independent reports even from differently situated participants are no substitute for observations by outside observers (see Silverman, 1971; Barnsley, 1972, pp. 206–18; and Hoff and Grueneisen, 1977a).

There has been little new research on the relationship between parental values and behavior since the book was published, and what work has been done suffers from the same limitation of being based on reported, not observed, behavior. The one major study directly in point is the Gecas and Nye (1974) study of middle- and working-class parents' differential responses to their children's misbehavior, depending on the presumed intent of the child. Though hardly definitive, it is consistent with our findings and supportive of my interpretation. (See also Erlanger, 1974.)

Nor has there been much evidence on the crucial next link in the causal chain: from parental values and childrearing practices to the personality and behavior of the child. Campbell's (1977) finding of a decided relationship between parents' social status, maternal valuation of self-direction or conformity, and children's independent reports about their own behavior when ill is indeed encouraging; but much more evidence, over a wider range of children's behaviors, is needed.

Nowhere in *Class and Conformity* or in my subsequent work have I spelled out an adequately complex model of the processes by which parents' life conditions directly and indirectly affect the personality development of their children (see Gecas, 1977; Bertram, 1976b). This is a task for the future. For now, there are two pertinent issues worth noting.

Some efforts to hypothesize linkages between parental life-conditions and children's personality seem to me to place undue weight on the quality of the parent-child relationship, treating the quality of that relationship as the antecedent, rather than as an intervening, variable. The principal antecedent variables in any social-structural analysis must be the actual conditions under which parents live. The degree to which these conditions, mediated through parental values and practices, actually affect the personality development of the child may depend on the quality of the parent-child relationship, but the primary antecedent variables for any such analysis must be social-structural conditions.

Many authors have seen my analysis of parental values and practices as pertinent to processes of social mobility. In the main, their logic follows that briefly outlined in my Chapter 11: parents train children for the world as they, themselves, experience it, and this training tends to equip the children for the parents' station in life, thus serving as a brake on mobility. But occasionally people read into my analysis something that is just not there—an implication that people of higher social-class position value their children's achievement more than do people of lower social-class position, and that hence, in some extrapolations, children from families of higher social-class position should have a greater "need for achievement." Our data suggest, though, that there is no relationship between social class and parental valuation of the child's "trying hard to succeed." I think that achievement motivation is at most a weak link from parental experience to parental values to the social mobility of the child. I would look instead (no surprise to anyone who has read this far) to parental emphasis on self-direction or conformity to external authority.

OCCUPATIONAL SELF-DIRECTION AND THE CLASS-VALUES RELATIONSHIP

The heart of the thesis of *Class and Conformity* is that the class-values relationship can be interpreted as resulting from class-associated conditions of life, occupational conditions in particular.  The crucial occupational conditions are those that determine how self-directed one can be in one's work—namely, freedom from close supervision, substantively complex work, and a nonroutinized flow of work. These occupational conditions are empirically tied to valuing self-direction and to having an orientation to oneself and to the outside world consonant with this value.

Everything we have learned from our research since the publication of the book confirms the utility of the concept "occupational self-direction," not only for explaining the relationships between social class and values and orientation but also for explaining the impact of occupational structure on psychological functioning. Our further work has, however, led us to modify terminology and to refine indices for two of the three occupational conditions that we see as determinative of occupational self-direction.

"Closeness of supervision" remains unchanged—a Guttman Scale based on five questions about how much latitude the supervisor allows and how supervisory control is exercised. We still see closeness of supervision as a limiting condition. To be closely supervised precludes the exercise of occupational self-direction, but not being closely supervised does not necessarily mean that one is self-directed in one's work; it depends on the nature of the work.

We now prefer the term "routinization" to the more cumbersome "complexity of organization of the work," but the new term refers to the same dimension and is based on the same questions about the repetitiveness of work tasks and the complexity of the "units" of which work is comprised. Although we have not been able to get away from the subjectivity of these questions, we have at least been able to combine them into a single index, which is useful for a wider range of statistical analyses (see Kohn and Schooler, 1973).

The central concept, "the substance of work with data, things, and people," has also been renamed. Since our focus is not on the type of work that is done, but on the complexity of that work, we now use the term "the substantive complexity of the work" (or of the job). The index of substantive complexity continues to be based on detailed questioning of each respondent about what he does in his work with things, with data or ideas, and with people. Here, too, we have developed a single index, based on factor analysis (see Kohn and Schooler, 1973, n. 15). To validate this index, which is specifically tailored to each respondent's description of his own job, we have compared it to assessments of the average level of complexity of work with things, with data, and with people for the entire occupation, as given in the *Dictionary of Occupational Titles* (U.S. Department of Labor, 1965). The multiple correlation between our index of substantive complexity and the independently coded *Dictionary* ratings is 0.78—sufficiently high to assure us that our appraisals of substantive complexity accurately reflect the reality of people's work.

Because this correlation is so high, we have been able to use the *Dictionary*'s ratings to develop an approximate measure of substantive complexity. This approximate index, reflecting as it does the average level of substantive complexity for an entire occupation rather than the precise level of substantive complexity of a particular job, is not as powerful as our detailed index. But, used cautiously, it can provide a serviceable index of substantive complexity in studies where adequate information with which to construct a detailed index is lacking.

Replications

There have been several attempts to test the central finding, that occupational self-direction plays a crucial role in explaining the relationships between social class and values and orientation. None of these studies comes close to being an exact replication, yet all are instructive.

The first, by Stephen Olsen (1971), confirmed in Taiwan the correlation between social class and parental valuation of self-direction or conformity to external authority, both for fathers and for mothers. But when Olsen statistically controlled the conditions determinative of occupational self-direction, he found that the correlations were not appreciably reduced. Four interpretations are possible: (1) Olsen's indices of the pertinent occupational conditions are insufficient. His index of substantive complexity, for example, is simply the respondent's evaluation of the relative importance in his job of work with things, with data, and with people; and he has no index of routinization. (2) In the very different occupational structure of partially industrialized Taiwan, dimensions of occupation other than closeness of supervision, substantive complexity, and routinization are more important for a person's having control over the essential conditions of his job. (3) In Taiwan, life-conditions other than occupational—perhaps economic, perhaps political, perhaps still others—are the bridge between class position and values. (4) Middle-class Taiwanese have adopted Western values while working-class Taiwanese still hold traditional, Confucian values. Olsen's data do not permit one to choose among these alternatives with any degree of confidence. All we can conclude is that occupational self-direction, Western style, may not be important for explaining the class-values relationship in Taiwan.

The second study, conducted in Peru by Scurrah and Montalvo (1975), found correlations between social class and such aspects of orientation as fatalism, trust, and anxiety similar to those we had found. They then asked whether these could be explained by class-correlated differences in occupational self-directon. To some degree they could: statistically controlling indices of substantive complexity and closeness of supervision reduced the correlations by from 19 to 28 percent. These reductions are smaller than those we had found. Perhaps this means that occupational self-direction is of lesser importance in a country at an early stage of industrialization than in a more industrialized country. Or perhaps it simply reflects Scurrah and Montalvo's reliance on our approximate index of substantive complexity and their lack of an index of routinization. Or perhaps it is just that their sample is limited to workers employed in retail stores. The data do not permit us to judge. But again doubt is raised whether occupational self-direction is as important for explaining the relationships between social class and values and orientation in partially industrialized as in more fully industrialized societies.

The third study, conducted in the United States by St. Peter (1975), utilized data that had been collected for a replication of Stouffer's study of communism, conformity, and civil liberties. St. Peter found social class to be correlated with the two pertinent aspects of orientation measured in those data—"internalization of locus of control" (based on Rotter, 1960, 1966) and the desirability of "behavioral conformity" in children. The correlations are of a magnitude similar to those we had found for correlations between class and similar aspects of orientation. He did not assess the reductions in the class-orientation correlations when occupational self-direction is statistically controlled. But he did assess the reductions in the correlations between occupational status and orientation (with education already statistically controlled) when substantive complexity is statistically controlled. Using his own approximate measure of substantive complexity, he found that the correlation of occupational status with "locus of control" is reduced by only 22 percent and that with "behavioral conformity" not at all. Again we are faced with the problem of evaluating evidence based on weak indices. St. Peter had no index of closeness of supervision or of routinization, and his approximate index of substantive complexity appears to be even weaker than our own approximate index. Does this study suggest that substantive complexity is less important for explaining the relationships between social class and values and orientation than I had concluded? Or does it simply indicate that weak indices pick up only faint traces of powerful phenomena? If the latter, then it is premature to draw any inferences about differences between partly and fully industrialized societies from the Stephen Olsen and Scurrah-Montalvo studies.

If the preceding studies suffer from the use of too weak an index of substantive complexity, then Bertram's (1976a) suffers from use of an inappropriate index. His study is based on interviews with parents of third-grade children in West Germany, mainly in Düsseldorf. Although his psychological variables are somewhat different from ours, focussing on the moral development of children, the study is pertinent because he employs our conceptualization of occupational self-direction. But he lacks comparable data on occupational conditions; in particular, he lacks detailed descriptive data from which to develop an index of substantive complexity. Where the previously discussed studies used approximate indices, he substitutes for substantive complexity an index of intrinsic or extrinsic orientations toward work. His correlations between what he calls autonomy (our occupational self-direction) and all psychological phenomena are thereby rendered tautological: his measure of occupational self-direction, instead of reflecting only the structural conditions of work, includes an unknown amount of subjective orientation. Taken at face value, his findings are consistent with ours, but one cannot be sure what they really mean.

Another West German study, by Hoff and Grueneisen (1977a, b), did develop occupational indices similar to our measures of occupational self-direction, and found these occupational conditions to be substantially related to parental values, particularly as these values guide parents' behavior in critical situations. But Hoff and Grueneisen did not address the question whether these occupational conditions help explain why social class is related to values and orientation. So this study confirms the importance of occupational self-direction for values in a highly industrialized society, but provides no information about the degree to which occupational self-direction explains the relationship between class and values in that society.

Finally, a Canadian study by Coburn and Edwards (1976) provides confirmatory evidence that closeness of supervision is related to fathers' valuation of self-direction or conformity to external authority. They employed a concept, "job control," that is roughly equivalent to our "closeness of supervision," even though it includes not only control over one's own job, but also control over other people. The magnitude of the correlation is approximately the same as we had found it to be.

Clearly needed is further research on the interrelationship of social class, occupational self-direction, and values and orientation—both in industrialized and in less industrialized societies. To be most useful, the research should employ indices of occupational self-direction based on detailed descriptive data about actual job conditions. I know of three such studies currently in process. One, by Słomczynski, Koralewicz-Zebik, and Janicka, builds our methods of inquiry and indices of occupational self-direction into a comparative study of social stratification in Poland. This study is designed to see if social stratification and occupational conditions have the same psychological effects in that socialist society as in capitalist America. The second study, by Lempert, uses our index of substantive complexity in a longitudinal study of occupational self-direction and psychological functioning of young machinists in West Berlin. Lempert intends to validate the index of substantive complexity against ratings of actual job conditions by trained observers. Finally, Hynes has recently collected data in Ireland on the core issue of whether the class-parental values relationship can be attributed to occupational self-direction. Very preliminary analyses (Hynes, 1977) provide encouraging indications that it can.

Other Uses of the Concepts

The concepts "occupational self-direction" and the "substantive complexity of the work" have been the subject of much research that goes considerably beyond the interpretive problems addressed in *Class and Conformity*. Many writers have adopted the concepts and used them for such diverse purposes as reinterpreting the status-attainment model (Spaeth, 1976), proposing a new method of classifying the occupational structure of the U.S. economy (Temme, 1975), reassessing the psychological impact of complex role-sets (Coser, 1975), interpreting the effects of fathers' occupational experiences on their sons' occupational choices (Mortimer, 1974 and 1976), and searching out the sources of powerlessness (Tudor, 1972). The concepts have even broader theoretical implications than I had realized.

THE DIRECTION OF CAUSAL EFFECTS

Again and again throughout the book I acknowledged that correlations do not prove causality. I argued that class-correlated occupational conditions probably do have a causal effect on values and orientation—conditions of work that foster thought and initiative tend to enlarge men's conceptions of reality, while conditions of constraint tend to narrow them. But I had to admit that the findings might simply reflect the propensity of men who value self-direction to seek out jobs that offer them opportunity to be self-directed in their work and, once in a job, to maximize whatever opportunities the job allows for exercising self-direction.

The only argument I then could offer against the latter interpretation was a priori: We know that occupational choice is limited by educational qualifications, which in turn are greatly affected by the accidents of family background, economic circumstances, and available social resources. Moreover, the opportunity to exercise greater or lesser self-direction in one's work is circumscribed by job requirements. Thus, an executive must do complex work with data or with people; he cannot be closely supervised; and his tasks are too diverse to be routinized; hence, to be an executive requires some substantial degree of self-direction. Correspondingly, to be a semi-skilled factory worker precludes much self-direction. The substance of one's work cannot be especially complex; one cannot escape some measure of supervision; and if one's job is to fit into the flow of other people's work, it must necessarily be routinized. The relationship between being self-directed in one's work and holding self-directed values would seem to result not just from self-directed people acting according to their values, but also from job experiences affecting these very values.

It was a plausible argument, but only that. A more definitive argument clearly requires empirical evidence. In subsequent research, Schooler and I have attempted to produce such evidence.

The evidence is of two types. The more extensive but less conclusive evidence comes from analysis of the cross-sectional data of the national study (Kohn and Schooler, 1973; Kohn, 1976b). Social scientists have long recognized that one cannot make inferences about the direction of causal effects from cross-sectional data unless some of the described phenomena clearly preceded others in their time of occurrence. But where one can realistically assume reciprocal effects

—that *a* affects *b* and *b* also affects *a*—it is possible to assess the magnitude of these reciprocal effects, using econometric techniques for solving simultaneous equations. Using one such technique, we have assessed the reciprocal effects of the substantive complexity of work and many facets of psychological functioning: occupational commitment, job satisfaction, parental valuation of self-direction, anxiety, self-esteem, receptiveness or resistance to change, standards of morality, authoritarian conservatism, intellectual flexibility, the intellectual demandingness of leisure-time activities, and three types of alienation—powerlessness, self-estrangement, and normlessness. The substantive complexity of work affects each of these facets of psychological functioning more—in most cases, much more—than that facet of psychological functioning affects the substantive complexity of work. This evidence is not conclusive, for only longitudinal studies of real change in real people can be conclusive, but it does establish a strong prima facie case that the substantive complexity of work has a meaningful effect on a very wide range of psychological processes.

More definitive, albeit less extensive, evidence comes from a follow-up study we have conducted with a representative subsample of men in the national study (Kohn and Schooler, in press). Analyses of longitudinal data are immensely difficult, because they require the development of "measurement models" that separate unreliability of measurement from real change in the phenomena studied. We have thus far constructed such measurement models for substantive complexity and for intellectual flexibility, the latter deliberately chosen because it appeared to offer us the greatest challenge: intellectual flexibility is obviously pertinent to job placement, and it might be expected to be the most stable of all the psychological phenomena we have studied.

Stable it certainly is. The correlation between the men's intellectual flexibility at the time of the original study and their intellectual flexibility ten years later, shorn of measurement error, is 0.93. Nevertheless, the effect of the substantive complexity of work on intellectual flexibility is striking—on the order of one-fourth as great as the effect of the men's earlier levels of intellectual flexibility. Considering that we are assessing men no younger than 26 years of age who are at least ten years into their occupational careers, the effect of the substantive complexity of the job on intellectual flexibility is indeed impressive.

The longitudinal analysis demonstrates also something that no cross-sectional analysis could show—that, over time, the relationship between substantive complexity and intellectual flexibility is truly reciprocal. As we have noted, substantive complexity has an ongoing and continuous effect on intellectual flexibility: today's job demands affect today's thinking processes. Intellectual flexibility, by contrast, has a delayed effect on substantive complexity: today's intellectual flexibility has scant effect on today's job demands, but it will have a sizeable effect on the further course of one's career. The cross-sectional analysis portrayed only part of this process, making it seem as if the relationship between the substantive complexity of work and psychological functioning is mainly unidirectional, with work affecting psychological functioning but not the reverse. The longitudinal analysis portrays a more intricate and more interesting, truly reciprocal, process.

We have thus shown, more definitively than ever before, that occupational conditions have a continuing and substantial effect on psychological functioning. Although the focus of the inquiry has thus far been limited to but one dimension of occupational structure and one dimension of psychological functioning, the data demonstrate, beyond reasonable doubt, what heretofore could be stated as only a plausible thesis buttressed by supportive evidence—that people's occupational conditions substantially affect their off-the-job psychological processes. The principal speculative link in the thesis of *Class and Conformity*—that class-correlated occupational conditions really do affect values, orientation, and psychological functioning—has thereby been given a strong evidentiary basis.

THE ROLE OF EDUCATION

Although *Class and Conformity* posited that the educational component of social class has both direct effects on values and orientation and indirect effects, mediated through job conditions, the analyses of Chapter 10 focused on only the direct effects. The principal hypothesis was that education matters, aside from its impact on job conditions, "insofar as education provides the intellectual flexibility and breadth of perspective that are essential for self-directed values and orientation." An empirical confirmation of this hypothesis demonstrated that statistically controlling an index of intellectual flexibility substantially reduces the correlations between the specifically educational component of social class and values and orientation.

Our subsequent analyses suggest that the indirect effects of education may be even more important than the direct effects. The very reason we had looked to such occupational conditions as substantive complexity, closeness of supervision, and routinization as possible keys to understanding the relationships between social class and values and orientation is that "few other conditions of life are so closely bound up with education and with occupational position." This thesis was developed further in analyses (Kohn and Schooler, 1973 and in press) that assessed the effects of education on occupational conditions at each stage of career. Education is a prime determinant, for example, of the substantive complexity of the job; and the substantive complexity of the job, in turn, has an appreciable effect on values and orientation. It is precisely because education is crucial for the very occupational conditions that most strongly affect values and orientation that education is so powerful; its indirect effects add greatly to its direct effects.

Although our analyses clearly indicate that education is an important determinant of job conditions, they do not enable us to distinguish between education as prerequisite to the job, in the sense of providing necessary intellectual skills and training; education as providing credentials for the job; and education as teaching values and forms of behavior appropriate to the job. That education has important direct and indirect effects on values and orientation seems unequivocal. But how it exercises these effects remains to be explained.

Two important studies (Rosenbaum, 1976; Bowles and Gintis, 1976) advance our understanding of these processes considerably. Both investigations imaginatively extrapolate from our analyses of the processes by which occupational conditions affect values and orientation, applying the same analytic logic to the educational sphere.

EXTENSIONS OF THE THESIS

In addition to research bearing directly on the main thesis of *Class and Conformity,* there has also been a great deal of work extending that thesis beyond the interpretive issues to which the book is addressed. My review of these studies is limited to a few of the most direct extensions—work that has spelled out personality consequences of class differences in values and orientation, or examined the psychological impact of facets of occupational structure other than those directly tied into the stratificational system, or applied the mode of analysis developed in the book to dimensions of social structure other than class itself. To keep this essay within reasonable bounds, I refrain from discussing parallel developments in such fields as sociolinguistics (see especially the important work of Bernstein, 1971 and 1973) and anthropology (see, for example, the discussion in Lee, 1977, Chapter 9).

Schizophrenia

Class and Conformity begins and ends with speculation about the relationship between social class and schizophrenia. I have since elaborated an interpretation of the interrelationship of class, stress, and genetic predisposition in the production of schizophrenia (Kohn, 1972; see also Kohn, 1973, 1976c, 1976d). My theme is that people of lower social class position experience conditions of life that foster conceptions of social reality so limited and so rigid as to impair their ability to deal resourcefully with the problematic and the stressful. This impairment, if it occurs in conjunction with a genetic vulnerability to schizophrenia and the experience of great stress, could be disabling. Since both genetic vulnerability and stress appear to occur disproportionately at lower social class levels, people in these segments of society may be in triple jeopardy.

Whether or not this particular formulation will prove to be correct, it does illustrate a type of interpretive model more adequate to the complexities of the current and rapidly accumulating evidence than were earlier models. Those models tried, unsuccessfully, to attribute schizophrenia to a single causal variable—genetics, family relationships, social class, stress, and so forth. An interactive model of the type I have proposed can deal with the evidence that no one factor explains schizophrenia and that some combination of relevant conditions must be present for schizophrenia to occur.

Occupational Structure

In Schooler's and my further research, our interest in occupational conditions has gone considerably beyond an initial concern with their role in explaining the psychological effects of social class, to a broader interest in occupational structure. There have been three major analyses, one focused on the psychological effects of employment in bureaucratic organizations, the second on occupational sources of alienation, and the third addressed more generally to the psychological effects of occupational structure.

Bureaucratization

Observers of bureaucracy, impressed by its need to coordinate many people's activities, have assumed that a primary effect of employment in bureaucratic organizations must be the suppression of individuality. Chapter 10 of *Class and Conformity* confirmed that employees of bureaucratic organizations are more closely supervised than are the employees of nonbureaucratic organizations and that being closely supervised is conducive to having conformist values and orientation. And yet, employment in bureaucratic organizations is associated with having somewhat more self-directed values and orientation. What is there about bureaucratization that makes for self-directed values and orientation? Answering this question has required a refinement of the index of bureaucratization, accomplished by combining the size and supervisory structure of the firm or organization to index the hierarchical organization of authority (Kohn, 1971).

The data indicate that the effect of bureaucracies' supervising employees closely is more than offset by their providing employees substantively more complex work than do nonbureaucratic firms and organizations. The psychological effects of bureaucratization are thus somewhat contradictory. In providing substantively complex work, bureaucracies offer their employees conditions that are conducive to having self-directed values and orientation. But in denying their employees freedom from close supervision, bureaucracies have the opposite effect. And although they provide a wide variety of complexly interrelated jobs to their white-collar workers, they tend to entrap their blue-collar workers in a routinized flow of simply organized tasks. The net result is that employees of bureaucratic organizations have somewhat more opportunity for occupational self-direction than do other people of comparable educational background. Hence, they are more self-directed in their values and orientation than are employees of nonbureaucratic organizations, but the difference is not great.

Another reason for employees of bureaucratic organizations being more self-directed in their values and orientation is that they have greater job protection. Bureaucracies must ensure that superordinate officials are limited in what facets of their subordinates' behavior they are allowed to control and how they may exercise that control; superordinates cannot dismiss subordinates at will, and questionable actions can sometimes be appealed to adjudicatory agencies. The power of nonbureaucratic organizations over their employees is more complete and may be more capricious. Thus, the alternative to bureaucracy's circumscribed authority is generally, not less authority, but personal, potentially arbitrary authority. What is notable about bureaucratic practice is not how closely authority is exercised but how effectively it is circumscribed. In providing their employees protection from arbitrary authority, bureaucracies make self-directed values and orientation more feasible.

The Occupational Sources of Alienation

In a further analysis of the data of the national study, I have appraised two related hypotheses derived from Marx's analysis of the occupational sources of alienation (Kohn, 1976b). One hypothesis, emphasizing loss of control over the products of one's labor, posits that ownership and hierarchical position are of crucial importance for alienation, and also ascribes an important, albeit secondary, role to division of labor. The other hypothesis, emphasizing loss of control over the process of labor, suggests that, at least within an industrialized, capitalist society, such determinants of occupational self-direction as closeness of supervision, routinization, and substantive complexity overshadow ownership, hierarchical position, and division of labor in their effects on alienation. The data show that ownership, hierarchical position, and division of labor have less effect on such facets of alienation as powerlessness, self-estrangement, and normlessness than do the occupational conditions determinative of whether or not one can exercise self-direction in one's work. These findings are entirely consonant with the basic Marxian analysis of the alienating effects of workers' loss of control over their essential job conditions. In this large-scale, capitalist economy, though, the type of control that is most important for alienation is control, not over the product, but over the process of one's work.

Much of the theoretical literature attributes alienation to conditions stemming directly from capitalism or bureaucracy or both. The data used here are far from adequate for dealing with these issues; the research was limited to one country, capitalist and heavily bureaucratized. Yet the data do bear on these themes, and insofar as they do, they consistently imply that neither capitalism nor bureaucracy is the primary source of alienation in this industrial society. Being or not being an owner is of at most minor importance for alienation. Moreover, people employed in profit-making enterprises are no more alienated than are those who work for government or for nonprofit enterprises. And as for bureaucratization, its effects are opposite to what would be expected by those who see it as a source of alienation. My findings suggest, instead, that the principal occupational sources of alienation are conditions that impinge directly and immediately on the worker, in particular, his opportunities to exercise self-direction in his work.

The Psychological Effects of Occupational Structure

In *Class and Conformity* I examined the psychological impact of many occupational conditions, but always with a primary interest in seeing whether a given occupational condition might help explain the relationships between social class and values and orientation. In later analyses using the national study data, Schooler and I have looked at occupational structure more generally (Kohn and Schooler 1973). We found that nearly all of the more than fifty occupational conditions we had inventoried are correlated with at least some of the several aspects of values, self-conception, social orientation, and intellectual functioning that we had measured. But most of these statistical relationships reflect the interrelatedness of occupational conditions with one another and with education. Only twelve of the occupational conditions we studied appear to have any substantial impact on people's psychological functioning independently of education and of all other pertinent occupational conditions. Few though they are, these twelve occupational conditions are sufficient to define the "structural imperatives of the job," in that they identify a person's place in the organizational structure, his opportunities for occupational self-direction, the principal job pressures to which he is subject, and the principal uncertainties built into his job. Of all these occupational conditions, those that determine occupational self-direction prove to be the most important: they are significantly related to all facets of psychological functioning, in most cases more strongly so than any other occupational condition. But organizational locus, job pressures, and job uncertainties all make some independent contribution to the overall relationship between the structural imperatives of the job and psychological functioning.

These findings buttress and extend our earlier conclusions about the social-psychological importance of conditions that facilitate or inhibit the exercise of occupational self-direction. We can now say that, in addition to its relevance for explaining the social-psychological impact of class, occupational self-direction has the most potent and most widespread effects of all the occupational conditions we have examined. To put the matter a little more generally, these findings emphasize the social-psychological importance of the structural imperatives of the job—those aspects of the job that impinge on a person most directly, insistently, and demandingly. Not only the conditions that determine occupational self-direction, but all structural imperatives of the job that elicit effort and flexibility, are conducive to positive evaluations of self, an open and flexible orientation to others, and effective intellectual functioning. People thrive in meeting occupational challenges.

These findings also bear on the issue of whether people similarly located in the structure of society come to share beliefs and values because they experience similar conditions of life or because of some interpersonal process of value-transmission. The structuralists would have us believe that the former is basic; theorists as diverse as the "human relations in industry" and "culture of poverty" schools stress the latter. Our findings point to the importance of the structural imperatives of the job and suggest that interpersonal relatedness is of relatively minor importance; they thus support the argument of the structuralists. A person's job affects his perceptions, values, and thinking processes primarily because it confronts him with demands he must try to meet. These demands, in turn, are to a great extent determined by the job's location in the larger structures of the economy and the society. It is chiefly by shaping the everyday realities people must face that social structure exerts its psychological impact.

Other Dimensions of Social Structure

In *Class and Conformity* social class is consistently treated as one aspect of a larger and more encompassing social structure, and the psychological impact of social class as illustrative of the more general impact of social structure. Several chapters describe relationships between aspects of social structure other than class—race, national background, religion, and urbanicity, among others—and values and orientation. But interpreting how and why these facets of social structure affect values and orientation was beyond the purview of the book. Schooler has subsequently analyzed the data of the national study much more thoroughly, to interpret the psychological effects of several major dimensions of social structure other than social class. His is a fundamental interpretation parallel to, but going considerably beyond, our interpretation of class alone.

Schooler (1972) began by examining what the various dimensions of social structure have in common as they impinge on a growing child: they all add to, or subtract from, what he calls a complex, multifaceted environment. By this term, he means an environment in which the individual is expected to make a wide range of decisions, is exposed to numerous models of behavior, and can see as plausible a wide range of goals. Concretely, the younger the person, and the more liberal the religious denomination in which he was raised, and the more educated his father, and the more urban the locale in which he was raised, and the further removed this locale from the Old South, the more complex and multifaceted his childhood environment. Schooler hypothesized, and then confirmed, that adults who had been raised in complex environments are more likely to see themselves as relatively autonomous and to be intolerant of external constraints on their behavior. Moreover, adults who had been raised in such environments are motivated to develop their intellectual capacities as fully as possible and to develop a form of subjectivism based on the belief that one's own thoughts and feelings are of primary importance.

In an analysis of the effects of national background on values and orientation, Schooler (1976) added an historical dimension to the study of social structure. He posited that the major European nationalities can be thought of as falling along a continuum that reflects the time of the release of their peasantry from serfdom. Such a continuum ranks countries according to the degree of self-direction and the number of behavioral options that were available in the recent historical past to the agricultural sector of the population, the very segment from which most immigrants to America came. In line with his expectations, Schooler found that belonging to a nationality that has had a long history of freedom from serfdom has the same general empirical relationships with intellectual functioning, attitudes toward authority, and moral standards as does working in a substantively complex job. Both conditions seem to produce persons who are intellectually more effective, who believe that they have some control over their lives, and who feel that the ultimate locus of ethical responsibility is within themselves, rather than in authorities, the law, or other external enforcers of conformity.

There is yet another extension of the interpretive scheme from social class to social structure, this by Nancy Olsen (1974). Olsen noted that in a large number of the world's societies, the ideal form of domestic arrangement is the patrilineally extended family, and in many of these, young women are subject to the authority and direction of their mothers-in-law. Thus, there is a basic similarity between the situation of a daughter-in-law in this type of three-generation family and that of the typical working-class man; in both cases, rewards are contingent upon following the directions of one's superior, rather than upon organizing and carrying out work on one's own. Mothers in three-generation households should therefore resemble working-class men in placing a high value upon their children's conformity, while mothers in nuclear families should place more emphasis on self-direction. To test this hypothesis, Olsen carried out a comparative study of two- and three-generation families in Taiwan. She used an ingenious research design, which permitted her to control statistically for urbanicity, social class, size of family, sex of the child, and ordinal position of the child. Her analysis clearly showed that living in a three-generation household affects a woman's values in much the same way as close supervision on the job affects the values of a man. She also showed that this finding does not depend on women who value conformity being more likely to marry into households that contain mothers-in-law. She was even able to show that her findings do not result from higher valuation of the traditional Chinese ethic by women living in extended households.

Schooler and Olsen have demonstrated the usefulness of extending the interpretive scheme employed in *Class and Conformity* from social class in particular to social structure in general. The key in looking at any dimension of social structure is to ask how a person's position in the larger social structure affects the conditions of life that directly impinge on him. The interpretive bridge is from position in the larger social structure to directly impinging conditions of life to values, orientation, and intellectual functioning.

OPEN QUESTIONS FOR FUTURE ANALYSIS

Research done in the eight years since the original publication of *Class and Conformity* has strengthened its thesis: by confirming the relationships between social class and values and orientation; by buttressing the argument that class-correlated occupational conditions not only are associated with, but have a causal impact on, values, orientation, and intellectual functioning; and by extending the thesis to new areas, some of them going far beyond those discussed in the book. Still, many of the most important questions raised by the interpretive thesis remain unanswered. We have already noted some of these unanswered questions—for example, those pertaining to the role of education and to the processes by which education affects values and orientation; and those pertaining to the links between values and behavior. There are others.

Women

There is, to begin, the question of whether occupational conditions have the same psychological impact on women as on men. Schooler and I had originally intended to extend the national study to women, but were not able to do so. Now, in our follow-up study, we have secured interviews with the wives of a subsample of the men in the original study. Admittedly, this sample of wives is not optimum for studying the effects of occupation on women, not only because a sample of wives is not representative of all women, but also because the age-range of the women in our sample is somewhat restricted: they are all married to men who were, at the time of the reinterview, between the ages of 26 and 65. Nevertheless, if these sample biases are kept firmly in mind, much can be learned from such an inquiry. These data are useful both for analyzing the effects of occupational conditions on women's values and orientation, and for addressing the related question of whether the relationships between social class and values and orientation (not just parental values) are the same for women as for men. The data are pertinent as well to the subsidiary but important question of how best to conceptualize and to index women's social class positions.

Cross-effects

Another important open question is whether (and if so, how) men's occupational conditions affect their wives' values and orientation, and whether (and if so, how) women's occupational conditions affect their husbands' values and orientation. The Turin study showed that men's occupational conditions are meaningfully and apparently causally related to their wives' values. But this study gave no information about the processes involved, nor did it examine the corresponding effects of women's occupational experiences on their husbands' values. The parallel interviews with husbands and wives in the follow-up study should enable us to do both.

Housework

Many people—wives in particular—do not have jobs outside the home. But most "unemployed" wives do a substantial amount of household work. Does household work have psychological effects comparable to those of jobs outside the household? In the follow-up study, we are treating household work as an occupation, to be analyzed in much the same way as any other occupation. Since, presumably, any person, man or woman, who spends much time at housework is affected by the conditions of this work, we are asking the questions about housework of all respondents, men and women, whether or not they are employed outside the home. We hypothesize that the psychological effects of occupational conditions encountered in housework are much the same as those encountered in other types of work; but we cannot predict whether the magnitude of these effects will be as great.

Behavioral Indicators

With the notable exception of parental disciplinary practices and parental support and constraint of children, our data and our analyses have focused almost entirely on people's subjective beliefs and intellectual processes rather than on their behavior. In our more recent work (e.g., Kohn, 1971; Kohn and Schooler, 1973) we have analyzed one facet of (reported) behavior—the intellectual demandingness of leisure-time activities. We are only now beginning to analyze our data on other aspects of leisure-time activities to see if there are parallels, as we hypothesize, between job demands and how people spend their leisure time. But these data tap only a small portion of the behavioral realm. Much more extensive behavioral data are needed for a systematic understanding of the interrelationship of class, occupation, and people's behavior in other-than-occupational areas of life.

Processes of Learning and Generalization

Other important questions concern the processes by which the lessons of work are generalized to other realms of life. Our findings (see Kohn and Schooler, 1973; Kohn, 1976b) argue for a simple learning-generalization model—the direct translation of the lessons of the job to outside-the-job realities—in contrast to a reaction-formation or compensatory model (see Breer and Locke, 1965). Thus, for example, men who do substantively complex work come not only to exercise their intellectual prowess on the job, but also to engage in intellectually demanding leisure-time activities. They become more open to new experience. They come to value self-direction more highly. In short, the lessons of work are directly carried over to nonoccupational realms. But our data are far from definitive on this score; other studies, including longitudinal studies addressed specifically to this issue, are needed.

A closely-related issue is whether occupational conditions affect all people similarly or whether their effect is mediated by a person's own needs, values, and abilities—the so-called "fit" hypothesis. Our analyses suggest the former. We repeatedly find, for example (see Kohn, 1976b), that the substantive complexity of the work has much the same effects regardless of whether men value intrinsic or extrinsic aspects of their work more highly. But these analyses have been broad-gauge, and more detailed analyses of pertinent subpopulations might require us to modify our views. Moreover, our analyses of this issue have thus far not been longitudinal, and only longitudinal assessments can be conclusive; as our data demonstrate, people's values and even their abilities are affected by their job conditions.

Deliberately Instituted Change

Our interpretation implies that deliberately instituted change in pivotal occupational conditions would actually affect people's values, orientation, and intellectual functioning. But would it? Would alienation, for example, be alleviated by occupational rearrangements, by worker participation in "management" decisions, or by the organization of work teams? Although experiments in the restructuring of work are being conducted in several countries, I know of none that really answers this question. Some seem not even to recognize that the most important work conditions are embedded in larger social and economic structures. Our findings imply that experiments that fail to give the worker meaningful control over the conditions that impinge directly on his opportunities to exercise initiative, thought, and independent judgment in his work would not decrease alienation. On the other hand, I should certainly expect experiments that do increase workers' control over the conditions of their work to decrease alienation (see Kahn, 1975). One interesting question is how large a measure of individual control, as against a share in group decision-making, is required for a worker to feel in sufficient command over his essential occupational conditions that he not feel alienated. The answer, of course, may not be the same in all cultures or in all political systems.

Cultural, Economic, and Political Contexts

The findings of the national study with respect to social class and occupational conditions, although based on a large and representative sample, cannot safely be generalized beyond the United States or even beyond the time the data were collected. The relative importance of various occupational conditions may be affected by economic conditions: 1964 was a time of relatively great economic security in the United States; occupational self-direction might be less important and, say, job security more important at times of greater economic uncertainty. Moreover, as we have seen from the Stephen Olsen study of Taiwan and the Scurrah-Montalvo study of Peru, it is an open question whether occupational self-direction has the effects on values and orientation in less industrialized societies that it has in the United States. Finally, we do not know whether occupational effects would be the same in different cultural, economic, or political contexts. Studies now in progress may help answer all these questions.

Washington, D.C.   Melvin L. Kohn
March, 1977

BIBLIOGRAPHY

Barnsley, John H.
1972 *The Social Reality of Ethics: The Comparative Analysis of Moral Codes.* London: Routledge and Kegan Paul.

Bernstein, Basil
1971 *Class, Codes, and Control.* Vol. 1. *Theoretical Studies toward a Sociology of Language.* London: Routledge and Kegan Paul.
1973 *Class, Codes, and Control.* Vol. 2. *Applied Studies toward a Sociology of Language.* London: Routledge and Kegan Paul.

Bertram, Hans
1976a Gesellschaftliche und Familiäre Bedingungen Moralischen Urteilens. Doctoral dissertation, Universität Düsseldorf.
1976b Probleme einer sozialstrukturell orientierten Sozialisationforschung. *Zeitschrift für Soziologie* 5 (April): 103-17.
1977 Personal communication (unpublished data).

Blalock, Hubert M., Jr.
1963 Correlated independent variables: The problem of multicollinearity. *Social Forces* 42 (December): 233-37.
1964 *Causal Inferences in Nonexperimental Research.* Chapel Hill: University of North Carolina Press.

Bowles, Samuel and Herbert Gintis
1976 *Schooling in Capitalist America: Educational Reform and the Contradictions of Economic Life.* New York: Basic Books.

Breer, Paul E. and Edwin A. Locke
1965 *Task Experience as a Source of Attitudes.* Homewood, Illinois: The Dorsey Press.

Campbell, John D.
1977 The child in the sick role: Contributions of age, sex, parental status, and parental values. *Journal of Health and Social Behavior* (in press).

Clausen, John A.
1974 Value transmission and personality resemblance in two genera-

tions. Paper presented to the annual meeting of the American Sociological Association, Montreal, August 27.

Coburn, David and Virginia L. Edwards
1976 Job control and child-rearing values. *Canadian Review of Sociology and Anthropology* 13 (August): 337-44.

Coser, Rose Laub
1975 The complexity of roles as a seedbed of individual autonomy. Pp. 237-63 in Lewis A. Coser (Ed.), *The Idea of Social Structure: Papers in Honor of Robert K. Merton.* New York: Harcourt Brace Jovanovich.

Di Palma, Giuseppe
1971 Review of *Class and Conformity. American Journal of Sociology* 77 (November): 615-16.

Erlanger, Howard S.
1974 Social class and corporal punishment in childrearing: A reassessment. *American Sociological Review* 39 (February): 68-85.

Farrar, Donald E. and Robert R. Glauber
1967 Multicollinearity in regression analysis: The problem revisited. *The Review of Economics and Statistics* 49 (February): 92-107.

Franklin, Jack I. and Joseph E. Scott
1970 Parental values: An inquiry into occupational setting. *Journal of Marriage and the Family* 32 (August): 406-9.

Gabennesch, Howard
1972 Authoritarianism as world view. *American Journal of Sociology* 77 (March): 857-75.

Gecas, Viktor
1977 The influence of social class on socialization. In W. R. Burr, R. Hill, I. L. Reiss, and F. I. Nye (Eds.), *Theories about the Family.* New York: The Free Press.

Gecas, Viktor and F. Ivan Nye
1974 Sex and class differences in parent-child interaction: A test of Kohn's hypothesis. *Journal of Marriage and the Family* 36 (November): 742-49.

Gordon, Robert A.
1968 Issues in multiple regression. *American Journal of Sociology* 73 (March): 592-616.

Hoff, Ernst-Hartmut and Veronika Grueneisen
1977a Arbeitserfahrungen, Erziehungseinstellungen, und Erziehungsverhalten von Eltern. In H. Lukesch und K. Schneewind (Eds.), *Familiäre Sozialisation: Probleme, Ergebnisse, Perspektiven.*

Stuttgart: Klett. In press.
1977b   Personal communication (unpublished data).

Hynes, Eugene
1977   Personal communication (unpublished data).

Kahn, Robert L.
1975   In search of the Hawthorne effect. Pp. 49–63 in *Man and Work in Society: A Report on the Symposium Held on the Occasion of the 50th Anniversary of the Original Hawthorne Studies, Oakbrook, Illinois, November 10–13, 1974.* New York: Van Nostrand Reinhold.

Kelman, Herbert C. and Janet Barclay
1963   The F Scale as a measure of breadth of perspective. *Journal of Abnormal and Social Psychology* 67 (December): 608–15.

Kohn, Melvin L.
1971   Bureaucratic man: A portrait and an interpretation. *American Sociological Review* 36 (June): 461–74.
1972   Class, family, and schizophrenia: A reformulation. *Social Forces* 50 (March): 295–304, 310–13.
1973   Social class and schizophrenia: A critical review and a reformulation. *Schizophrenia Bulletin,* no. 7 (Winter), pp. 60–79.
1976a   Social class and parental values: Another confirmation of the relationship. *American Sociological Review* 41 (June): 538–45.
1976b   Occupational structure and alienation. *American Journal of Sociology* 82 (July): 111–30.
1976c   Looking back: A 25-year review and appraisal of social problems research. *Social Problems* 24 (October): 94–112.
1976d   The interaction of social class and other factors in the etiology of schizophrenia. *American Journal of Psychiatry* 133 (February): 177–80.

Kohn, Melvin L. and Carmi Schooler
1973   Occupational experience and psychological functioning: An assessment of reciprocal effects. *American Sociological Review* 38 (February): 97–118.
in press   The reciprocal effects of the substantive complexity of work and intellectual flexibility: A longitudinal assessment. *American Journal of Sociology.*

Lee, Gary R.
1977   *Family Structure and Interaction: A Comparative Analysis.* Philadelphia: Lippincott.

Le Masters, E. E.
1975   *Blue-Collar Aristocrats: Life-Styles at a Working-Class Tavern.*

Madison: University of Wisconsin Press.

Martinussen, Willy
1971   Review of *Class and Conformity*. *Acta Sociologica* 14, no. 3: 199-200.

Miller, Daniel R.
1971   Review of *Class and Conformity*. *Psychiatry* 34 (November): 439-42.

Mortimer, Jeylan T.
1974   Patterns of intergenerational occupational movements: A smallest-space analysis. *American Journal of Sociology* 79 (March): 1278-99.

1976   Social class, work, and the family: Some implications of the father's occupation for familial relationships and sons' career decisions. *Journal of Marriage and the Family* 38 (May): 241-56.

Olsen, Nancy J.
1974   Family structure and socialization patterns in Taiwan. *American Journal of Sociology* 79 (May): 1395-417.

Olsen, Stephen Milton
1971   Family, Occupation, and Values in a Chinese Urban Community. Ph.D. dissertation. Cornell University.

Otto, Luther B.
1975   Class and status in family research. *Journal of Marriage and the Family* 37 (May): 315-32.

Perron, Roger
1971   *Modèles D'Enfants, Enfants Modèles*. Paris: Presses Universitaires de France.

Platt, Jennifer
n.d.   Social class and childrearing norms in Britain and the U.S.A. Manuscript, University of Sussex.

Porter, John
1970   Review of *Class and Conformity*. *Science* 170 (December 11): 1183-85.

Roof, Wade Clark
1974   Religious orthodoxy and minority prejudice: Causal relationship or reflection of localistic world view? *American Journal of Sociology* 80 (November): 643-64.

Rosenbaum, James E.
1976   *Making Inequality: The Hidden Curriculum of High School Tracking*. New York: John Wiley and Sons.

Rotter, Julian B.
  1960 Some implications of a social learning theory for the prediction
        of goal directed behavior from testing procedures. *Psychological
        Review* 67 (September): 301-16.
  1966 Generalized expectancies for internal versus external control of
        reinforcement. *Psychological Monographs,* vol. 80, no. 1, whole
        no. 609.

St. Peter, Louis Glenn
  1975 Fate Conceptions: A Look at the Effects of Occupational Tasks
        on Human Values. Ph.D. dissertation, University of Nebraska.

Schooler, Carmi
  1972 Social antecedents of adult psychological functioning. *American
        Journal of Sociology* 78 (September): 299-322.
  1976 Serfdom's legacy: An ethnic continuum. *American Journal of
        Sociology* 81 (May): 1265-86.

Scurrah, Martin J. and Abner Montalvo
  1975 *Clase Social y Valores Sociales en Perú.* Lima, Peru: Escuela de
        Administración de Negocios Para Graduados (Serie: Documento
        de Trabajo No. 8).

Sennett, Richard and Jonathan Cobb
  1973 *The Hidden Injuries of Class.* New York: Alfred Knopf.

Silverman, Sydel
  1971 Review of *Class and Conformity. American Anthropologist* 73
        (April): 332-33.

Simpson, Miles
  1972 Authoritarianism and education: A comparative approach. *Socio-
        metry* 35 (June): 223-34.

Spaeth, Joe L.
  1976 Cognitive complexity: A dimension underlying the socioeconomic
        achievement process. Pp. 103-31 in William H. Sewell, Robert
        M. Hauser, and David L. Featherman (Eds.), *Schooling and
        Achievement in American Society.* New York: Academic Press.

Temme, Lloyd V.
  1975 *Occupation: Meanings and Measures.* Washington, D.C.: Bureau
        of Social Science Research, Inc.

Tudor, Bill
  1972 A specification of relationships between job complexity and
        powerlessness. *American Sociological Review* 37 (October): 596-
        604.

United States Department of Labor
1965   *Dictionary of Occupational Titles.* 3d ed. Washington, D.C.:
         U.S. Government Printing Office.
Weslowski, W.
1969   The notions of strata and class in socialist society. Pp. 122–45
         in Andre Beteille (Ed.), *Social Inequality: Selected Readings.*
         Harmondsworth, Middlesex, England: Penguin Books, Ltd.
Wright, James D. and Sonia R. Wright
1976   Social class and parental values for children: A partial replication
         and extension of the Kohn thesis. *American Sociological Review*
         41 (June): 527–37.

PART I

Class, Values, and Orientation

CHAPTER 1

Introduction

It is a commonplace among social scientists that, no matter what the subject of study, we should always measure people's social class positions, for class is nearly always significantly involved. Remarkable though it seems, one aspect of social structure,[1] hierarchical position, is related to almost everything about men's lives—their political party preferences, their sexual behavior, their church membership, even their rates of ill health and death.[2] Moreover, the correlations are not trivial; class is substantially related to all these phenomena.

These facts are abundant and beyond dispute. What is not at all clear, though, is why class has such widespread ramifications. How do these impressive and massive regularities come about? What, specifically, is it about "class" that makes it important for so much of human behavior?

This question is too broad to be answered in a single empirically based book. We therefore focus on the relationship of class to one strategic realm of human experience, values and orientation. The heart of our work is an exploration of class and parental values for children. We describe the impact of class on parental values, trace the consequences for parental behavior of class differences in values, and then attempt to interpret why class matters for values. As we describe, and then again as we interpret, the relationship of class to

---

[1] By social structure we mean patterned, predictable regularities in behavior (cf. Williams, 1960: 20-22). In this book, the emphasis will be on those regularities associated with major lines of social demarcation for society as a whole—such as class, race, religion, and national background—rather than those that occur within component parts of the society.

[2] So many references could be cited to support these assertions that it would be pretentious to list them. We offer only a few that demonstrate the great range of class effects. On political party preference and voting behavior: Lazarsfeld, *et al.,* 1948; Berelson, *et al.,* 1954; Campbell, *et al.,* 1960: 333-380; Lipset, 1960; Valen and Katz, 1964. On sexual behavior: Kinsey, *et al.,* 1948, 1953. On church membership: Pope, 1948; Yinger, 1957; Lipset, 1960; Demerath, 1965. On rates of ill health and death: Scotch and Geiger, 1963; Geiger and Scotch, 1963; Antonovsky, 1967, 1968; Kohn, 1968.

For much more comprehensive bibliographies, see Barber, 1957; Kahl, 1957; Svalastoga, 1959; Berelson and Steiner, 1964: 474-490; Hodges, 1964.

parental values, we shall broaden the inquiry to show that what is true for parental values is equally true for values and orientation in general.

In discovering and interpreting the effects of social class upon parent-child relationships, our point of departure is explicitly sociological. That is, we take as given the existing social structure of class, religion, national background, and the like and trace its probable impacts on parental values and behavior. The opposite procedure could be followed, starting with one or another aspect of parental behavior and searching back for things that might explain it. We believe that working forward from a known social setting within which families operate is a more promising approach for our purposes. Our immediate problem, then, is to trace the effects of social class upon parent-child relationships.

STABILITY AND CHANGE

Any analysis of the effects of social class upon parent-child relationships should start with Bronfenbrenner's (1958) analytic review of the studies conducted in this country up to the late 1950's. From the seemingly contradictory findings of a number of studies,[3] Bronfenbrenner discerned not chaos but orderly change. Re-examining the apparent "inconsistencies" in research evidence, he inferred that there had been changes in the child-training techniques employed by middle-class parents during the 25 years covered by the research. Similar changes had been taking place in the working class, but working-class parents consistently lagged behind by a few years. While middle-class parents had once been more "restrictive" than working-class parents, by the late 1950's they had become the more "permissive."

---

[3]Since we are, in effect, using Bronfenbrenner's analysis as a review of the research literature on class and family, it is desirable to cite the principal studies on which he relied: Anderson, 1936; Baldwin, *et al.,* 1945; Duvall, 1946; Davis and Havighurst, 1946; Klatskin, 1952; Maccoby and Gibbs, 1954; McClelland, *et al.,* 1955; Boek, *et al.,* 1957; Littman, *et al.,* 1957; Sears, *et al.,* 1957; White, 1957; Miller and Swanson, 1958; Strodtbeck, 1958; Bayley and Schaefer, 1960; Miller and Swanson, 1960. (Where Bronfenbrenner relied on studies that had not then been published, we cite the eventual publication.)

Several important later studies (notably Bronfenbrenner, 1961b; Elder, 1962; McKinley, 1964) are consistent with the main themes of Bronfenbrenner's analysis. Also, several outstanding studies carried out in other countries (which Bronfenbrenner excluded from his analysis) are consistent with his, and our, conclusions. See, in particular, Spinley, 1953; Oeser and Hammond, 1954; Himmelweit, 1957.

These conclusions are necessarily limited by the particular questions asked by the investigators whose work Bronfenbrenner reviewed. The studies deal largely with a few specific techniques of child rearing, especially those involved in caring for infants and very young children, and say little about parents' overall relationships with their children, particularly as the children grow older. There is clear evidence that the quarter-century saw change, even faddism, with respect to the use of breast feeding or bottle feeding, scheduling or not scheduling, spanking or isolating. But when we generalize from these specifics to talk of a change from restrictive to permissive *practices*—or, worse yet, of a change from restrictive to permissive *parent-child relationships*—we may impute to these child-rearing practices and techniques a far greater importance than they probably have, either to parents or to children.[4]

Actually, there is no evidence that faddism in child-training techniques is symptomatic of major changes in the relations of parents to children in either the middle class or working class. What evidence we do have, as Bronfenbrenner notes on pages 420-422 and 425, points in the opposite direction: The overall quality of parent-child relationships did not seem to change very much in either class. In all probability, parents changed techniques in service of much the same values, and the changes were quite specific. These changes must be explained, but the enduring characteristics of the underlying parent-child relationships are probably even more important.

Why the changes? Bronfenbrenner's interpretation is ingeniously simple. He notes that the changes in techniques employed by middle-class parents closely paralleled those advocated by presumed experts, and he concludes that middle-class parents changed their practices because they are responsive to changes in what the experts tell them is right and proper. Working-class parents, being less educated and thus less directly responsive to printed communication, followed later.

This interpretation probably is correct, as far as it goes, in asserting that middle-class parents have followed the lead of presumably expert opinion. But why have they done so? It is not

---

[4]Furthermore, these concepts employ a priori judgments about which the various investigators have disagreed radically. See Sears, *et al.*, 1957: 444-447; Littman, *et al.*, 1957: 703.

sufficient to assume that the explanation lies in their greater degree of education. This might explain why middle-class parents are more likely than are working-class parents to read books and articles on child rearing, as we know they do.[5] But they need not follow the experts' advice. We know from various studies of the mass media that people generally search for confirmation of their existing beliefs and practices and tend to ignore or, in one way or another, to evade contradictory information.

From all the evidence at our disposal, it seems that middle-class parents not only read what the experts have to say but also actively search out a wide variety of other sources of information and advice. They are more likely than are working-class parents to discuss child rearing with friends and neighbors, to consult physicians on these matters, to attend Parent-Teacher Association meetings, and to discuss with the teachers their children's behavior.[6] Middle-class parents seem to regard child rearing as more problematic than do working-class parents. More than simply a matter of reading, this difference must be rooted in the conditions of life peculiar to each of the social classes.

Nearly everything about working-class parents' lives—most notably their comparative lack of education and the more routinized nature of their jobs—is conducive to their retaining familiar methods.[7] Furthermore, even if they are receptive to change, they are less likely than middle-class parents to find the experts' writings appropriate to their wants, for the experts' advice is predicated on middle-class values. Middle-class parents' conditions of life, on the other hand, are conducive to their looking for new methods to achieve their goals. They look to the experts, to other sources of relevant information, and to each other not for new values but for more serviceable techniques.[8] And judged within the limits of our present scanty

---

[5]This was noted by Anderson (1936) in the first major study of social class and family relationships conducted in the United States and has repeatedly been confirmed. The Washington study provides one of many confirmations.

[6]These statements are based on data from the Washington study.

[7]The differences between middle- and working-class conditions of life will be discussed more fully in subsequent chapters.

[8]Certainly middle-class parents do not get their values from the experts. In the Washington study, we compared the values of parents who say they read Spock, Gesell, or other books on child rearing, to those who read only magazine and newspaper articles, and those who say they read nothing at all on the subject. In the middle class, these three groups have substantially the same values. In the working class, the story is different. Few working-class parents claim to read books or even articles on child rearing. Those few who do have values much more akin to those of the middle class. But these are atypical

knowledge about means-ends relationships in child rearing, the experts often have provided practical and useful advice. It is not so much that educated parents slavishly follow the experts but rather that the experts have provided what the parents have sought.

If parents, in fact, have sought out new approaches because they really wanted them, their child-rearing practices must spring in some considerable part from their own basic goals and standards. To look at the matter this way is to put it in a perspective quite different from that assumed in many earlier studies. The focus becomes not specific techniques nor changes in the use of specific techniques, but rather parents' values for their children and for themselves.

A REFORMULATION

Understanding the nature of the ties between social class and parent-child relationships is part of the more general problem of understanding the effects of social structure upon behavior. We believe that social class has proved to be so useful a concept because it embodies more than simply one or another of the items used to index it—such as education or occupational position—and more than any of the large number of social, cultural, and psychological variables with which it is correlated. The concept, "class," captures the reality that the intricate interplay of all these variables creates different basic conditions of life at different levels of the social order. Members of different social classes, by virtue of enjoying (or suffering) different conditions of life, come to see the world differently—to develop different conceptions of social reality, different aspirations and hopes and fears, different "conceptions of the desirable."

The last is particularly important for present purposes, for from people's conceptions of the desirable—especially of what characteristics are desirable in children—we can discern their objectives in child rearing. Thus, conceptions of the desirable—that is, *values*—become the key concept for this analysis, the bridge between position in the larger social structure and the behavior of the individual. The intent of the analysis is to trace the effects of social class position on values and the effects of values on behavior.

---

working-class parents who are eager to attain middle-class status. One suspects that for them the experts provide a sort of handbook to the middle class; even for them, it is unlikely that the values come out of Spock and Gesell.

In doing this, we follow an old tradition in sociological inquiry, but apply it to a subject matter where it has not much been used, with methods often thought foreign. The tradition is the "sociology of knowledge," the effort to trace the underpinnings of belief, value, and ideology to men's positions in the social structure. It is based on the works of the giants—Marx, Weber, Durkheim, Veblen, Tawney, and Mannheim.[9]

The subject matter, parent-child relationships, is customarily approached from a psychodynamic perspective. We mean our perspective to be, not antithetical to that, but complementary. We do not underestimate the consequences for children of class differences in parent-child relationships, but our focus is explicating why there are class differences.

The methods are those of survey research, with all the statistical trimmings. Sociological classicists may shudder at the thought of despoiling a classical tradition of inquiry with statistical significance levels, correlation coefficients, and the like, but we think these modern methods are appropriate to the old, important problems.

PLAN OF THE BOOK

There are three major parts to this book, corresponding to the three major points of our basic thesis. In the first part (Chapters 2-5), we describe the relationship of class to parental values and, more generally, to orientation. The argument will be that class is pervasively related to men's valuation of self-direction or of conformity. In the second part (Chapters 6-7), we look at parental behavior. The argument is that class differences in parental valuation of self-direction or conformity provide a necessary key for understanding class differences in parental behavior. Finally, in the third part (Chapters 8-11), we attempt to interpret why class is related to values and orientation. The argument centers on the importance of

---

[9]Some of the principal works in this tradition are Marx's *Capital* (1906), *Eighteenth Brumaire of Louis Bonaparte* (1964), and, with Engels, *The German Ideology* (1932); Weber's *Essays in Sociology* (Gerth and Mills, Eds., 1946) and *Law in Economy and Society* (Rheinstein, Ed., 1954); Durkheim's *Elementary Forms of the Religious Life* (1954); Veblen's *The Higher Learning in America* (1957); Tawney's *Religion and the Rise of Capitalism* (1926); Mannheim's *Ideology and Utopia* (1936) and *Man and Society in an Age of Reconstruction* (1941). (The dates given above are not necessarily those of first publication, but may refer to the English translation or to a recent edition.)

For a cogent review, see Merton (1949).

occupational experience, particularly of occupational self-direction, in molding men's values and orientation.

At the risk of demanding too much of the reader's forbearance, we shall shuttle back and forth among the three studies on which our research is based, pursuing ideas to whatever body of data they lead us, rather than discussing the studies one at a time. Thus, a brief description of the essential facts about these studies is now in order. A more complete discussion can be found in the Appendixes.

THE STUDIES

— Father occup.
— mother respons.

The Washington study, conducted in 1956-57, is based on interviews with 339 mothers, from families broadly representative of the white middle and working classes, but deliberately not representative of the city of Washington. All the mothers had a child in the fifth grade of a local public or parochial school. In a random subsample of 82 families, the father and the fifth-grade child were interviewed, too, using interview schedules comparable to that used for the mothers. The interviews focused on parental values, disciplinary practices, and the major dimensions of parent-child relationships.

The Turin study, conducted by Leonard Pearlin in 1962-63, was designed to be comparable to the Washington study. Thus it, too, is based on samples broadly representative of the middle and working classes, but deliberately not representative of the city of Turin. It is limited to families having children equivalent in school grade (and age) to those in the Washington study. The children themselves were not interviewed in this study, but there is a much larger sample of fathers (341) and a larger sample of mothers (520). The interviews covered the same subjects as did those in Washington, with some important additions—notably, questions asked of fathers about their occupational circumstances.

men only

The National study, conducted in 1964, is based on interviews with 3,101 men, chosen to be representative of all men employed in civilian occupations in the United States. No women or children were studied. The sample is broadly representative of men at all socioeconomic levels except the very lowest, the unemployed. There are no restrictions on race, region, paternity, or any other condition except that the respondents be men, employed, and civilian. The interviews dealt not only with parental values and practices, but also with men's general orientations, and—rather exhaustively—with their occupational experiences.

In general, we discuss the *concepts and indices* developed in these studies as they become relevant to the substantive analysis. The one exception is social class—which is of such great importance that it had best be presented here at the outset.

SOCIAL CLASS

Our conception of social class follows closely that of Williams, as defined in *American Society* (1960: 98):

> In principle, we can show with great precision the distribution of [power, privilege, and prestige] among the individuals or other social units within any given social system.It can be expressed in objective, statistical terms once we know what the relevant privileges are. Groupings or strata derived from such measurements are not necessarily real social groups, however, but may represent simply the more or less arbitrary classification of the investigator. The distribution of privileges . . . begins to take on full sociological meaning only when it is related to *prestige rankings, social-interaction groupings,* and *beliefs and values held in common.* We shall use the term "social class" to refer to an aggregate of individuals who occupy a broadly similar position in the scale of prestige. . . . There is no doubt that the several major bases for stratification tend to go along together. Power or authority can bring wealth; wealth is often associated with power; high income frequently means also high prestige. But we must not make the elementary mistake of confusing correlation with identity. Many prestigeful occupations do not pay particularly well. A general with a moderate income may have vastly more authority than a wealthy stockmarket operator. History is full of impoverished aristocrats, as well as of the new wealth that does not yet command high prestige. As a matter of fact, some of the most interesting problems in the analysis of stratification have to do precisely with the *relations* among the various types of rank-orders.

Williams's definition allows a certain necessary flexibility for variation, from society to society and historical epoch to historical epoch, in precisely which dimensions of power, privilege, and prestige are most important for defining particular class systems. At the same time, it emphasizes that all relevant dimensions must be fairly consistent, if the stratificational system is to hold together.

The latter point is clearly enunciated by Barber (1968: 292):

> To say that the several dimensions of stratification are independent of one another, both theoretically and empirically, does not mean that they are not also interdependent—that is, that they affect one another to some extent and yet retain a measure of autonomy. For example, the dimensions of occupational

prestige, power, income, and education are to some extent independent. That is to say, in some measure occupational prestige is respected regardless of the amount of power or income. Contrariwise, power or income may achieve goals despite low occupational prestige. But the different dimensions also affect or limit one another because of their interdependence. A certain level of educational attainment may not be able to express itself without a certain level of income. And a certain level of occupational prestige may find itself ineffective because it does not have a certain amount of power. One of the important tasks for a multidimensional theory is to conduct research that leads to more and more precise statements, probably in quantified form, of the various measures of independence and interdependence that the several dimensions of stratification have in regard to one another.

In this book, we use a multidimensional index of class, based on the two dimensions of stratification that appear to be the most important in contemporary American society—occupational position and education. We also index two other dimensions of social stratification—income and subjective class identification. Later, we shall examine the independent contributions of each of these dimensions to the total effect of social class on men's values and orientations.[10]

Implicit in the foregoing are the ideas that class is an abstraction from a complex reality, that in all probability power, privilege, and prestige are continuously distributed in society, and that it is an oversimplification to speak of any given number of social classes. It is often useful, nevertheless, to deal in oversimplifications. For some purposes, Marx's division of society into a bourgeoisie and a proletariat is an adequate approximation to reality; for other purposes, the poll-takers' division of the population into upper, middle, and lower classes is sufficient.

For convenience, we temporarily adopt an oversimplified model, one implicit in most research on social class and family relationships in the United States. This model conceives of society as divided into four relatively discrete classes: a "lower class" of unskilled manual workers, a "working class" of manual workers in semiskilled and skilled occupations, a "middle class" of white-collar workers and professionals, and an "elite," differentiated from the middle class not so much in terms of occupation as of wealth and lineage. The middle class can be thought of as comprising two distinguishable segments:

---

[10]For an alternative approach that deliberately limits analyses of class to a single dimension—power—see Dahrendorf, 1959.

an upper-middle class of professionals, proprietors, and managers, who generally have at least some college training, and a lower-middle class of small shopkeepers, clerks, and salespersons, generally with less education.

The sampling methods of the Washington and Turin studies require that we use some such model. Since we do not have data for the entire range of social classes, we must have descriptive terms for part of the range—the working and middle classes. But with the data of the National study, we shall show that it is actually more fruitful to think of a continuous distribution of power, privilege, and prestige.

INDICES OF CLASS

In both American studies, social class position has been indexed by Hollingshead's two-factor "Index of Social Position," a weighted combination of occupational position and education.[11] In the Italian study, Hollingshead's classification of occupational position was used alone, for occupational levels in Italy are quite comparable to those in the United States, but educational levels are not (see Appendix B).

In the Washington study, our sampling methods were designed to exclude the highest and lowest socioeconomic strata (see Appendix A). Thus, most of the families fall naturally into the second, third, and fourth of the five socioeconomic levels into which Hollingshead divides the population. In analyzing these data, we consider the first three of Hollingshead's levels to be middle class and the remaining two to be working class. (Dividing the Washington sample into the middle and the working class by this procedure results in virtually

[11]Hollingshead classifies occupational positions into seven categories, education into another set of seven categories, then weights the occupational scores by seven and the educational scores by four, adds the two, and finally divides the resulting composite scores into five socioeconomic levels.

The major occupational categories are: (1) Higher executives, proprietors of large concerns, and major professionals. (2) Business managers, proprietors of medium-sized businesses, and lesser professionals. (3) Administrative personnel, proprietors of small independent businesses, and minor professionals. (4) Clerical and sales workers, technicians, and owners of little businesses. (5) Skilled manual employees. (6) Machine operators and semiskilled employees. (7) Unskilled employees.

The educational categories are: (1) Professionally trained. (2) College graduate. (3) Some college. (4) High school graduate. (5) 10-11 years of school, some high school. (6) 7-9 years of school, approximately grade school graduate. (7) Less than 7 years of school, approximately some grade school.

Hollingshead has not, to our knowledge, published his detailed occupational classification, but it has been included in a compilation of sociological indices by Bonjean, *et al.*, 1967: 441-448. See also Hollingshead and Redlich, 1958: 387-397.

the same dichotomization of the sample as if we used the U.S. Census classification of occupations—treating professionals, proprietors, clerks, and salesmen as middle class; foremen, skilled, semiskilled, and unskilled workers as working class.)

It must be emphasized that the working-class sample is composed preponderantly of stable working class rather than of lower class families—in the sense that the men have steady jobs, and that their education, income, and skill levels are above those of the lowest socioeconomic stratum.

Since the Turin study was designed to be comparable to the Washington study, it too excludes the highest and lowest socioeconomic strata. Thus, a similar dichotomization of the sample into a working class and a middle class is appropriate, with the dividing line falling between blue- and white-collar workers.

In the National study, the sample is representative of the class distribution of the United States, excluding only the unemployed (see Appendix C). Here, we can and do talk of the full range of social classes. In this usage, we treat Hollingshead's division of the population into five classes as having no substantive importance, as being simply a convenient (but for our purposes, arbitrary) approximation to a continuous distribution.

ADEQUACY OF THE HOLLINGSHEAD INDEX

There are two primary issues that must be considered in evaluating the adequacy of the Hollingshead index of social class. One is the justification for basing an index of class on education and occupational position. This issue can best be pursued later when we examine their separate effects on values and orientation and see if anything has been lost by leaving out income and subjective class identification.

The other issue is the adequacy of Hollingshead's particular classification of occupational position. His classification is a modification of Edwards's system (1938), long used by the U.S. Census. Hollingshead made a number of useful changes, two principal ones being to distinguish among various professions that are combined in the Census, and to classify businesses according to their size. On the face of it, Hollingshead's changes are entirely appropriate for research on social class and are a considerable improvement on the original.

To validate his classification, Hollingshead conducted a survey of 522 households in New Haven, Connecticut, collecting detailed information on the full range of socioeconomic characteristics of each family (cf. Hollingshead and Redlich, 1958: 387-397). Then he and another sociologist, Jerome Myers, independently rated each family on a five-point scale—having previously decided that the New Haven community could most accurately be thought of as comprising five social classes. They agreed 96 percent of the time, indicating that, whatever the basis of their judgment, it was reliable.

The correlation of the family's class position, as judged by Hollingshead and Myers, to the head of household's occupational score was 0.88, sufficiently high to indicate that the two indices were measuring much the same thing. (The multiple correlation of occupational position and education with class position is a bit higher, 0.91, which is why Hollingshead decided to include education in his index of class.) Thus, one can conclude that Hollingshead's classification of occupations is a good indication of how knowledgeable sociologists, having very complete data at their disposal, would judge men's social class positions. The occupational classification is as valid (or nearly as valid) as is informed sociological judgment.

An alternative approach to validating an index of occupational position is to rely, not on the judgment of sociologists, but on the judgments of society at large. Ever since the National Opinion Research Center (NORC) study of 1946, we have known that there is remarkable agreement in people's judgments about the relative prestige of occupations (Hatt, 1950; North and Hatt, 1953; Reiss, *et al.*, 1961; Gusfield and Schwartz, 1963). Moreover, these judgments are quite stable over time (Hodge, *et al.*, 1964) and differ little from country to country (Inkeles and Rossi, 1956; Tiryakian, 1958; Svalastoga, 1959: 60-68, 79-102; Thomas, 1962; Hodge, *et al.*, 1966; Haller and Lewis, 1966).

Several investigators have used these facts as the basis for constructing scales of occupational position. Each of them started with the occupations that had been included in the 1946 study, and by one or another method interpolated scores for the many occupations that had not been included. Until recently, though, there has been no well-justified basis for such interpolations. Duncan (1961a, b) solved this problem by demonstrating a high multiple correlation between the prestige of those occupations that had been included in the 1946 survey, and the educational and income levels of the corresponding U.S. Census occupational categories.[12] By using the appropriate weights from that multiple correlation, he assigned scores to the many occupations in the Census listing that had not been included in the survey.

The difficulty is that Duncan's method is dependent on the sometimes imprecise distinctions employed in the Census classification (cf. Hodge and Siegel, 1966). We would prefer to use Hollingshead's more precise distinctions. Fortunately, the correlation between Duncan's and Hollingshead's classifications (in a random sample of 90 men in the National study) is 0.89, high enough to conclude that they are measuring essentially the same thing. [13] Furthermore, where the two indices differ, the disparity generally results from Duncan's use of one of the grosser Census categories; the Hollingshead measure almost always seems more appropriate. We thus retain Hollingshead's classification of occupational position, in effect having validated it against Duncan's conceptually well-buttressed but less precise alternative.

For now, we leave the discussion with the conclusion that Hollingshead's Index is an appropriate measure with which to begin the research. We recognize that some important issues remain to be dealt with: How much do the various dimensions of class contribute to the effects we credit to class? Are the dimensions of class consistent with one another? Is it more realistic to conceive of discrete classes or of a socioeconomic continuum? Although these fundamental issues cannot be completely resolved empirically, there are some highly relevant facts that we shall bring into the discussion later. It is sufficient at this point that we have a sound basis for the use of the Hollingshead Index as our measure of class.

Accordingly, we are free to turn to the first major substantive question—what is the relationship of social class to parental values?

---

[12]Forty-five occupations in the NORC list have close equivalents in the U.S. Census classification of occupations. Using these 45 occupations, Duncan showed that the multiple correlation of the age-adjusted educational and income levels of their members to the prestige of the occupations (as measured by the NORC data) is 0.91. This is high enough to provide an eminently reasonable basis for interpolation.

In calculating educational and income levels for the occupations, Duncan found it efficacious to use measures more sensitive to extremes than the median or other measures of central tendency—specifically, the proportion of men in each occupation who are high school graduates and the proportion reporting incomes of $3,500 or more in 1949.

[13]This result is hardly surprising, since both systems are based on Edwards's classification. Moreover, it has been known for some time that most currently used measures of socioeconomic status are highly intercorrelated (cf. Kahl and Davis, 1955).

CHAPTER 2

Social Class and Parental Values — The Washington Study

Despite its importance to social policies and to sociological theory, there has been relatively little empirical study of values,[1] even less on the relationship of social stratification to values,[2] and almost none on the relationship of class to parental values.

Prior to the present research, only two studies (of which we know) had dealt explicitly with the relationship of social class to parental values. The Lynds, in their now-classic community study, *Middletown,* asked mothers to "score a list of fifteen habits according to their emphases upon them in training their children" and discovered that working-class mothers put greater emphasis on obedience than do mothers of higher social class position (1929: 143). Some 17 years later, Duvall (1946) characterized working-class (and lower middle-class) mothers' values as "traditional"—these mothers want their children to be neat and clean, to obey and respect adults, to please adults. In contrast to this emphasis on how the child comports himself, middle-class mothers' values are more "developmental"— they want their children to be eager to learn, to love and confide in the parents, to be happy, to share and cooperate, to be healthy and well. Duvall's traditional-developmental dichotomy does not describe the difference between middle- and working-class parental values quite exactly, but it does point to the essence of the difference, a concern with external conformity or with internal process.

----

[1]Among the relatively few empirical studies, some of the most notable are cross-cultural studies that have much in common with our social class comparisons (cf. Kluckhohn and Strodtbeck, 1961; Caudill and Scarr, 1962).

[2]One of the most important studies is Hyman's (1953) provocative reanalysis of a number of public opinion polls that had been conducted in various parts of the Western world. Most relevant is his conclusion that lower-class individuals, in effect, erect barriers to their own upward mobility by holding values that de-emphasize both success and the traditional ladders to success, especially education.

It is our purpose to pursue the problem posed by the Lynds and Duvall—to study the relationship of social class to parental values —and then to see what implications class differences in parental values might have for child-rearing practices. But before we can carry out such studies it is necessary to have an adequate index of parental values. This, in turn, requires that we be clear about what we mean by the concept, "value."

☀ DEFINING AND INDEXING PARENTAL VALUES

We conceive of values as standards of desirability—criteria of preference. Our conception of value is close to that proposed by Williams (1968: 283):

. . . we look first to the common features of all value phenomena. It seems that all values contain some congnitive elements (although some definitions do not include this), that they have a selective or directional quality, and that they involve some affective component. Values serve as criteria for selection in action. When most explicit and fully conceptualized, values become criteria for judgment, preference, and choice. When implicit and unreflective, values nevertheless perform *as if* they constituted grounds for decisions in behavior. Men do prefer some things to others; they do select one course of action rather than another out of a range of possibilities; they do judge the conduct of other men. . . .

In ordinary speech the term "value" is used interchangeably in two senses that must be kept separate here. In one meaning, we refer to the specific *evaluation* of any object, as in "industrialized countries place a high value on formal education" or "governmental regulation is worthless." Here we are told how an object is rated or otherwise appraised, but not what standards are used to make the judgments. The second meaning of value refers to the *criteria, or standards in terms* of which evaluations are made, as in "education is good because it increases economic efficiency." Value-as-criterion is usually the more important usage for purposes of social scientific analysis.

By parental values we mean the values that parents would most like to see embodied in their children's behavior—the characteristics they consider most desirable to inculcate in their children.

How does one measure parental values? No approach is completely satisfactory. To ask people to tell us their values is obviously subject to the risk that they may not really know or at any rate may not be able to formulate them in terms that we shall understand; moreover, they may not wish to be altogether frank. But inferring values from observed behavior may not be satisfactory either, for we cannot be certain that we are correctly distinguishing the normative from other components of action. Actions may deceive as well as words; one often misinterprets people's intent.

Our solution, in the Washington study, was to take the most straightforwardly naive course—to *ask* parents what they value—and then to subject their assertions to critical examination. Instead of simply assuming that their stated values matter for their behavior, we shall go on to see whether or not these values bear a meaningful relationship to how they act.

From the preceding discussion, it is clear that a central manifestation of value is to be found in *choice*. It tells us little to know merely that a parent values honesty for his child; the critical question is whether he values honesty more or less than self-control, or obedience, or some other valued characteristic. It is also clear that if we are to make valid comparisons of middle- to working-class parental values, the index of values must put no premium upon articulateness or imagination, which may be primarily reflective of formal education.

Both considerations can be satisfied by the device of presenting all parents with a list of characteristics known to be generally valued and asking them to choose those few that they value most of all. This we did. The list was compiled from the suggestions made by parents interviewed during the development and pretesting of the interview schedule. In those interviews we searched for any and all characteristics the parents thought desirable for their 10- or 11-year-old children. The 17 that seemed most generally valued by parents having children of this age were:

That he is honest.	That he is a good student.
That he is happy.	That he is neat and clean.
That he is considerate of others.	That he is curious about things.
That he obeys his parents well.	That he is ambitious.
That he is dependable.	That he is able to defend himself.
That he has good manners.	That he is affectionate.
That he has self-control.	That he is liked by adults.
That he is popular with other children.	That he is able to play by himself.
	That he acts in a serious way.

From this list, the parents were asked to choose the three characteristics that they considered to be the most important in a boy or girl of their fifth-grader's age. (Here, as throughout the interview, parents were asked the questions with reference to a specific child, the fifth-grader. If that child was a boy, we asked about the characteristics most desirable for a boy of his age; if a girl, we asked about the characteristics most desirable for a girl of her age.)

This, then, is the index of parental values: the choice of 3 of these characteristics as more desirable than the other 14 for a 10- or 11-year-old boy or girl. Later, we shall subject the index to closer scrutiny. But first, let us see what it yields. Do middle- and working-class parents assert different values for their children? We turn to the data of the Washington study for an answer.

CLASS AND VALUES

Middle- and working-class mothers share a common, but by no means identical, set of values (Table 2-1). There is considerable

TABLE 2-1
Mothers' Values, by Social Class and Sex of Child

	For Boys		For Girls		Combined	
	Middle Class	Working Class	Middle Class	Working Class	Middle Class	Working Class
Proportion who value:						
That he is honest	.44	.57	.44	.48	.44	.53
That he is happy	.44 *	.27	.48	.45	.46 *	.36
That he is considerate of others	.40	.30	.38 *	.24	.39 *	.27
That he obeys his parents well	.18 *	.37	.23	.30	.20 *	.33
That he is dependable	.27	.27	.20	.14	.24	.21
That he has good manners .	.16	.17	.23	.32	.19	.24
That he has self-control . . .	.24	.14	.20	.13	.22 *	.13
That he is popular with other children	.13	.15	.17	.20	.15	.18
That he is a good student .	.17	.23	.13	.11	.15	.17
That he is neat and clean . .	.07	.13	.15 *	.28	.11 *	.20
That he is curious about things	.20 *	.06	.15	.07	.18 *	.06
That he is ambitious	.09	.18	.06	.08	.07	.13
That he is able to defend himself	.13	.05	.06	.08	.10	.06
That he is affectionate . . .	.03	.05	.07	.04	.05	.04
That he is liked by adults .	.03	.05	.07	.04	.05	.04
That he is able to play by himself	.01	.02	.00	.03	.01	.02
That he acts in a serious way	.00	.01	.00	.00	.00	.01
Number of cases . . .	(90)	(85)	(84)	(80)	(174)	(165)

* Social-class differences statistically significant, $p < 0.05$, using the t test for the difference between two proportions.

agreement in what is highly valued in the two social classes. In both classes, happiness and such standards of conduct as honesty, consideration, obedience, dependability, manners, and self-control are most highly ranked for both boys and girls of this age. Standards of conduct outrank all other requisites except happiness.

Although there is agreement on this broad level, middle-class mothers differ from working-class mothers in which of these values they emphasize.[3] Middle-class mothers give higher priority to values that reflect *internal dynamics*—the child's own and his empathic concern for other people's. Specifically, they are significantly[4] more likely than are working-class mothers to value happiness (in particular, for sons), consideration, self-control, and curiosity. Working-class mothers, by contrast, give higher priority to values that reflect *behavioral conformity*—obedience and neatness.

It must be repeated that the class differences are variations on a common theme, most of the highest rated values reflecting respect for the rights of others. The middle-class variant focuses on the internal processes of self-direction and empathic understanding,

---

[3]The mode of analysis we use here is to focus on *differences* in the proportions of middle- and working-class mothers who choose each characteristic. The *absolute* proportions are so much a function of how we asked the question that they have no clearly interpretable meaning. (Had we asked parents to choose 12 of the 17 characteristics, the proportions would have been higher, had we asked them to choose only 1, the proportions would have been correspondingly lower. In fact, less than half of the sample chose even the most heavily-endorsed item, less than a fifth chose the median item.)

The *magnitude of the difference* in the proportions of middle- and working-class parents who endorse any item must also be viewed in light of the restricted choices. A 10 or 15 percent difference is more impressive if only 20 or 30 percent of the sample choose an item. To be safe, we focus on the question of whether or not any given difference is statistically significant, leaving an assessment of the magnitude of the differences for later chapters, when we shall have less restrictive data with which to work. (But see Johnsen and Leslie, 1965: 350-352.)

[4]For the sake of those readers who have no special interest in methods of statistical analysis, we shall wherever possible relegate information about statistical procedures, levels of confidence, and the like to footnotes, where they can be ignored by the uninterested and read by the concerned.

Except where explicitly indicated, all findings discussed in this book are statistically significant at the 0.05 level of confidence or better. Of course, the fact that a finding is statistically significant does not necessarily make it socially important; in the National study, with its large sample, many trivial findings are statistically significant at levels of confidence much more impressive than 0.05. That a finding is *not* statistically significant, on the other hand, does not make it unimportant. We take the conservative position, though, that when a finding is not significant at the 0.05 level or better, one is well advised to treat it with extreme caution, no matter how well it fits one's preconceptions.

The tests of statistical significance used in this chapter are chi-squared (and its equivalent, the *t* test for the difference between two proportions) and, where there are few cases in a comparison, Fisher's exact test.

while the working-class variant focuses on conformity to externally defined standards.

The difference between the classes is illustrated anew by the sex distinctions mothers do or do not make. Middle-class mothers' conceptions of the desirable are much the same for boys and for girls. But working-class mothers distinguish between the sexes: They are more likely to regard dependability, school performance, and ambition as important for boys, and to regard happiness, neatness and cleanliness, and good manners as important for girls. We think this difference in mothers making or not making a sex distinction reflects the differential emphasis on self-direction and behavioral conformity. If the focus is internal dynamics, the same values should apply to boys and to girls. But if the focus is externally imposed standards, then what is appropriate for boys is different from what is appropriate for girls. Working-class mothers draw precise distinctions between what is behaviorally proper for boys and for girls; these distinctions are irrelevant to middle-class mothers.

As for fathers: Judging from our small sample of 82 fathers, their values are similar to those of mothers (Table 2-2). Essentially the same rank order of choices holds for fathers as for mothers, with one exception—fathers rank daughters' happiness lower than do mothers. Moreover, among fathers, too, consideration and self-control are more highly valued in the middle class, and obedience is more highly valued in the working class. There are two additional class differences for fathers: Dependability is more highly regarded in the middle class, and the ability to defend oneself, in the working class.

The question of whether or not working-class fathers make the same sex distinctions that mothers do must be answered equivocally, for our sample of working-class fathers of girls is very small. There are no statistically significant differences, but with so small a sample, that is hardly definitive.

In any event, the class differences in fathers' values are consistent with those in mothers' values. We take this to indicate that middle-class parents (fathers as well as mothers) are more likely to ascribe predominant importance to children's acting on the basis of internal standards of conduct, while working-class parents ascribe greater importance to compliance with parental authority.[5]

---

[5]Compare this conclusion to Bronfenbrenner's (1958: 423): "In this modern working class world there may be greater freedom of emotional expression, but there is no laxity or vagueness with respect to goals of child training. Consistently over the past twenty-five

TABLE 2-2
Fathers' Values, by Social Class and Sex of Child

	For Boys		For Girls		Combined	
	Middle Class	Working Class	Middle Class	Working Class	Middle Class	Working Class
Proportion who value:						
That he is honest	.60	.60	.43	.55	.52	.58
That he is happy	.48	.24	.24	.18	.37	.22
That he is considerate of others	.32	.16	.38	.09	.35 *	.14
That he obeys his parents well	.12 *	.40	.14	.36	.13 *	.39
That he is dependable	.36 *	.12	.29	.00	.33 *	.08
That he has good manners .	.24	.28	.24	.18	.24	.25
That he has self-control ...	.20	.08	.19	.00	.20 *	.06
That he is popular with other children	.08	.16	.24	.45	.15	.25
That he is a good student .	.04	.12	.10	.36	.07	.19
That he is neat and clean ..	.16	.20	.14	.09	.15	.17
That he is curious about things	.16	.12	.10	.00	.13	.08
That he is ambitious	.20	.12	.14	.00	.17	.08
That he is able to defend himself	.04	.16	.00	.18	.02 *	.17
That he is affectionate ...	.00	.04	.05	.18	.02	.08
That he is liked by adults .	.00	.08	.00	.09	.00	.08
That he is able to play by himself	.00	.08	.05	.00	.02	.06
That he acts in a serious way	.00	.04	.00	.00	.00	.03
Number of cases ...	(25)	(25)	(21)	(11)	(46)	(36)

* Social-class differences statistically significant, $p < 0.05$, using the t test for the difference between two proportions or, where the number of cases is small, Fisher's exact test.

But what does it mean to say that parents ascribe predominant importance to one value over another? We have found, for example, that working-class parents value neatness and cleanliness more highly than do middle-class parents. Offhand, this seems strange, for neatness and cleanliness are such stereotypically middle-class values. Perhaps middle-class parents simply take them for granted.

The issue is central to any effort at measuring values. In essence, the argument is that middle-class parents think neatness and cleanliness are important,[6] but not as problematic as some other

years, the parent in this group has emphasized what are usually regarded as the traditional middle class virtues of cleanliness, conformity, and [parental] control, and although his methods are not so effective as those of his middle class neighbors, they are perhaps more desperate."

[6]It is not crucial to the argument, but it may well be that middle-class parents do not

values. In the circumstances of middle-class life, neatness and cleanliness are easily enough attained to be of less immediate concern than are other values. (Conversely, working-class mothers may be less likely than middle-class mothers to value happiness for their sons, not because they think it less important that their sons be happy, but because other concerns are more pressing.) Parents rate values, not only in terms of intrinsic desirability, but also in terms of how problematic is their realization.

To put the matter more generally, we believe that there are two main elements in people's ratings of values. One element is their judgment of *intrinsic importance*—which essentially means their judgment of where any given value would rank in a hierarchy of values if all other relevant considerations were equal. Second is their judgment of the *probability of realization* of the value—if it is 100 percent certain of attainment, it will be rated down in comparison to values whose attainment is problematic.

Parents are most likely to accord high priority to those values that seem important, in that failure to achieve them would affect the children's futures adversely, and problematic, in that they are difficult to achieve. Our index of parental values measures conceptions of the *important, but problematic*. In judging what is important but problematic, middle-class parents give higher priority to children's acting on the basis of internal standards of conduct, while working-class parents give higher priority to their conforming to parental authority.

AN APPRAISAL OF THE INDEX OF VALUES

Before accepting these findings, we must ask whether they mean what they seem to mean. These questions must be answered: Is the list of 17 values sufficiently comprehensive? If not, our findings might overemphasize the importance of some values simply because more highly rated alternatives were not made available to the parents. Is it possible for parents to make value-choices independently of their appraisals of their own children's strengths and

---

think that neatness and cleanliness are as important as do working-class parents. Our unsystematic observations in the homes we visited suggested that, by and large, the working-class children were dressed more neatly. This was particularly true of the girls—the working-class girls were turned out in spotlessly clean starched dresses, the middle-class girls in not quite so clean and certainly not so starched blue jeans.

weaknesses? If not, our findings might reflect class (and sex) differences in children's behavior. Do the words used to describe the values have the same meaning for middle- and working-class parents? If not, some apparent differences (and some apparent similarities) might be deceptive.

The form in which the question on values was asked set the same ground rules for all parents. No premium was put on imaginativeness or articulateness. But limiting parents' choice to these particular characteristics meant that we denied them the opportunity to select others that they might have regarded as even more desirable. However, we had previously asked each parent: "When you think of a boy (or girl) of (child's) age, are there any things that you look for as most important or most desirable?" Only three additional characteristics were suggested by more than a handful of parents.

The first, suggested by a larger proportion of middle- than of working-class parents, was self-reliance or independence—a result entirely consistent with the rest of this study. The second, variously labeled friendliness, cooperativeness, or ability to get along well with others was also primarily a middle-class concern. It indicates that we may have underrepresented middle-class parents' valuation of children's ability to relate to others. Finally, several parents (of both social classes) said that they considered it desirable that the child not act too old, too young, nor be effeminate (in a boy) or masculine (in a girl). There seems to be a certain concern, not adequately indexed by our question, that the child conform to the appropriate age and sex role.

Of course, parents might have selected other characteristics as well, had we suggested them. These possible limitations notwithstanding, it appears that the index is reasonably comprehensive.

More important than the question of comprehensiveness is whether it is really possible for parents to select characteristics as desirable independently of the way that they rate their own children's behavior. Fortunately, we can check out this possibility. Each parent was later asked to *rate his own child's performance with respect to each characteristic*—which means that we can compare the ratings given by parents who chose a particular characteristic with those given by parents of the same social class who did not choose it. Parents who chose each characteristic were no more and no less likely to describe their children as excelling in that characteristic; nor were they any more or less likely than other parents to feel that their children were deficient. Evidently, the parents did not impute desirability to the characteristics that they felt represented their children's strengths or deficiencies. Values are independent of estimates of children's performance.

The final question about the index of values is the most difficult to answer. Do these rather abstract words—honesty, consideration, curiosity—have different meanings for middle- and working-class parents?

The possibility is real, and there are two ways of coping with it. First, we tried through intensive preliminary interviews (before the survey was launched) to select words whose meaning was as invariant as could be found. Insofar as we failed to find invariant terms, the remaining variations are instructive. Here we have an opportunity to study differences in parents' conceptions of what these words mean, and thereby to learn something more about values. The method we use is to search for class differences in how the choice of any one characteristic is related to the choice of each of the others.[7] This

---

[7]A logical procedure for examining these patterns of choice is to compare the proportions of parents who choose any given characteristic, B, among those who do and who do not choose another characteristic, A. Since a parent who selects characteristic A has exhausted one of his three choices, the a priori probability of his selecting any other characteristic is only two thirds as great as the probability that a parent who has not chosen A will do so. (A straightforward application of probability considerations to the problem of selecting 3 things from 17 when one is interested only in the joint occurrence of 2, say, A and B, shows that we can expect B to occur 2/16 of the time among those selections containing A and 3/16 of the time among those not containing A.) This, however, can be taken into account by computing the ratio of the two proportions: p_1, the proportion of parents who choose B among those who choose A, and p_2, the proportion who choose B among those who do *not* choose A. If the ratio of these proportions (p_1/p_2) is significantly larger than two thirds, the two are positively related; if significantly smaller, they are negatively related.

The test of statistical significance is based on the confidence interval on a ratio, originally given by Fieller, with the modification that we deal here with the ratio of two independent proportions whose variances under the null hypothesis (chance) are known and whose distribution we assume to be normal. The 95 percent confidence interval on the true ratio, R, of the two proportions, p_1 and p_2, that hold for any given A and B, is given by:

$$R = \frac{r \pm (1/8p_2) \sqrt{(28/n_1) + (39r^2/n_2) - [(28 \times 39)/64n_1 n_2 p_2^2]}}{[1 - (39/64n_2 p_2^2)]}$$

where p_1 and p_2 are the observed sample proportions, $r = p_1/p_2$, n_1 = the number of persons selecting A, and n_2 = the number of persons who do not select A.

The logic of the testing procedure is as follows: If the interval contains the null hypothesis value of $R = 2/3$ implied by chance selection, then we assume no association between B and A. If the interval excludes 2/3 such that the lower limit is larger than 2/3, we conclude that the true R is greater than we expect on the basis of randomness and hence that B is positively associated with A. On the other hand, if the upper limit of the interval is smaller than 2/3, then we conclude that the true R is smaller than 2/3 and hence B and A are negatively related. *(Footnote Continues.)*

analysis is limited to the mothers, for the sample of fathers is too small.

The main thing we learn is that *honesty,* the highest ranked value for parents of both social classes, has quite different associations with the other value-choices in the middle and working classes (Table 2-3). For middle-class mothers, honesty appears to be at the core of one or more sets of standards by which the child should govern his behavior.[8] That is, the choice of honesty is positively related to the choice of other standards for behavior (consideration, dependability, and manners), and negatively related to the choice of popularity. For working-class mothers, though, honesty is associated with characteristics that represent, not standards for behavior, but the enjoyment of good fortune. Although the choice of honesty is positively related to the choice of manners (albeit not as strongly as in the middle class), it is not related to the choice of consideration or dependability. It is, however, positively related to the choice of popularity and of happiness, and negatively related to valuing the child's being a good student. Although both middle- and working-class mothers are very likely to value honesty, this apparent similarity masks a real difference in values.

The relationship between the choice of honesty and of popularity is noteworthy, for the two are related negatively in the middle class and positively in the working class. Moreover, honesty is the only standard of behavior that is positively related to working-class mothers' choice of popularity; such other standards as obedience, manners, and neatness are all negatively related to popularity. The implication is that working-class mothers see honesty less as a specific standard for behavior and more as a general attribute of the person.

There are a few other things one can learn from this method of analysis, despite the diminishing number of statistically significant relationships as one deals with less frequently chosen characteristics. One such additional item of information is that valuing curiosity is positively associated with valuing happiness in the middle class, but not in the working class. Another finding is that obedience seems

---

This procedure was suggested by Samuel W. Greenhouse. For the derivation of the test see Fieller, 1944; Sukhatme, 1954: 158-160.

[8]Honesty may be at the core of two distinguishable sets of standards—one consisting of honesty, consideration, dependability, and self-control; the other of honesty, manners, and neatness. (The choice of consideration is positively related to the choice of self-control, and the choice of manners tends to go with a choice of neatness; but manners and dependability appear to be negatively related.)

TABLE 2-3
The Relationship Between Mothers' Valuation of One Characteristic and Their Valuation of Other Characteristics[a]

Characteristic B	Middle-Class Mothers Characteristic A								Working-Class Mothers Characteristic A							
	Honesty	Happiness	Consideration	Obedience	Dependability	Manners	Self-Control	Popularity	Honesty	Happiness	Consideration	Obedience	Dependability	Manners	Self-Control	Popularity
Honesty	–	.00	.45*	.05	.38*	.54*	.16	-.43*	–	.26*	.08	-.05	.18	.26*	-.03	.55*
Happiness	.00	–	-.04	.02	-.10	.00	-.05	.33*	.22*	–	.02	.01	-.22	-.18	.22	.42*
Consideration	.47*	-.07	–	-.29*	.02	-.11	.38*	-.12	.02	-.01	–	.00	.08	.41	-.03	-.58*
Obedience	.00	-.04	-.34*	–	-.24	.59	-.08	-.12	-.12	-.01	.02	–	.07	.30	.27	-.41*
Dependability	.42*	-.19	.00	-.26	–	-.46*	.05	-.07	.11	-.29	.06	.03	–	-.35	.19	-.24
Manners	.71*	-.06	-.17	.61	-.45	–	-.31	-.29	.21	-.20	.37	.29	-.35	–	-.34	-.67*
Self-control	.09	-.15	.42*	-.09	.04	-.32	–	-.04	-.17	.19	-.07	.26	.19	-.36	–	-.04
Popularity	-.50*	.33	-.20	-.14	-.08	-.32	-.04	–	.76*	.45	-.58*	-.46*	-.22	-.67*	.11	–
Good student	-.14	-.14	-.20	.76	.54	-.50	.14	.08	-.37*	-.31	.27	.16	.39	.05	.15	.64
Neatness	-.42	.02	-.24	.33	-.53	2.33*	-.29	.06	-.09	-.02	-.19	.33	-.42	.54	.00	.00
Curiosity	-.25	.97*	-.05	-.53*	.51	-.44	-.17	.16	-.59	-.29	2.08	-.10	1.73	-.24	.16	-.67
N_1[b] =	(77)	(80)	(68)	(35)	(41)	(33)	(39)	(26)	(88)	(59)	(44)	(55)	(34)	(40)	(22)	(29)
N_2 =	(97)	(94)	(106)	(139)	(133)	(141)	(135)	(148)	(77)	(106)	(121)	(110)	(131)	(125)	(143)	(136)

* Indicates $p < 0.05$, using Fieller's test (cf. footnote 7).

[a] Entries represent $p_1/p_2 - 0.67$, where p_1 is the proportion of mothers who choose characteristic B among those who choose characteristic A, p_2 is the proportion who choose characteristic B among those who do not choose characteristic A, and 0.67 is the value of p_1/p_2 under the null hypothesis.

[b] N_1 refers to the number of mothers who choose characteristic A, N_2 to the number of mothers who do not.

inconsistent with curiosity and consideration—for middle-class mothers, but not for working-class mothers. Working-class mothers do, however, see some conflict between obedience to parents and respect from peers.

Our conclusion is that class differences in parental values are not just an artifact of different meanings attributed to the concepts by middle- and working-class parents. On the contrary, the more we learn about the probable differences in middle- and working-class parents' conceptions of what the words mean, the more impressive do the differences in their values seem to be.

CLASS, ITS COMPONENTS AND ITS CORRELATES

In discussing the relationships of social class to values we have talked as if American society were composed of two relatively homogeneous groupings, manual and white-collar workers, together with their families. Yet it is likely that there is considerable variation in values, associated with other bases of social differentiation, within each class. If so, it should be possible to differentiate the classes in such a way as to specify more precisely the relationships of social class to values.

Class and Status

Consider, first, the use we have made of the concept, social class. Are the differences we have found between the values of middle- and working-class mothers a product of this dichotomy alone, or do values parallel class gradations more generally? Given the method of sample selection used in this study, only an approximate answer can be given; our samples from the highest and lowest of Hollingshead's five classes are inadequate. Tentatively, we conclude that variations in mothers' values (there are too few fathers to do a comparable analysis for them) parallel their socioeconomic levels rather closely. The *higher* a mother's socioeconomic status, the higher the probability that she will choose consideration, curiosity, self-control, and happiness as highly desirable. The *lower* her status, the higher the probability that she will select obedience, and neatness and cleanliness; it appears, too, that mothers in the lowest stratum are more likely than are those in the highest to value honesty (Table 2-4).

The Hollingshead Index, of course, is based on the husband's occupational and educational status. Mothers' values are also directly

TABLE 2-4
Mothers' Values, by Socioeconomic Level

	Socioeconomic Level				
	1	2	3	4	5
Proportion of mothers who value:					
Obedience	.14	.19	.25	.35	.27
Neatness, cleanliness	.06	.07	.16	.18	.27
Consideration	.41	.37	.39	.25	.32
Curiosity	.37	.12	.09	.07	.03
Self-control	.24	.30	.18	.13	.14
Happiness	.61	.40	.40	.38	.30
Honesty	.37	.49	.46	.50	.65
Number of cases	(51)	(43)	(80)	(128)	(37)

related to their own occupational positions and educational attainments, whatever their families' class status.

Even in families classified as working class (on the basis of the husband's occupation and education) a considerable proportion of the mothers hold white-collar jobs. Those who do are closer to middle-class mothers in their values than are other working-class mothers (Table 2-5). And those who hold manual jobs are further from middle-class mothers in their values than are working-class mothers who do not have jobs outside the home.[9]

TABLE 2-5
Mothers' Values, by Own Occupation
(working class only)

	White-Collar Job	No Job	Manual Job
Proportion of mothers who value:			
Obedience	.26	.35	.53
Neatness, cleanliness	.16	.18	.42
Consideration	.39	.21	.05
Curiosity	.10	.04	.00
Self-control	.13	.14	.11
Happiness	.33	.40	.26
Number of cases	(69)	(77)	(19)

---

[9]No middle-class mothers have manual jobs, so the comparable situation does not exist. Those middle-class women who do work (at white-collar jobs) are less likely to value neatness and cleanliness and more likely to value obedience and curiosity than are other middle-class mothers.

The mothers' own educational attainments matter, too. In both social classes, the more educated mothers are more likely to value consideration, curiosity, self-control, and happiness; the less educated are more likely to value obedience, and neatness and cleanliness (Table 2-6). Many of the differences are not statistically significant, because the numbers of cases are small, but almost all are consistent. At the extremes are the middle-class mothers of highest educational attainments and the working-class mothers of lowest educational attainments.

Thus, even when we restrict ourselves to considerations of social status and its various ramifications, we find that values vary

TABLE 2-6
Mothers' Values, by Social Class, Mothers' Education, and Sex of Child

	Middle-Class Mothers					
	For Boys		For Girls		Combined	
	At Least Some College	High School Graduate or Less	At Least Some College	High School Graduate or Less	At Least Some College	High School Graduate or Less
Proportion who value:						
Obedience	.11	.22	.13	.29	.12 *	.25
Neatness, cleanliness .	.03	.09	.03 *	.23	.03 *	.16
Consideration	.47	.35	.41	.37	.44	.36
Curiosity	.31 *	.13	.31 *	.06	.31 *	.09
Self-control	.33	.19	.19	.21	.26	.20
Happiness	.50	.41	.59	.40	.54	.41
Number of cases .	(36)	(54)	(32)	(52)	(68)	(106)

	Working-Class Mothers					
	For Boys		For Girls		Combined	
	At Least High School Graduate	Less than High School Graduate	At Least High School Graduate	Less than High School Graduate	At Least High School Graduate	Less than High School Graduate
Obedience	.29	.43	.28	.32	.29	.38
Neatness, cleanliness .	.12	.14	.21	.35	.17	.23
Consideration	.32	.27	.33 *	.14	.32	.21
Curiosity	.07	.05	.12 *	.00	.10 *	.02
Self-control	.22 *	.07	.16	.08	.19 *	.07
Happiness	.27	.27	.47	.43	.37	.35
Number of cases .	(41)	(44)	(43)	(37)	(84)	(81)

* Difference between mothers of differing educational status statistically significant, $p < 0.05$, using the t test for the difference between two proportions.

appreciably within each of the two broad classes. And, as one would expect, variation in values proceeds along other major lines of social demarcation as well.

Other Major Lines of Social Demarcation

Religious background is particularly appropriate as a criterion for distinguishing relatively distinct groups within the social classes. It is not so highly related to values that Protestant mothers differ significantly from Catholic mothers of the same social class (Table 2-7). (Even when the comparison is restricted to Catholic mothers whose children attend Catholic school versus Protestant mothers of the same social class, there are no significant differences.)

TABLE 2-7
Mothers' Values, by Social Class and Religious Background

	Middle-Class Protestant	Middle-Class Catholic	Working-Class Protestant	Working-Class Catholic
Proportion of mothers who value:				
Obedience	.17	.25	.33	.36
Neatness, cleanliness	.08	.15	.17	.27
Consideration	.36	.38	.26	.29
Curiosity	.24	.12	.07	.05
Self-control	.28	.15	.15	.09
Happiness	.47	.42	.38	.30
Number of cases . . .	(88)	(52)	(107)	(56)

But the combination of class and religious background does enable us to isolate groups that are more homogeneous in their values than are the social classes *in toto*. There is an ordering, reasonably consistent for all class-related values, proceeding from middle-class Protestant mothers, to middle-class Catholic, to working-class Protestant, to working-class Catholic. (Jewish mothers—almost all, middle class—are very similar to middle-class Protestant mothers in their values.) Middle-class Protestants and working-class Catholics constitute the two extremes whose values are most dissimilar.

Another relevant social distinction is between urban and rural background.[10] As with religious background, we can arrange the

---

[10]We classified as having a rural background all mothers who, prior to age 15, had lived on a farm for some time other than simply summer vacations.

mothers into four groups delineated on the basis of class and rural-urban background in an order that is reasonably consistent for all class-related values. The order is: middle-class urban, middle-class rural, working-class urban, working-class rural. The extremes are middle-class mothers raised in the city and working-class mothers raised on farms.

It would be valuable to examine the effects of a number of other major lines of social demarcation upon parental values, but the Washington sample does not permit this. We cannot, for example, compare whites to blacks, people of one region of the country to those of another, small-town residents to large-city residents. We cannot take adequate account of national background, because the sample is too small to permit comparisons among the various national backgrounds—although we do find that mothers who are at least second-generation American-born do not differ appreciably in their values from mothers who are not.

For now, we tentatively conclude that it is possible to specify the relationship between social class and values more precisely by subdividing the social classes on the basis of other lines of social demarcation—but that social class seems to provide the single most potent line of demarcation.

Correlates of Class

There are a large number of other variables, each of them correlated with social class, that might possibly account for the class-values relationships. We have reexamined the relationship of class to values, controlling each of a large number of possibly relevant correlates of social class. *None* of them differentiates mothers of the same social class into groups having decidedly different values or affects the relationship of class to values. These variables include the size of the family, the mother's age, the ordinal position of the child in the family, the length of time the family has lived in the neighborhood, the social class composition of the neighborhood, whether or not the mother has been socially mobile (from the status of her childhood family), and her class identification. It should be especially noted that class differences in mothers' values do not result from the relatively large proportion of families of government workers included in the sample. Wives of government employees do not differ from other mothers of the same social class in their values.

In sum, we find that these correlates of social class do *not* explain the relationship of class to values.

Aspirations

One other issue worth considering here is the possible relevance of parents' aspirations for their children. The issue arises because working-class values seem so stereotypically middle class that one wonders whether working-class parents may be expecting their children to be socially mobile. But working-class parents are considerably less likely than are middle-class parents to expect (or even to want) their children to go on to college and the middle-class jobs for which a college education is required. Moreover, those working-class mothers who do want and expect their children to go to college tend disproportionately to be the more highly educated. They think of themselves as upwardly mobile, but in fact are likely to have married down. One gets the impression that, for many of them, the child's upward mobility represents an opportunity to recoup the status that they, themselves, have lost.

In any event, working-class parents who do expect their children to go on to college have much the same values as do working-class parents who have lower expectations. It is not that working-class parents expect their children to lead middle-class lives, but that we have had an inadequate grasp of what are working-class values.

CONCLUSION

The first conclusion must be that parents, whatever their social class, deem it very important indeed that their children be honest, happy, considerate, obedient, and dependable. Middle- and working-class parents share values that emphasize, in addition to children's happiness, their acting in a way that shows a decent respect for the rights of others. All class differences in parental values are variations on this common theme.

Middle-class parents, however, are more likely to emphasize children's *self-direction*, and working-class parents to emphasize their *conformity to external authority*. This basic tendency is apparent in the greater propensity of middle-class parents to choose consideration and self-control, and of working-class parents to choose obedience and neatness, as highly desirable. It is apparent, too, in the differential meanings that seem to be attributed to honesty and in the generally different patterns of association in choice of values. It is even discernible in middle-class mothers valuing the same characteristics for boys and for girls, while working-class mothers—more attuned to the manifestly appropriate and less to children's intent—value more masculine characteristics for boys, more feminine characteristics for girls.

On the Meaning of Self-Direction and Conformity

We conclude that middle-class parents are more likely to value self-direction; working-class parents are more likely to value conformity to external authority. Throughout the rest of this book, we shall verify, extend, elaborate, and search out the implications of this finding. Since the terms self-direction and conformity have many connotations, some of which we do not intend, we must make clear precisely what we mean by them. In a sense, this gets us ahead of the story, for the concepts take on richness as the data unfold. Nevertheless, it is better to proceed with clear definitions than to run the risk of misinterpreted meanings.

The essential difference between the terms, as we use them, is that self-direction focuses on *internal* standards for behavior; conformity focuses on *externally* imposed rules. (One important corollary is that the former is concerned with intent, the latter only with consequences.) Self-direction does not imply rigidity, isolation, or insensitivity to others; on the contrary, it implies that one is attuned to internal dynamics—one's own, and other people's. Conformity does not imply sensitivity to one's peers, but rather obedience to the dictates of authority. To make these definitions as precise as possible, we shall try to show how our use of self-direction and conformity is similar to and different from the concepts used in some important analyses of related issues.

The distinctions made by Piaget in his study of the moral development of children come very close to those that we intend. In *The Moral Judgment of the Child* (n.d.), Piaget defines *moral realism* as the belief that a person should be held responsible for the consequences of his acts regardless of his intent in acting as he does. The morally good consists of rigid obedience to authority; the letter rather than the spirit of the law is to be observed; and responsibility is "objective"—conformance to established rules rather than motive is what counts. This closely resembles our concept, conformity, in its emphasis on adherence to externally imposed rules rather than internal standards.

Piaget does not define a single concept in contradistinction to moral realism, but instead uses a number of terms that together connote his meaning—"autonomy" is the principal one; "reciprocity," "cooperation" and "mutual respect" are others. The focus of them all is the replacement of preoccupation with the external elements of a situation by an awareness of internal elements. The emphasis on consequences is superseded by considerations of intent. "Objective" responsibility diminishes in importance and "subjective" responsibility gains correlatively. These are the precise differences that are at issue in distinguishing conformity from self-direction.

Piaget further reasons—and we agree—that attending to the internal does not imply being isolated or asocial. On the contrary, self-direction implies being attuned not only to one's own internal dynamics, but also to other people's. Again like Piaget, we see an emphasis on the external (conformity), not as implying sensitivity to other people, but as limiting the focus of attention to the external aspects of things, to consequences rather than intent, to the forms of action rather than the reasons for acting.

Our concepts can be further clarified by distinguishing them from those employed by Riesman in *The Lonely Crowd* (1950). Despite the apparent similarities, self-direction is meant to be quite different from Riesman's term, "inner-directed," and conformity is not at all the same as Riesman's "other-directed." He uses the term inner-directed to describe behavior based on rigid principles derived from childhood training. We imply nothing of the kind, intending instead that self-direction implies thinking for oneself, making one's own decisions, in short—flexibility. His term, "autonomous," is actually closer to what we mean by self-direction, but it implies more than we intend. We do not mean rising to some height of lonely moral independence, but thinking for oneself rather than following the dictates of authority.

Riesman's term, other-directed, implies a sensitivity to, a wish to conform to the practices of, and a desire to be liked by *one's peers*. Conformity, in our usage, implies nothing about sensitivity or wanting to be liked, and it is quintessentially a matter of conforming to *authority*. Moreover, it suggests, not imitating but obeying authorities—which can be very different indeed. Finally, the other-directed man, as Riesman depicts him, is intent on getting ahead; our conformist is intent on staying out of trouble.

From this discussion, it should be clear that our use of the term conformity differs also from the meaning it has in most experimental studies, where the conformity studied is acquiescence to majority opinion of a small group in face-to-face contact (cf. Asch, 1952; Jahoda, 1959). Rather, we mean *conformity to authority,* often a distant and sometimes a diffuse authority. A face-to-face group may take on the reality of authority, but that is a special case, and not the focus of this study.

Many of the implications of self-direction and conformity are only vaguely discernible in the data presented thus far; they will become more explicit as we proceed.

The class difference in parental valuation of self-direction and conformity is potentially important—both for helping us understand class differences in how parents raise children, and as an indication of the broader relationship of class to values and orientation. But is the difference in parental values a general fact, or is it somehow peculiar to the time and social circumstances of the Washington study? To answer that, we turn to the Turin study.

CHAPTER 3

A Cross-National Comparison – The Turin Study

The central problem for this chapter is whether the relationship of social class to parental values is specific to the historical, cultural, and economic circumstances of Washington, D.C., in the late 1950's, or is a more general phenomenon. Is high valuation of conformity by working-class parents a response peculiar to the affluence and economic security of that place and time? If so, we must confine our interpretation to those limited circumstances; if not, it will be more appropriate to interpret the relationship of class to values in terms of conditions that are generally characteristic of industrial societies.

In the absence of definitive evidence about the "typicality" of the Washington findings, two alternative interpretations seem plausible. The first assumes that the relationship of class to values was especially pronounced under the conditions of affluence that obtained when the Washington study was conducted. It emphasizes that, with the end of mass immigration, there has emerged in the United States a stable working class, largely derived from the manpower of rural areas, uninterested in mobility into the middle class, but very much interested in security, respectability, and a decent standard of living (cf. Miller and Riessman, 1961a). This working class has come to enjoy a standard of living formerly reserved for the middle class, but has not chosen a middle-class style of life. In effect, the working class has striven for, and partially achieved, an American dream distinctly different from the dream of success and achievement. In an affluent society, it is possible for the worker to be the traditionalist—politically, economically, and, most relevant here, in his values for his children. Working-class parents may want their children to conform to external authority because the parents themselves accept the status quo; they are willing to defer to authority, in return for security and respectability.

The alternative interpretation of the relationship of class to values assumes its generality. From this perspective, what needs to be explained is not so much that working-class parents value conformity as that middle-class parents value self-direction. In all modern societies, middle-class parents can—and must—instill in their children a degree of self-direction that would be less appropriate to the conditions of life of the working class. Although there is substantial truth in the characterization of the middle-class way of life as one of great conformity, it is nevertheless true that, relative to the working class, middle-class conditions of life require more independent action. Furthermore, the higher levels of education enjoyed by the middle class make possible a degree of internal scrutiny difficult to achieve without the skills in dealing with the abstract that formal education can provide. Finally, the economic security of many middle-class occupations, the level of income these occupations provide, and the status they confer, permit their incumbents to focus on the subjective and the ideational. Middle-class conditions of life both allow and demand a greater degree of self-direction than do those of the working class.

Which is it? Do the Washington findings indicate what happens to a working class when it becomes affluent, or do they reflect differences in conditions of life that are built into the social structure of other, perhaps all, industrial societies? There is little in the research literature to help us answer this question. We cannot assess whether or not the relationship of class to values has been stable over time, for all directly pertinent data are of fairly recent vintage. Even the Lynds' (1929) study goes back only to the late 1920's.[1] As for stability from place to place, there is one limited but important piece of information: From public opinion polls in a number of different countries, Inkeles (1960) ingeniously gleaned data showing that working-class parents consistently place greater emphasis on obedience than do middle-class parents. The implication is that class differences in parental values are not a phenomenon specific to Washington, D.C. or even to the United States. But these data are hardly definitive.

A more certain basis for choosing between the two interpretations

---

[1]Indirectly relevant is Riesman's (1950) conclusion that there have been important changes in American values since the early days of this country. But he does not talk directly about the relationship of class and values. Moreover, there is impressive contrary evidence in Lipset's (1961, 1963) and Furstenberg's (1966) works.

requires at least one study comparable to that done in Washington—in a place that offers a different cultural and historic context, less affluence, and less economic security. Turin, Italy was chosen to be that place.

NATION, CLASS, AND VALUES

No single comparative study can tell us whether the relationship of class to values is universal. But even one study that demonstrates a similar relationship of class to parental values in a sufficiently dissimilar context would have significance for establishing the generality of the relationship. Turin seemed a good place to conduct such a study, especially because there we could be confident not only of cultural dissimilarity and much less affluent economic conditions, but also of a politically more radical working-class tradition.

The question then becomes: Is social class related to parental values in Turin, Italy in much the same way as in Washington, D.C.—despite the great differences in history, culture, and material conditions of life? Is working-class parents' high valuation of obedience a result of circumstances peculiar to the United States? Or is the necessity of conforming to external authority so built into the conditions of working-class life that even in a markedly dissimilar political, economic, and social context, working-class parents would have their children learn to conform to external standards?

To answer these questions requires an examination of the relationship of both nationality and class to parental values (Table 3-1). Italian and American parents of the same social class differ more in their value priorities than do middle- and working-class parents of either country. One indication of this is that the rank order of value-choices differs much more from country to country than from class to class in either country.[2] Another indication is that the percentage differences[3] associated with nationality are greater

---

[2]The rank order correlations for the value-choices of Italian and American parents are: (1) among middle-class mothers: 0.37; (2) among working-class mothers: 0.43; (3) among middle-class fathers: 0.44; and (4) among working-class fathers: 0.43. The rank order correlations for the value-choices of middle- and working-class parents are: (1) among Italian mothers: 0.79; (2) among American mothers: 0.88; (3) among Italian fathers: 0.73; and (4) among American fathers: 0.47. (The last of these is based on too few cases to be taken literally.)

[3]The statistical tests employed in this chapter are the *t* test for the difference between two proportions and chi-squared.

TABLE 3-1

Parental Values, by Social Class and Sex of Parent—Turin, Italy, Compared to Washington, D. C.

| | Italy | | | | | | United States | | | | | |
| | Fathers | | | Mothers | | | Fathers | | | Mothers | | |
Proportion who value:	Middle-Class		Working-Class	Middle-Class		Working-Class	Middle-Class		Working-Class	Middle-Class		Working-Class
That he is honest	.54	*	.54	.55		.55	.52		.58	.44		.53
That he has good manners	.32	*	.44	.44		.51	.24		.25	.19		.24
That he obeys his parents well	.31	*	.45	.36	*	.48	.13	*	.39	.20	*	.33
That he acts in a serious way	.25		.18	.18		.20	.00		.03	.00		.01
That he has self-control	.23	*	.11	.16	*	.08	.20	*	.06	.22	*	.13
That he is dependable	.23	*	.13	.21	*	.10	.33	*	.08	.24		.21
That he is able to defend himself	.21		.14	.17	*	.08	.02	*	.17	.10		.06
That he is ambitious	.19		.17	.21		.19	.17		.08	.07		.13
That he be happy	.14	*	.07	.16		.14	.37		.22	.46	*	.36
That he be considerate of others	.11		.09	.10	*	.03	.35	*	.14	.39	*	.27
That he is affectionate	.10		.12	.13		.12	.02		.08	.05		.04
That he is neat and clean	.09		.14	.07	*	.14	.15		.17	.11	*	.20
That he is popular with other children	.09		.07	.06		.04	.15		.25	.15		.18
That he is a good student	.08	*	.24	.13	*	.24	.07		.19	.15		.17
That he is liked by adults	.04		.09	.05		.09	.00		.08	.05		.04
That he is curious about things	.03		.01	.02		.01	.13		.08	.18	*	.06
That he is able to play by himself	.01		.02	.00		.01	.02		.06	.01		.02
Number of cases	(160)		(148)	(263)		(205)	(46)		(36)	(174)		(165)

* Social class difference statistically significant, $p < 0.05$, using the t test for the difference between two proportions.

Note: Italian parents who did not answer the question completely have been excluded from this Table.

than those associated with class. In either social class, American parents are more likely to value happiness, popularity, and consideration; Italian parents are more likely to value manners, obedience, and seriousness. American parental values seem to be focused more on the child *qua* child, Italian parental values more on the child as proto-adult.[4]

Despite the differences between Italian and American parental values, almost all the class relationships noted in the United States are found in Italy, too. Of the eight characteristics significantly related to social class in Washington, six are significant in Turin, too—obedience and neatness being more highly valued by the working class in both places, self-control, dependability, happiness, and consideration by the middle class in both places. (The two that are not related to class in Turin as they are in Washington are curiosity and the ability to defend oneself; we suspect imprecisions of translation.[5]) In addition, there are two class differences in Turin that were not significant in Washington: Italian working-class parents value manners more than do middle-class parents—which is obviously consistent with other indications of their higher valuation of conformity. They also value children's being good students more highly than do middle-class parents. This fact is at first puzzling—until we remember that "good student" implies conformity to school requirements, in contrast to the intellectuality implied in "curiosity."

The preceding discussion assumes that the index of parental values is as exhaustive of the range of parental values for Italians as for Americans. Fortunately, the pretest interviews indicated that it is. This was confirmed by the survey itself: When parents were asked if there were any characteristics not on this list that they considered important, nothing substantively different was suggested.

Taking all the evidence together, we conclude that in both Italy and the United States, middle-class parents are more likely to value

---

[4]One other difference between the two countries is not shown in Table 3-1. Italian mothers make virtually no distinction between what is desirable for boys and for girls. In fact, the sex of the child makes no difference for any of the analyses of the Turin data presented in this book. Thus, for simplicity of presentation, the data will not be presented separately for boys and for girls.

[5]In the case of curiosity, we could find no Italian equivalent that was free of the connotation of voyeurism. As for ability to defend oneself, we think that to working-class American fathers it connoted protecting oneself in physical combat, but to Italian fathers it connoted looking out for oneself in a potentially hostile world.

characteristics that bespeak self-direction; working-class parents are more likely to value characteristics that bespeak conformity to external standards.

It must be stressed that few of the differences in proportions of middle- and working-class parents who value any given characteristic are large. What is impressive is that the relationship of social class to parental values is consistent in the two countries—despite the cultural differences.

One thing is especially clear: A high valuation of obedience is not something peculiar to the American working class. On the contrary, obedience is more highly valued by working- than by middle-class parents in either country, and by Italians more than by Americans in either social class. The cumulative effect of nationality and class is that obedience is valued more highly by Italian working-class parents than by any of the other groups.

THE RELATIONSHIP OF SELF-CONTROL TO OBEDIENCE

For Italian, as for American parents, the crux of the class difference in values seems to lie in the distinction between self-control and obedience. In one sense, these two values are antithetical; one stresses control from within and the other from without. Yet in another respect they are similar: Although the locus of control is different, both stress control; they stand as one, in contrast, for example, to happiness. Does the class difference in parental valuation of self-control and obedience result primarily from differential valuation of control, whatever its source, or from wanting the locus of control to be internal or external?

The Turin study provides a way to answer this question. In this study, we asked parents not only to select 3 characteristics as the most important of the 17, but also to judge each of the others as important or unimportant. This enabled us to classify each parent as valuing a particular characteristic highly (selecting it as one of the three most important), moderately (not selecting it as one of the three most important, but judging it to be important), or not at all (judging it unimportant).

Using this classification, we can examine the interrelationship of fathers' valuations of self-control and obedience. (We focus on fathers, because that will be more relevant to subsequent analyses. The picture is essentially the same for mothers.) There are two basic ways to analyze the interrelationship of these values. The first ignores the source of control, treating self-control and obedience as equally indicative of an emphasis on control. It asks: Are middle-class fathers any more or less likely than working-class fathers to emphasize control? The answer is unequivocally "no." Class differences in the valuation of self-control and obedience are not at all a result of a differential emphasis on control *per se* (Table 3-2).

TABLE 3-2
Fathers' Valuation of Self-Control and Obedience, by Social Class

	Middle Class	Working Class
Proportion of fathers who:		
Value both self-control and obedience highly	.04	.03
Value either self-control or obedience highly, the other moderately	.15	.13
Value either self-control or obedience highly, the other not at all	.29	.35
Value both self-control and obedience moderately .	.17	.10
Value either self-control or obedience moderately, the other not at all	.09	.12
Value neither self-control nor obedience	.26	.27
Total	1.00	1.00
Number of cases...................	(167)	(158)

The second way to examine the interrelationship of self-control and obedience is to focus on the differential emphasis on internal or on external sources of control, as indicated by the relative emphases given to self-control and to obedience (Table 3-3). This makes it

TABLE 3-3
Fathers' Differential Valuation of Self-Control and Obedience, by Social Class

	Middle Class	Working Class
Proportion of fathers who:		
Value self-control highly	.22	.10
Value self-control moderately	.29	.25
Value neither self-control nor obedience	.26	.26
Value obedience moderately and self-control not at all	.04	.09
Value obedience highly and self-control not at all	.19	.30
Total	1.00	1.00
Number of cases...................	(167)	(158)

$\chi^2 = 14.2$, 4 d.f.
$p < 0.01$

possible to specify the difference between middle- and working-class fathers' values more precisely. Although fathers of both social classes value obedience, working-class fathers are more likely than are middle-class fathers to value obedience highly and exclusively, and to regard self-control as altogether unimportant. Obedience is valued throughout the culture; what differentiates the middle from the working class is that, in the middle class, self-control has come to be valued too.

CONCLUSION

Even though there are impressive differences between Italian and American parental values, the relationship of social class to parental values is much the same in both countries. In Italy and in the United States, middle-class parents put greater emphasis on children's self-direction, working-class parents on their conformity to external standards. There is something intrinsic to social stratification that yields similar results in the two countries.

Class differences in parental values are not a function of the conditions of affluence characteristic of the United States in the late 1950's; nor are they attributable to idiosyncrasies of the particular population studied in Washington, D.C. Not only are the patterns of values associated with social class much the same in Italy; more than that, the conservatism apparent in American working-class parental values, far from being a peculiarly American phenomenon, is even more apparent in Italian working-class values.

To this limited degree, we have established the generality of the relationship of social class to parental values: We know that it holds in two dissimilar locales. But we have hardly begun to explore the extent of this generality. Both the Washington and Turin studies were confined to middle- and working-class samples; but does the relationship of class to values apply to the entire range of social classes? Although the two cities are very different—Washington, the seat of government; Turin, a major manufacturing center—they certainly do not exhaust the range of urban diversity. If we interpret them strictly, both studies tell us about parents' values for 10- and 11-year-old children; but is the relationship of class to parental values the same for children of all ages? Most important: Is the relationship of class to values essentially the same in all major segments of society? We turn to the National study for answers to these questions.

CHAPTER 4

The Generality of the Relationship — The National Study

Our primary objective in this chapter is to assess the generality of the essential finding of the Washington and Turin studies—that higher class position is related to greater valuation of self-direction and lower class position is related to greater valuation of conformity to externally imposed standards. A first test of generality is to see whether or not the relationship will be found in a sample representative of fathers in all social classes and all major segments of the society. More definitive tests of generality come from determining whether the relationship is equally strong no matter what the age and sex of children, regardless of race, religion, and national background, in all regions, in communities large and small, and in families of varying size, composition, and functional pattern.

A secondary objective, which can be pursued at the same time, is to assess the magnitude of the class-values relationship.

The data for this analysis come from the National study—which provides a representative sample of some 1,500 fathers of children from ages 3 through 15, living at home (see Appendix C).

REVISED INDEX OF PARENTAL VALUES

The basic rationale of our index of values—asking parents to choose the three most desirable from a longer list of generally valued characteristics—had proved its worth in the Washington and Turin studies, but the index could be improved. For the National study, the five least chosen characteristics were dropped. A sixth—happiness—was eliminated, despite its importance to many parents, because it seemed to be on a different plane from all the rest, implying a desired goal rather than behavior. Four characteristics were modified, to broaden their connotations: dependable was changed to responsible; popularity to getting along well with other

47

children; curious about things to interested in how and why things happen; and ambitious to tries hard to succeed. Two characteristics were added: acts like[1] a boy should (or, for girls: acts like a girl should) and good sense and sound judgment.

The result was this list of 13 values—enough to offer a sizeable range of choice, but not too many to be readily comprehended:

That he is considerate of others.
That he is interested in how
    and why things happen.
That he is responsible.
That he has self-control.
That he has good manners.
That he is neat and clean.
That he is a good student.

That he is honest.
That he obeys his parents well.
That he has good sense and sound judgment.
That he acts like a boy
    (she acts like a girl) should.
That he tries hard to succeed.
That he gets along well with other children.

This time, we asked fathers to choose not only the three most desirable characteristics, but also the one most desirable of all. We asked them also to choose the three least important (even if desirable), and the one least important of all. This information provides a basis for classifying each father's valuation of each characteristic along a five-point scale:

5 = The most valued of all.
4 = One of the three most valued, but not the most valued.
3 = Neither one of the three most nor one of the three least valued.
2 = One of the three least valued, but not the least valued.
1 = The least valued of all.

This classification is our index of parental values.[2]

CLASS AND VALUES

The first test of the generality of the Washington and Turin findings is embodied in this hypothesis: For fathers generally, higher social class position will be associated with valuing characteristics

[1]Our apologies for this disservice to the English language.

[2]It would be cumbersome, in using this index, to continue talking of the proportion of fathers who value a given characteristic, for we should always have to deal simultaneously with the proportions who value it as the most desirable of all, as one of the three most desirable, as one of the three least, and as the least desirable of all. It is descriptively simpler to talk of the mean valuation of a given characteristic—that is, the average of the above scores.

There is a further and greater advantage to using means; it makes available a flexible and powerful armamentarium of statistical tools—analysis of variance and of covariance, correlation, canonical correlation, and factor analysis. But one has to pay for everything.

indicative of self-direction, and lower social class position will be associated with valuing characteristics indicative of conformity to external standards.

On the basis both of their manifest content (reflecting either self-direction or conformity) and of the empirical findings of the Washington and Turin studies, specific predictions can be made for 9 of the 13 characteristics. Four characteristics that reflect self-direction—consideration, an interest in how and why things happen, responsibility, and self-control—should be more highly valued by fathers of higher social class position. Five characteristics that reflect conformity—manners, neatness and cleanliness, being a good student, honesty, and obedience[3]—should be more highly valued by fathers of lower social class position.

We find (Table 4-1) that there is a statistically significant,[4] linear[5]

The greater flexibility of these statistical techniques can be enjoyed only when one makes the assumption that this index of parental values can be thought of as an interval scale. It is no longer sufficient to assume that someone who chooses some characteristic values it more highly than someone who does not; we now have to assume that the distances between adjacent points on the one-to-five scale of valuation are equal. The assumption is obviously untestable and probably false. But the amount of error introduced by acting as if it were true is both small and incommensurate with the gains. (Cf. Blalock, 1964: 94; Labovitz, 1967; Cohen, 1965.)

For more general discussions of the logical bases of our statistical procedures, see: Blalock, 1960, Chapters 15-21; Cohen, 1968.

[3]It is self-evident why we think that consideration, an interest in how and why things happen, responsibility, and self-control reflect self-direction, and why we think that manners, neatness, and obedience reflect conformity to external standards. But one might question the assumptions that honesty and being a good student reflect conformity. The assumption that the choice of honesty reflects valuation of conformity is based on the analysis, in Chapter 2, of the meaning of honesty; since there is only a minority of middle-class men in the sample, we expect that honesty will not have the middle-class connotation of being a standard for self-directed behavior. (This is, in fact, confirmed by a factor analysis that will be presented shortly.)

The assumption that being a good student reflects conformity is based on a comparison of its manifest content with that of its alternative, an interest in how and why things happen. The former stresses school performance, including such nonintellectual aspects of performance as deportment and pleasing the teacher; the latter is more precisely addressed to intellectual process.

For the empirical bases of the predictions, see Chapter 2, Tables 1, 2, and 4; and Chapter 3, Table 1.

[4]This and all subsequent analyses of variance are based on the computer program initially developed by Dean J. Clyde, Elliot M. Cramer, and Richard J. Sherin (cf. Clyde, *et al.*, 1966) and further developed by Cramer. The test of statistical significance is the F ratio.

All of the significant relationships in Table 4-1 would also be significant if the mode of analysis were contingency tables (as in previous chapters) and the test, chi-squared.

[5]The computer program that we used for the analysis of variance makes it possible to measure separately the variation in some dependent variable that is attributable to the *linear* component of an independent variable and the variation attributable to other components. Since our hypothesis asserts linear relationships of class to values, only the former is directly relevant.

TABLE 4-1
Parental Values, by Social Class

	Considerate of Others	Interested in How and Why Things Happen	Responsible	Self-Control	Good Manners	Neat and Clean	Good Student	Honest	Obeys His Parents	Good Sense and Sound Judgment	Acts as a Boy (Girl) Should	Tries to Succeed	Gets Along with Other Children	Number of Cases
Mean scores for:														
Social class 1	3.40[a]	3.12	3.07	2.95	2.84	2.23	2.53	3.58	3.43	3.16	2.81	2.92	3.07	(74)
Social class 2	3.36	3.00	3.05	2.90	2.94	2.40	2.47	3.54	3.61	3.09	2.77	2.71	3.32	(192)
Social class 3	3.24	2.69	2.85	2.87	3.13	2.70	2.54	3.81	3.64	3.12	2.74	2.65	3.21	(431)
Social class 4	3.06	2.56	2.72	2.84	3.26	2.84	2.70	3.87	3.68	3.03	2.82	2.75	3.16	(580)
Social class 5	2.95	2.39	2.72	2.77	3.40	2.90	2.85	3.76	3.70	3.01	2.74	2.92	3.20	(222)
Degree of association η (eta)														Canonical correlation
Linear component of social class	0.20**	0.18**	0.14**	0.06*	0.20**	0.20**	0.12**	0.09***	0.06*	0.05	0.00	0.04	0.02	0.38**
All components of social class	0.21**	0.19**	0.16**	0.06	0.20**	0.21**	0.13**	0.13**	0.07	0.05	0.04	0.11**	0.07	0.38**

*Indicates $p < 0.05$
**Indicates $p < 0.01$
[a] High valuation is indicated by a score of 5, low by a score of 1.

relationship, in the appropriate direction, between social class and fathers' valuation of all nine characteristics. But, although class is significantly related to them all, the magnitude[6] of the relationships is not great[7]—the correlations being no larger than 0.20. (A more general estimate of the relationship of class to the entire set of values—as given by the canonical correlation[8]—is a somewhat more impressive 0.38.) We are once again reminded that class differences in parental values are variations on a common theme. What makes them impressive is not their magnitude but their consistency.

It is instructive to note two pairs of closely related characteristics that are oppositely related to social class. Manners, with its emphasis on the proper forms of behavior, is more highly valued at lower class levels; consideration, with its emphasis on an empathic concern for the other person, at higher class levels. Being a good student, with its emphasis on how one's performance is judged by others, is more highly valued at lower class levels; an interest in how and why things happen, with its emphasis on intellectual curiosity, at higher class

---

[6]The measure of association that we use is the correlation coefficient most easily obtained from an analysis of variance, η *(eta)*. It is the square root of the ratio of (a) the "between groups" sum of the squared deviations from the mean, to (b) the total sum of the squared deviations from the mean. η is directly analogous to the product-moment correlation coefficient, in that it represents the square root of the proportion of the variation in the dependent variable that can be attributed to the independent variable. When one deals with the linear component of the independent variable (as we most often do), η is identical to the product-moment correlation coefficient, except that its sign is always positive—it does not indicate the direction of relationship. The advantage of η is that it can be used in the many situations where the ordinary correlation coefficient is inappropriate because the independent variable is not linear.

When used with small samples, η may overestimate the degree of association. This can be corrected. With the large number of cases in our analyses, however, a correction is unnecessary. (Cf. Blalock, 1960: 266-269; Cohen, 1965; Peters and Van Voorhis, 1940: 312-324 and 353-357.)

The computational formula for η is:

$$\eta = \sqrt{\frac{df_b F}{df_b F + df_w}}$$

where df_b is the number of degrees of freedom associated with the numerator of the F ratio, F is the F ratio, and df_w is the number of degrees of freedom associated with the denominator of the F ratio. The formula is applicable both to total and to partial correlations. (Cf. Cohen, 1965: 105; Costner, 1965.)

[7]This conclusion may be overly cautious. The forced-choice index imposes an arbitrary limitation on both the upper and lower limits of the magnitudes of relationship between the choice of these characteristics and other variables. We have, in effect, guaranteed that there be some relationship, but we have also severely limited the maximum possible relationship by restricting the number of valued (and disvalued) alternatives. In all probability, we have understated the relationships of social class to the individual values, but it is better to err on the side of caution.

[8]The canonical correlation is a multiple correlation of one or a set of independent variables to a set of dependent variables. More precisely, it is the maximum correlation between linear functions of the two sets of variables. (Cf. Cooley and Lohnes, 1962: 35.)

levels. These two pairs of manifestly similar but connotatively opposite characteristics nicely illustrate the differential emphases on internal process and external form that lie at the heart of class differences in fathers' values.

Two other characteristics—good sense and sound judgment and acts as a boy (or girl) should—were not in the previous studies; therefore, we have no *empirical* basis for predictions about them. Judging from apparent meaning, good sense seems indicative of self-direction, and acting as a boy should seems indicative of conformity. (But without further analysis, we cannot be certain that these are the meanings that parents impute to the terms.) Class is not related to fathers' valuation of either characteristic. But this finding is deceptive; as we shall soon see, more refined analysis shows the expected class relationship for fathers whose children are of an appropriate age and sex.

The remaining two characteristics—tries hard to succeed and gets along well with other children—are useful for specifying what is and what is not involved in the class-values relationship. A success orientation is not integral to valuing either self-direction or conformity. Peer acceptance is irrelevant both to parental valuation of self-direction and to parental valuation of conformity to adult authority. We have no reason to expect social class to be linearly related to fathers' valuation of either characteristic; nor do we in fact find linear relationships. (But, for reasons that we cannot explain, striving for success is valued more highly at the two ends of the class hierarchy than in the middle.)

Overshadowing all the particular findings from this first level of analysis is the central conclusion, which we repeat: The higher their social class position, the greater is fathers' valuation of characteristics that bespeak an emphasis on self-direction; the lower their social class position, the greater is their valuation of characteristics that bespeak an emphasis on conformity to externally imposed standards.

THE AGE AND SEX OF THE CHILD

No further analysis is needed to demonstrate that the relationship of social class to parental values is real. But further analysis[9] could

---

[9]In the following analyses, we use two complementary procedures. Where possible, we do separate analyses of the relationship of class to values in each of the relevant segments of the population, to see if the magnitude of the relationship is approximately the same in

show limits to its generality—and that would be important for interpreting why class is related to values. We now know, for example, that the class-values relationship is not limited to values for 10- and 11-year-old children, the ages on which we focused in the Washington and Turin studies, but that it applies to children from 3 through 15. Perhaps, though, it is more pronounced for children of some ages, and weak or nonexistent for children of other ages. Self-direction and conformity might be especially pertinent issues for fathers of preadolescents but less so for fathers of younger or older children.

First, consider the relationship of children's age to fathers' valuation of the 13 characteristics—controlling on social class and children's sex[10] (Table 4-2). The age relationships cut across the distinction between self-direction and conformity. The older the children, the more highly do fathers value responsibility, being a good student, honesty, and good sense and sound judgment; and the less highly do they value an interest in how and why things happen, manners, obedience, acting as a boy (or girl) should, and getting along well with other children.[11] In addition, fathers value self-control most highly for the youngest and oldest children, least highly for intermediate ages.[12]

---

each. This procedure becomes cumbersome (and the figures unreliable) when the population is divided into many segments. We turn then to the more generally applicable procedure of statistically controlling other social variables, to see if the relationship of class to values is thereby reduced.

Our usual method of statistical control is to use the other social variables as "factors" in an analysis of variance, attributing all possible variation in parental values to them, and then testing the relationship of social class to the residual variation in parental values. This procedure is not quite as satisfactory as examining the relationship of class to values separately for each segment of the population, because it does not tell us whether the class-values relationship is of approximately equal magnitude in all segments—it might be stronger in some and weaker in others. But, by testing the "interaction" of class and the other social variables, we determine if the relationship is similar in the various segments; if it is much different, the interactions will be sizeable.

When the number of variables to be controlled is too great for the capacity of the computer program, we use covariation as the method of statistical control. It provides comparable results, except that only the linear components of the covariates are controlled, and the interactions between the covariates and the factors are not tested. These limitations are not serious when we have already ascertained that the linear component is preponderant, and have already examined the interaction terms in simpler models.

[10]For ease of presentation, we often leave it implicit that, whenever we refer to the relationship of any social variable to parental values, we have statistically controlled all other variables involved in that analysis.

[11]We have grouped the children into five age levels (3-4 years, 5-6, 7-9, 10-12, and 13-15). These categories most accurately reflect the picture given by a more detailed analysis using all 13 ages (that is, ages 3 through 15).

[12]Limitations of space prevent our routinely presenting the statistical tests for

TABLE 4-2
Parental Values, by Age of Child, Sex of Child, and Social Class

	Considerate of Others	Interested in How and Why Things Happen	Responsible	Self-Control	Good Manners
Mean scores[a] for age of child, adjusted for social class and sex of child					
Age 3-4	3.12	3.11	2.53	2.93	3.23
Age 5-6	3.14	2.83	2.68	2.78	3.30
Age 7-9	3.20	2.62	2.78	2.78	3.16
Age 10-12	3.16	2.50	2.93	2.84	3.14
Age 13-15	3.12	2.32	3.09	2.93	3.13
Mean scores for sex of child, adjusted for social class and age of child					
Boys	3.12	2.75	2.81	2.86	3.16
Girls	3.19	2.56	2.82	2.85	3.21
Mean scores for social class, adjusted for age and sex of child					
Class 1	3.41	3.09	3.09	2.95	2.84
Class 2	3.36	2.99	3.05	2.90	2.94
Class 3	3.24	2.69	2.85	2.88	3.13
Class 4	3.06	2.56	2.72	2.84	3.26
Class 5	2.95	2.42	2.70	2.77	3.41
Degree of association η (eta)					
Age (linear), controlled on social class and sex	0.01	0.25 **	0.25 **	0.01	0.06*
Sex, controlled on social class and age	0.05	0.09**	0.00	0.01	0.03
Social class (linear), controlled on age and sex	0.20 **	0.18**	0.16**	0.06 *	0.20**

* Indicates $p < 0.05$
** Indicates $p < 0.01$
[a] High valuation is indicated by a score of 5, low by a score of 1.
Note: Interactions not shown.

Neat and Clean	Good Student	Honest	Obeys His Parents	Good Sense and Sound Judgment	Acts as a Boy (Girl) Should	Tries to Succeed	Gets Along with Other Children	Number of Cases
2.71	2.00	3.44	3.87	2.93	2.97	2.71	3.52	(288)
2.63	2.47	3.71	3.79	2.89	2.95	2.70	3.30	(221)
2.70	2.87	3.82	3.65	3.06	2.70	2.70	3.21	(356)
2.77	2.91	3.91	3.52	3.10	2.69	2.82	3.03	(322)
2.78	2.81	3.97	3.49	3.31	2.67	2.80	2.99	(312)
2.54	2.67	3.84	3.64	3.04	2.84	2.84	3.17	(770)
2.92	2.61	3.72	3.66	3.09	2.71	2.66	3.23	(729)
2.26	2.55	3.59	3.42	3.18	2.79	2.91	3.06	(74)
2.40	2.48	3.55	3.61	3.10	2.77	2.72	3.32	(192)
2.69	2.55	3.82	3.63	3.12	2.74	2.65	3.20	(431)
2.84	2.70	3.87	3.68	3.03	2.82	2.75	3.16	(580)
2.90	2.81	3.74	3.72	3.00	2.75	2.92	3.23	(222)
								Canonical Correlation
0.05	0.32**	0.21**	0.17**	0.14**	0.11**	0.05	0.24**	0.51**
0.21**	0.04	0.07**	0.01	0.03	0.06*	0.10**	0.04	0.27**
0.20**	0.12**	0.08**	0.07**	0.05*	0.01	0.04	0.01	0.37**

Children's sex is also independently related to fathers' values, albeit not so strongly as is age. Fathers deem it more desirable that *boys* be interested in how and why things happen, be honest, and try hard to succeed, and that *girls* be neat and clean. They also consider it more important, until the children reach adolescence, that boys act as boys should than that girls act as girls should. For adolescents, however, conformity to sex role is thought to be more important for girls.

But even when all variation that can be attributed to the age and sex of children is so attributed, social class continues to be significantly related to fathers' valuation of the nine characteristics that are indicative of self-direction or of conformity. In fact, the magnitudes of the relationships of class to these values are much the same for children of all age levels and both sexes.[13]

Moreover, social class is meaningfully related to fathers' valuation of both good sense and acting as a boy or girl should—under limited conditions. The higher fathers' social class, the more highly do they value good sense and sound judgment for older children. The lower their social class, the more highly do they value girls, particularly older girls, acting as they should.

In general, though, the relationship of class to values is essentially invariant, whatever the children's age and sex.

DIMENSIONS OF VALUATION

Children's age, their sex, and fathers' social class—each is independently linked to values. One can think of three independent dimensions in the act of valuing—a "developmental" dimension, a dimension of masculinity-femininity, and a dimension of self-direction or conformity to external standards. A factor analysis should demonstrate that some or all of these dimensions do in fact pervade fathers' value-choices. Such a finding would hardly constitute a discovery, but it would be useful as a basis for constructing indices of the relevant dimensions.

---

curvilinear and higher order relationships. Where these are not significant, this is no great loss. Where they are, we discuss them in the text.

[13]The canonical correlations of class to values, for example, range from a low of 0.41 for 5- to 6-year-old girls to a high of 0.50 for 10- to 12-year-old boys.

A factor analysis[14] of the value-choices yields one factor easily identified as self-direction versus conformity to external standards, and a second that clearly reflects the developmental dimension. The third factor, however, does not represent masculinity-femininity, but rather striving for success. This suggests that masculinity-femininity is not a major dimension of valuation; in addition, it confirms our belief that striving for success is not integral to self-direction, but is an independent dimension of valuation. No useful purpose is served in basing an index on this factor, though, for it reflects little more than the single characteristic, tries hard to succeed.

Factor scores[15] based on the first two factors provide eminently serviceable indices of self-direction versus conformity and maturity versus immaturity. (Table 4-3 presents the correlations of all 13

---

[14]This was an orthogonal principal component factor analysis, rotated to simple structure through the varimax procedure, based on the computer program presented by Clyde, *et al.* (1966: 15).

Parallel analyses, one using unities and the other, communalities, in the diagonal of the correlation matrix, yield quite similar results. Our discussion is based on the former, since it is more appropriate for the construction of factor scores.

To see if self-direction/conformity has essentially the same meaning at higher and lower class levels, we performed two separate factor analyses, one for the three highest social classes, the other for the two lowest. These separate analyses yield self-direction/conformity factors similar to that for the sample as a whole. In particular, manners, neatness, self-control, consideration, and an interest in how and why things happen are equally strongly correlated with the factor in both segments of the population. But there are some noteworthy variations on the main theme: Good sense, responsibility, and obedience are more strongly correlated with self-direction/conformity at higher class levels, while being a good student is more strongly correlated with this factor at lower class levels.

From our analyses of mothers' value-choices in the Washington study—where we found honesty to be a standard for behavior in the middle class but not in the working class—we would expect honesty to be correlated with self-direction/conformity at higher class levels but not at lower class levels. This expectation is confirmed, but the correlation of honesty to self-direction/conformity in the higher social classes is rather weak—0.17. This results from the combination of a strong correlation within the two highest social classes (0.45) and a very weak correlation (0.04) in the third class. The correlation in the two lowest classes, as anticipated, is virtually zero (0.01).

[15]Factor scores were computed by multiplying three matrices—the rotated factor loadings (transposed), the inverse of the correlation matrix, and the matrix of standardized scores. This procedure preserves the orthogonality of the factors and yields correlations of the original variables to the factor scores that are identical to the "loadings" of these variables on the factors. (Cf. Ryder, 1965.)

In constructing the scores, we repeated the factor analysis, limiting the number of rotated factors to two. We left out 1 of the 13 values, so that no error in the computation of the inverse of the correlation matrix could result from linear dependency among the values. It makes little difference which value is dropped, so we chose the one that showed the smallest correlations with the first two factors (because it is so highly correlated with the third), tries hard to succeed.

values with these indices.) As would have to be the case, social class is more closely related to self-direction (Figure 4-1), and age to

TABLE 4-3

Correlations of Parental Values Factor Scores[a] with the 13 Parental Values

	Factors	
	Self-Direction/ Conformity	Maturity/ Immaturity
Parental values		
Considerate of others	0.43	0.07
Interested in how and why things happen	0.51	-0.40
Responsible	0.28	0.54
Self-control	0.29	0.01
Good manners	-0.56	-0.09
Neat and clean	-0.62	0.04
Good student	-0.35	0.37
Honest	-0.07	0.49
Obeys his parents	-0.34	-0.38
Good sense and sound judgment	0.30	0.42
Acts as a boy/girl should	-0.05	-0.41
Tries to succeed	0.07	0.09
Gets along with other children	0.17	-0.52
(N = 1499)		

[a] Factor scores based on a principal component factor analysis of 12 parental values (all except "tries hard to succeed"), using unities in the diagonal of the correlation matrix, rotated to simple structure through the varimax procedure, and limited to two factors.

FIGURE 4-1

Parental Values Factor Scores, by Social Class [a]

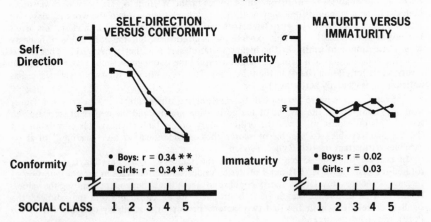

[a] Adjusted for Age of Child

**Indicates $p < 0.01$

maturity. Sex is significantly (but not greatly) related to fathers' valuation of self-direction—which is more highly valued for boys— and not at all to their valuation of maturity.

In the analyses that follow, the focus is the relationship of social class to fathers' valuation of self-direction or conformity. Since social class is not significantly related to the second factor, maturity, the index based on this factor is of secondary importance in these analyses; we refer to maturity only when some other social variable (religion proves to be the principal one) is related to it.

For simplicity of presentation, we discuss the 13 individual values only on those few occasions when something can be learned from them that is not apparent from analyses based on the factor scores.

OTHER MAJOR LINES OF SOCIAL DEMARCATION

Of all questions pertaining to the generality of the class-values relationship, the most important is whether the relationship is essentially the same in all major segments of the society—regardless of race, religion, and national background. We now examine that question, and at the same time assess the relevance for values of each of these lines of social demarcation.

Race

Is there any difference between the values of black and white fathers of roughly comparable social class position?[16] Is class as important for blacks as for whites? The first question cannot be answered definitively, for a given level of educational and occupational achievement may not indicate the same social class position for blacks as for whites in the United States today. But, assuming our index of class to be roughly comparable, we conclude that black fathers value conformity to external standards more than do whites of similar class position (Table 4-4). Nevertheless, the relationship of social class to fathers' valuation of self-direction or conformity is nearly as strong for blacks as for whites.

Thus, the relationships of class and race to fathers' values would appear to be essentially independent and additive. Of the two, class is

---

[16]In this analysis, we are (for reasons of numbers) leaving out Indian, Oriental, and a few other respondents.

TABLE 4-4
Parental Valuation of Self-Direction/Conformity, by Social Class and Race

	Mean Valuation of Self-Direction/Conformity[a]		
	Classes 1-3[b]	Class 4	Class 5
Whites	-0.32	0.18	0.33
	(668)[c]	(503)	(153)
Blacks	0.03	0.30	0.63
	(24)	(66)	(64)

Degree of association η (eta) with valuation of self-direction/conformity
Race, controlled on social class: 0.07**
Social class (linear), controlled on race: 0.31**
Interaction of social class (linear) and race: 0.01
Social class (linear)–whites only: 0.32**
Social class (linear)–blacks only: 0.25**

* Indicates $p < 0.05$
** Indicates $p < 0.01$
[a] High valuation of self-direction is indicated by a negative score, of conformity by a positive score.
[b] Since the sample contains only 2 black fathers in Class 1, 7 in Class 2, and 15 in Class 3, the mean scores for blacks in those three classes have been combined. For comparability, the same has been done for whites. The statistics, however, have been computed on the basis of all five social classes.
[c] Numbers in parentheses represent the number of cases on which means are based.

by far the more important, its correlation with fathers' valuation of self-direction being more than four times as large as that of race.

Religion[17]

There are two aspects of religion to be examined—religious background considered as a social fact, and religious practice. The former is easy enough to inquire about; although the latter is more difficult to measure, we have used the crude but serviceable index of frequency of church attendance.

Consider, first, religious background—not yet taking religious practice into account. A comparison of Catholics, Protestants, and Jews shows only that Jews value acting as a boy or girl should more highly than do Catholics or Protestants, and that Catholics value obedience more highly than do Protestants or Jews. A more refined classification further informs us that both honesty and self-control

---

[17]There is considerable research literature on the relationship of religion and values. Some of the most pertinent works are Weber, 1930; Tawney, 1926; Argyle, 1958; Lenski, 1961: 199-201; Williams, 1964: 57-61, 65.

are especially valued by men from those smaller Protestant churches that appear (to us) to be in transition from sect to denomination, and that getting along well with other children is most highly valued by men from fundamentalist Protestant backgrounds. The relationship of religious background to fathers' valuation of self-direction or conformity is not quite large enough to be statistically significant.[18] But religious background is significantly related to fathers' valuation of maturity—which is valued most highly by fathers from a miscellany of small, nonfundamentalist Protestant churches, least highly by men from fundamentalist Protestant churches (Table 4-5). Catholics, Jews, and men from all the larger Protestant denominations fall in between. Even when frequency of church attendance is controlled, the relationship of religious background to the valuation of maturity remains significant.

Church attendance is not at all related to fathers' valuation of maturity, but it is significantly related to their valuation of self-direction. This relationship is not quite linear: Men who go to church at least once a month but not as often as once a week value conformity most highly; men who go to church on rare occasions (but do not boycott churches altogether), value self-direction most highly. It is *approximately* correct to say that church attendance is positively associated with valuation of conformity. We conclude, then, that both religious background and practice matter for fathers' values, the former more for the valuation of maturity, the latter more for the valuation of self-direction or conformity.

Regardless of religious background and of religious practice, the higher their social class, the more highly men value self-direction and the less highly they value conformity to external authority. The magnitudes of the relationships of class—both to the set of values as a whole and to self-direction—are nearly as high when religious background and church attendance are statistically controlled as when they are not. Religious background and practice are potent variables, but independently of social class.

National Background

Since few men in our sample were born abroad, we cannot

[18]It does appear, though, that the relationship of class to fathers' valuation of self-direction or conformity is stronger for Jews ($r = 0.46$) than for Catholics ($r = 0.29$), with Protestants falling in between ($r = 0.34$).

TABLE 4-5
Parental Valuation of Self-Direction/Conformity and of Maturity/Immaturity,
by Social Class, Religious Background, and Frequency of Church Attendance

	Mean Valuation of Self-Direction/Conformity[a]		Mean Valuation of Maturity/Immaturity[b]		
	Adjusted for Social Class	Adjusted for Social Class and Frequency of Church Attendance	Adjusted for Social Class	Adjusted for Social Class and Frequency of Church Attendance	Number of Cases
Religious background:					
None	$-c$	–	–	–	(13)
Catholic	0.05	0.03	0.06	0.08	(415)
Jewish	-0.25	-0.20	0.06	0.02	(39)
Mixed Catholic and Protestant	–	–	–	–	(13)
Baptist	0.06	0.07	0.04	0.04	(292)
Lutheran	0.02	0.02	0.02	0.02	(141)
Methodist	-0.04	-0.02	0.00	-0.01	(190)
Presbyterian, Congregationalist, Unitarian, Episcopalian and other long-established denominations	-0.11	-0.10	-0.10	-0.11	(152)
Assembly of God, Disciples of Christ, and other churches in transition from sect to denomination	-0.11	-0.13	-0.13	-0.12	(90)
Fundamentalist sects	0.05	0.04	0.21	0.22	(31)
Other Christian churches	-0.09	-0.07	-0.22	-0.23	(98)
					(1474)

	Self-Direction/ Conformity	Maturity/ Immaturity
Degree of association η (eta) with valuation of		
Religious background, controlled on social class	0.12	0.13*
Religious background, controlled on social class and frequency of church attendance	0.10	0.13*
Frequency of church attendance (linear), controlled on social class	0.07*	0.02
Frequency of church attendance (linear), controlled on social class and religious background	0.06*	0.04
Social class (linear), controlled on religious background and frequency of church attendance	0.30**	0.03

* Indicates $p < 0.05$
** Indicates $p < 0.01$
[a] High valuation of self-direction is indicated by a negative score, of conformity by a positive score.
[b] High valuation of maturity is indicated by a negative score, of immaturity by a positive score.
[c] Means are not given where the number of cases is less than 20.
Note: Interactions are nonsignificant.

compare specific countries of origin. Overall, the foreign-born value conformity more than do men born in the continental United States.

To measure the effects of specific national background (other than American) requires going back two generations. We asked each man to state his country of birth, that of both parents, and that of each of his grandparents. If the man was born abroad, if only one parent was born abroad, if both parents were born in the same foreign country, or if all grandparents born abroad came from one country, there is only one possible predominant national background. If two or more countries were involved, we asked him to tell us which of them has had the greatest influence on him, and took this to be his predominant national background. That way we avoided giving priority to his paternal or maternal lineage; the choice was his to make.

Although national background is not significantly related to the entire set of 13 values, it is significantly related to the valuation of self-direction or conformity. Self-direction is most valued by men originating from Great Britain and countries populated by the British, from Ireland, and from Scandinavia; conformity, by men originating from Italy and from Latin America. (That conformity is valued highly by Americans of Italian descent accords nicely with the Turin finding that Italians value conformity more than do Americans.)

National background may be more relevant for the values of men who closely identify with their national origins than for other men. We tried to take this possibility into account by the (perhaps too simple) device of asking men to assess the importance of their predominant national background. These assessments do not appreciably change the picture.

It is no surprise that the relationship of class to values, particularly to the valuation of self-direction, is much the same for men of all national backgrounds.

The Combined Effects of Race, Religion, and National Background

The variation in values that is associated with race, religion, and national background taken all together is much greater than is apparent from examining them one at a time (Table 4-6). This can be seen most easily by examining the mean scores for self-direction.

TABLE 4-6
Parental Valuation of Self-Direction/Conformity,
by Race, Religious Background, and National Background

Group[a]	Mean Valuation of Self-Direction/Conformity (Adjusted for Social Class)[b]	Number of Cases
White		
U. S.—born to third generation		
Catholic	-0.02	(84)
Protestant	-0.03	(538)
English-speaking countries		
Catholic	-0.24	(44)
Protestant	-0.33	(71)
Scandinavian		
Protestant	-0.18	(77)
German, Austrian, Swiss		
Catholic	0.04	(58)
Protestant	-0.04	(118)
Central and Eastern European		
Catholic	0.10	(54)
Protestant	-0.08	(20)
Jewish	-0.45	(30)
Irish		
Catholic	-0.22	(49)
Italian		
Catholic	0.26	(68)
Black		
Protestant	0.38	(138)

Degree of association η (eta) with valuation of self-direction/conformity

Race, controlled on social class and religious background:	0.07*
Religious background, controlled on social class and race:	0.06
Religious background, controlled on social class and national background:	0.06
National background, controlled on social class and religious background:	0.13**
Social class (linear), controlled on race, religious background, and national background:	0.30**

* Indicates $p < 0.05$
** Indicates $p < 0.01$
[a]Means not given for groups having fewer than 20 cases. Total $N = 1423$.
[b]High valuation of self-direction is indicated by a negative score, of conformity by a positive score.
Note: Interactions are nonsignificant.

Jews of Eastern and Central European background are at one extreme in valuing self-direction most highly; they are followed by Protestants from Great Britain and British-populated countries (the "English-speaking countries"), Catholics from those same countries, Irish Catholics, and Scandinavian Protestants. At the other extreme, valuing conformity most highly, are black Protestants, followed by Italian Catholics, and then Central and Eastern European Catholics.

The differences among people from similar national backgrounds are best illustrated by the Central and Eastern Europeans: Jews from that region are extreme in their valuation of self-direction, Catholics in their valuation of conformity; Protestants fall in between. (But religious background makes less difference for people of other national backgrounds, witness the English-speaking countries.) The differences among people of the same religious background are best illustrated by the Catholics: English and Irish Catholics stand out for their valuation of self-direction, Italian Catholics for their valuation of conformity. Clearly, the combination of race, religion, and national background enables us to differentiate groups of considerable diversity in their valuation of self-direction and conformity.

The effect of all these variations on the relationship of class to values is slight. Even when controlled simultaneously on race, religion, and national background, the correlations of social class with each of the values, with the entire set of values, and with self-direction, remain nearly as large as before. However great the diversity in values associated with race, religion, and national background, taking them into account does not greatly affect the relationship of class to values.

DEMOGRAPHIC DIVISIONS

We shift now from relatively enduring personal characteristics to more easily modified demographic characteristics—region and rural or urban residence. These are not lines of social demarcation in the same social structural sense as are race, religion, and national background, but they do mark socially relevant axes along which values might vary. They provide further tests of the generality of the class-values relationship.

Region of the Country

For the analysis of possible regional variations in fathers' values, we used the nine geographic regions of the continental United States delineated by the U. S. Census—New England, the Middle Atlantic, South Atlantic, East North Central, West North Central, East South Central, West South Central, Mountain, and Pacific states.

The effects of region, thus indexed, are not large, but they are relevant. Fathers in the Pacific states—Washington, Oregon, and California—are most likely to value self-direction; fathers in the East South Central states—Kentucky, Tennessee, Mississippi, and Alabama—are most likely to value conformity to external standards.[19] (These variations do not result from the differing racial and religious compositions of the regions.) But the relationship of class to values is equally strong in the Pacific and in the East South Central states—and in all other parts of the United States.

Then, on the chance that the really important regional variations might result, not from where men presently live but from where they grew up, we asked them to name the state in which they had lived longest up to the time they were 16. The effects are much the same as those of the region in which men currently live.

Clearly, regional variations in values are only moderate, and the relationship of class to values is much the same in all regions of the country.

The Rural-Urban Continuum

The relationship of class to values might nevertheless apply only, or especially, to cities the size of Washington and Turin. This is easily tested. The results of this test must be treated cautiously, however, for size of community is the one variable we know to be related to the rate of nonresponse in this survey (Appendix C).

Our index here is less detailed than we should like; we used the National Opinion Research Center's classification of the areas from which they draw samples—metropolitan areas of over 2 million population, metropolitan areas of smaller population, nonmetropolitan counties with a major city of 10,000 or greater population, and nonmetropolitan counties without such a city.

Although it is questionable to treat this classification as an interval scale, we did test the linear relationship of size of community to values. The one significant result is that the smaller the community,

---

19This analysis could underestimate regional variations because it relies on a less than optimum classification of the states. So we repeated the analysis, regrouping the states into what seemed to be more meaningful categories: New England, Mid-Atlantic, Border, Southeast, Great Lakes, Great Plains, Southwest, Mountain, and Pacific states. The reanalysis adds no potency to region as a source of variation in fathers' values, but it does locate the source of regional variations more precisely. Self-direction is valued most highly in the Pacific states, conformity in the Border states.

TABLE 4-7
Parental Valuation of Self-Direction, by Social Class and Size of Community

	Mean Valuation of Self-Direction/Conformity[a]			
	Class 1-2	Class 3	Class 4	Class 5
Size of community				
Metropolitan areas of				
2,000,000 or more people ...	-0.71	-0.03	0.32	0.52
	(68)[b]	(109)	(146)	(29)
Smaller metropolitan areas	-0.62	-0.25	0.10	0.28
	(137)	(181)	(218)	(86)
Counties containing a city				
of 10,000 or more people	-0.50	-0.09	0.12	0.60
	(39)	(67)	(91)	(33)
Counties without a city of				
10,000 people	-0.39	0.00	0.32	0.49
	(22)	(74)	(125)	(74)

Degree of association η (eta) with valuation of self-direction/conformity
Size of community (linear), controlled on social class: 0.03
Size of community (total), controlled on social class: 0.09**
Social class (linear), controlled on size of community: 0.32**
Interaction of social class (linear) and size of community: 0.05

* Indicates $p < 0.05$
** Indicates $p < 0.01$
[a] High valuation of self-direction is indicated by a negative score, of conformity by a positive score.
[b] Numbers in parentheses represent the number of cases on which means are based.

the more highly is honesty valued—an empirical triumph for the folklore of rural virtue. Valuation of self-direction is related to size of community, but not linearly: It is most highly valued in metropolitan areas of less than 2 million people, next most in nonmetropolitan counties having a city of at least 10,000 population, then in the largest metropolises, and least in rural counties—a thoroughly scrambled pattern (Table 4-7). Nevertheless, in rural counties, huge metropolises, and communities of intermediate size, social class is consistently related to fathers' valuation of self-direction.

As a further test that the class-values relationship is not primarily an urban phenomenon, we can examine the size of the place where the men were raised. The principal lesson of this analysis is that self-direction is somewhat more highly valued by fathers who grew up in urban places—it hardly matters what size the city, or whether the city itself or its suburbs. Conformity is more highly valued by men who spent their childhoods in nonurban places—whether a farm or a village or a small town. The relationship of class to values, however, is only slightly diminished when one takes rural or urban background into account.

Clearly, the effects of social class are much the same however rural or urban men's present place of residence or past upbringing.

FAMILY STRUCTURE AND PROCESS

Now that we are assured that the relationship of social class to parental values is essentially the same throughout all major segments of the society, we must narrow the focus to the family itself. If the class-values relationship differs in families of varying size, composition, or functional pattern, our further analyses should be focused on intra-family processes specifically relevant to parental values. If not, we should expand our inquiry to social processes that are relevant not only to parental values but also to values more generally.

This analysis need not detain us long. Of the aspects of family that we studied, few prove to be related to fathers' values, when class is controlled, and none proves relevant to explaining the relationship of class to values. Since the weight of these conclusions is dependent on the comprehensiveness of our inquiry, we must review the variables that were analyzed.

They fall, more or less naturally, into four clusters. The first set relates to men's childhood families and their places in them—thought to be relevant because the lessons learned in childhood might mold men's views of what is appropriate for the families they now head. We considered their mothers' age when they were born; the number of brothers and sisters; ordinal position among the children; the sex composition of the sibship; whether or not the family stayed intact; and when, if ever, mothers started to work outside the home. All prove to be unrelated to men's present values.

The second set of variables deals with the structure of the present family and the place within it of the child on whom the inquiry is focused. Of particular interest here are family size and the child's ordinal position in the sibship; men's age, wives' age, and such interlocking variables as length of marriage; and the number of generations living in the household. These prove relevant to values only insofar as they reflect the age of the child.

Third are several aspects of family life from which we can infer patterns of family interaction. These include men's judgments of their marital happiness, their descriptions of whether or not their leisure-time activities include or exclude their wives, and their accounts of how much time they spend with wives, with children, and working around the house. None of these proves relevant to fathers' values, when social class is controlled. One variable that does correlate with fathers' values, independently of class, is their wives' employment status. Men whose wives have jobs outside the home are likely to value responsibility and are unlikely to value consideration and acting as a boy or girl should. (This difference does not result from the children being older.) Moreover, the higher their wives' occupational status, the more highly do men value self-direction and its constituent values. But the relationship of men's own class positions to their values is much the same whatever their wives' occupational status.

Finally, parental aspirations for children: The data for fathers give essentially the same results as did those for mothers in the Washington study. Fathers' educational aspirations and expectations for children are significantly—albeit weakly—related to their valuation of self-direction. Occupational aspirations and expectations are difficult to judge, since half the fathers were unwilling to express themselves; but, so far as we can tell, they do not have much bearing on fathers' values. Hence, aspirations and expectations do not much affect the relationship of class to values.

Even though this examination of family structure and process has not been exhaustive, its results have been so thin as to direct our attention to social processes external to the family.

THE COMBINED EFFECTS OF ALL SOCIAL VARIABLES

Our strategy has been to examine clusters of variables—age and sex of children, major lines of social demarcation, demographic divisions, and family patterns—for their relationship to values and for their effects on the relationship of class to values. Now we can consider all these variables together. We find that the effects of the relevant social variables are essentially additive. More important for the main theme of our analysis, controlling these other social variables, not only singly or in small clusters, but all together, has little effect on the relationship of class to values.

It is possible to control simultaneously the age and sex of children, race, region, size of community, religious background (to the extent of dividing the men into three major religious groups), frequency of church attendance, national background (grossly categorized), and men's assessment of the importance of their national background. [20] This we have done in Table 4-8, which compares the original relationships of class and values to the modified relationships when

TABLE 4-8

Comparison of Class-Values Correlations when Not Controlled and when Controlled Simultaneously on Age of Child, Sex of Child, Race, Region, Size of Community, Religious Background, Frequency of Church Attendance, National Background, and Importance of National Background

| | Class Correlations[a] | | |
	Not Controlled[b]	Controlled on All	Proportional Reduction
Individual values			
Considerate of others	.21**	.17**	.19
Interested in how and why			
things happen	.19**	.17**	.11
Responsible	.16**	.13**	.19
Self-control	.06*	.03	.50
Good manners	.21**	.16**	.24
Neat and clean	.19**	.16**	.16
Good student	.12**	.11**	.08
Honest	.08**	.07**	.13
Obeys his parents	.05*	.07*	.00
Good sense and sound judgment	.04	.07*	—[c]
Acts as a boy (girl) should	.02	.04	—
Tries to succeed	.05	.02	—
Gets along with other children	.03	.01	—
Canonical correlation with all values ...	.39**	.33**	.15
Factor scores			
Self-direction/conformity	.34**	.29**	.15
Maturity/immaturity	.02	.00	—

* Indicates $p < 0.05$
** Indicates $p < 0.01$
[a] η (eta) or the canonical correlation for the linear component of social class.
[b] These figures differ somewhat from those of Table 4-1, because they are based on those 1369 respondents for whom we had complete data on all the relevant variables.
[c] Proportional reduction not computed where original relationship is not significant.

---

[20]The computer program we used does not permit the simultaneous control of all the variables that are related to fathers' values, but it does permit a close approximation. This program is capable of handling up to 40 dependent variables and covariates, which is adequate for our purposes. The limitation is that it can accept no more than 100 nonzero cells in the factor structure. This limitation poses no problems where the control variables are essentially linear and thus can be handled as covariates; but such important variables as religion and national background are nonlinear and must be handled as factors. To encompass them within the allowable structure of 100 cells, religious background has to be combined into three categories and national background into four.

all these variables have been controlled. The correlations of social class, both to values in general and to men's valuation of self-direction in particular, are reduced remarkably little. The relationship of class to values is ubiquitous.

Let us return for a moment to the question of magnitude. The absolute magnitudes of the correlations of class to values are only moderate. But our analysis has shown that class is more powerfully related to values than is any other relevant social factor. In fact, class controlled on all other major social variables is more powerfully related to parental values than is the *totality* of such other major social variables as race, region, religion, and national background, controlled on class alone (Table 4-9).

TABLE 4-9
Comparison of Correlations with Parental Values
of Social Class and Other Major Social Variables

	Canonical Correlations with Set of 13 Values	Correlation η with Self-Direction/ Conformity
Social class (linear)		
Uncontrolled	0.38**	0.33**
Controlled on race, region, size of community, religious background, and national background	0.34**	0.29**
Other major social variables		
Race, religion, and national background		
Uncontrolled	0.25**	0.19**
Controlled on social class	0.19**	0.12**
Race, region, and size of community		
Uncontrolled	0.29**	0.25**
Controlled on social class	0.22**	0.16**
Race, region, religion, and national background		
Uncontrolled	0.26**	0.22**
Controlled on social class	0.20**	0.16**
(N = 1369)		

* Indicates $p < 0.05$
** Indicates $p < 0.01$

CONCLUSION

Social class is consistently related to fathers' values for children: The higher their class position, the more highly they value self-direction and the less highly they value conformity to externally imposed standards. This is true regardless of the age and sex of the children—even though age and sex are related to fathers' values.

Moreover, the relationship is much the same in all segments of the society—regardless of race, religion, national background, region of the country, and the size of community; in families large and small; for oldest children and for children of every other birthrank. In short, despite the heterogeneity of American society, the relationship of social class to fathers' values is remarkably pervasive and consistent.

The implications are impressive. In this exceptionally diverse society—deeply marked by racial and religious division, highly varied in economy, geography, and even degree of urbanization—social class stands out as more important for men's values than does any other line of social demarcation, unaffected by all the rest of them, and apparently more important than all of them together.

CHAPTER 5

Orientations to Work, Society, and Self

Implicit in parents' values *for their children* are values *for themselves;* we should certainly expect men of higher social class position to value self-direction for themselves, just as they do for their children. Moreover, values imply a great deal about conceptions of reality. Thus, if men value self-direction, they will tend to see the world and their own capacities in ways that make self-direction seem possible and efficacious. If they value conformity, they will tend to see the world and their own capacities in ways that make conformity seem necessary and appropriate. We therefore expect social class to be related, not only to men's values, but also to their conceptions of the external world and of self. (We call these conceptions "orientations," thereby emphasizing that they serve to define men's stance toward reality.) We shall examine men's orientations to three major aspects of reality—work, society, and self.

This analysis is based on data from the National study. It utilizes the entire sample of 3,100 men, fathers and non-fathers alike.

VALUES FOR SELF

To test our expectation that values for self are consistent with values for children, we use a similar index—modifying the characteristics to be more appropriate for adults (see Table 5-1 for the complete list). As anticipated, characteristics indicative of self-direction—an interest in how and why things happen, good sense and sound judgment, responsibility, self-reliance, the ability to face facts squarely, and the ability to do well under pressure—are more valued at higher social class levels.[1] There is evidence, too, that conformity is more valued at lower class levels. But this evidence is limited,

---

[1]The statistical procedures used in this chapter are the same as those of Chapter 4.

TABLE 5-1
Values for Self, by Social Class

	Interested in How and Why Things Happen	Good Sense and Sound Judgment	Responsible	Self-Reliant	Able to Face Facts Squarely	Able to Do Well under Pressure	Respectable	Able to Do Many Things Well	Truthful	Successful	Able to Get Along Well with People	Helpful to Others	Number of Cases
Mean scores for:													
Social class 1	2.83[a]	3.73	3.50	3.08	3.33	2.69	2.63	1.94	3.35	2.38	3.40	3.17	(138)
Social class 2	2.56	3.74	3.42	3.01	3.14	2.61	2.89	2.00	3.45	2.48	3.61	3.18	(332)
Social class 3	2.33	3.62	3.38	2.93	3.08	2.64	3.11	2.12	3.59	2.54	3.68	3.10	(887)
Social class 4	2.32	3.52	3.36	2.91	3.09	2.56	3.19	2.33	3.59	2.53	3.56	3.16	(1160)
Social class 5	2.28	3.47	3.21	2.83	3.01	2.47	3.12	2.50	3.57	2.65	3.78	3.24	(544)
													Canonical correlation
Degree of association η (eta)													
Linear component of social class	.10**	.10**	.09**	.07**	.06**	.06**	.13**	.16**	.05**	.06**	.05**	.04	.27**
All components of social class	.12**	.10**	.10**	.08**	.08**	.07**	.17**	.17**	.07**	.07**	.10**	.07**	.27**

* Indicates $p < 0.05$
** Indicates $p < 0.01$
[a] High valuation is indicated by a score of 5, low by a score of 1.

because in modifying the list, we substituted only one *adult* characteristic—respectability—for four *child* characteristics—manners, obedience, neatness, and good student. Moreover, we narrowed—perhaps distorted—the connotations of honesty by changing it to truthfulness. Thus, the only way men could endorse conformity was to choose respectability.[2] At lower class levels, more men did so—thereby providing the only possible evidence that conformity is more highly valued by men of lower social class position.

There is a second cluster of values associated with lower class position—centering around a high valuation of competence, as reflected in the ability to do many things well, success, and the ability to get along well with people. We think this represents an important theme, different from conformity, but also in contradistinction to self-direction.

This supposition is borne out by a factor analysis of the entire set of value-choices. Two factors embodying self-direction appear, one contrasting it to conformity, the other to competence. (The first factor is focused on *judgment,* contrasting reliance on one's own judgment with reliance on other people's judgments. The second is focused on *performance,* the contrast being between acting on the basis of one's own standards and acting competently.)[3] Both are significantly correlated with social class, albeit neither very strongly (Figure 5-1). It adds an essential modicum of information to have this evidence that the higher men's class positions, the more self-directed are their values, with reference both to thought and to action.

JUDGMENTS ABOUT WORK

It seems reasonable to assume that men judge jobs both in terms of the occupational conditions they might ideally want and in terms of the alternatives that are realistically open to them. Again, as with values, judgments about jobs are constrained by what is thought

---

[2] For this same reason—we think—the magnitude of the relationship of class to values for self is weaker than that to values for children (the canonical correlations being 0.27 and 0.38 respectively).

[3] The first factor contrasts an interest in how and why things happen ($r = 0.57$), good sense and sound judgment ($r = 0.45$) and the ability to face facts squarely ($r = 0.45$) with respectability ($r = -0.62$), truthfulness ($r = -0.43$), and success ($r = -0.33$). The second factor contrasts responsibility ($r = 0.52$) and self-reliance ($r = 0.40$) with the ability to get along well with people ($r = -0.68$) and the ability to do many things well ($r = -0.44$).

FIGURE 5-1
Values for Self Factor Scores,
by Social Class

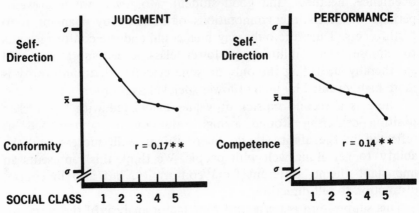

**Indicates $p < 0.01$

important and what is thought problematic. Consonant with their greater valuation of self-direction, men of higher social class position should be better able to take such extrinsic aspects of the job as pay and security for granted, and to focus instead on the possibilities that the job affords for self-expression and individual accomplishment. This expectation is given support in Inkeles's (1960: 9) analysis, which shows that among both Americans and refugees from the Soviet Union, men in higher status jobs are "more likely to be concerned about having a job which is 'interesting,' stimulating, challenging, permits self-expression, and so on."

To learn about orientations to work, we asked men to evaluate the importance of various occupational conditions. Our data (Table 5-2) confirm Inkeles's conclusion and extend it. Essentially, men of higher class position judge jobs more by intrinsic qualities, men of lower class position more by extrinsic characteristics. That is, the *higher* men's social class, the more importance they attach to how interesting the work is, the amount of freedom you have, the chance to help people, and the chance to use your abilities. The *lower* their class position, the more importance they attach to pay, fringe benefits, the supervisor, co-workers, the hours of work, how tiring the work is, job security, and not being under too much pressure.

That the extrinsic-intrinsic distinction is a central line of cleavage is substantiated by a factor analysis that differentiates an *intrinsic*

TABLE 5-2
Judgments about Work, by Social Class

	How Interesting the Work Is	Amount of Freedom	Chance to Help People	Chance to Use Abilities	Pay	Fringe Benefits	Supervisor	Co-Workers	Hours of Work	How Tiring the Work Is	Job Security	Not Being under Too Much Pressure	Chance to Get Ahead	How Clean the Work Is	How Highly People Regard the Job	Number of Cases	Canonical Correlation
Mean scores for:																	
Social class 1	2.91[a]	2.59	2.43	2.88	2.25	1.95	2.36	2.25	1.76	1.70	2.30	1.74	2.55	1.65	2.01	(133)	
Social class 2	2.90	2.47	2.47	2.91	2.30	2.04	2.36	2.27	1.79	1.74	2.32	1.88	2.68	1.74	1.99	(326)	
Social class 3	2.75	2.32	2.39	2.81	2.41	2.17	2.34	2.24	1.96	1.88	2.59	2.08	2.68	1.80	2.07	(858)	
Social class 4	2.55	2.25	2.32	2.69	2.59	2.39	2.40	2.28	2.05	1.94	2.76	2.25	2.62	1.75	1.98	(1148)	
Social class 5	2.48	2.31	2.39	2.58	2.66	2.42	2.50	2.35	2.20	2.08	2.71	2.36	2.59	1.83	2.03	(522)	
Degree of association η (eta)																	
Linear component of social class	0.25**	0.10**	0.04*	0.20**	0.21**	0.20**	0.06**	0.04*	0.16**	0.13**	0.23**	0.22**	0.03	0.03	0.01		0.46**
All components of social class	0.25**	0.13**	0.07**	0.20**	0.21**	0.21**	0.08**	0.05	0.16**	0.14**	0.26**	0.22**	0.07**	0.06	0.05		0.47**

* Indicates $p < 0.05$
** Indicates $p < 0.01$
[a] High importance is indicated by a score of 3, low by a score of 1.

from an *extrinsic* dimension in these judgments.[4] Social class is correlated with both dimensions (Figure 5-2). The correlation of class with men's interest in the extrinsic, though, is nearly twice as great as with their interest in the intrinsic. Class apparently matters

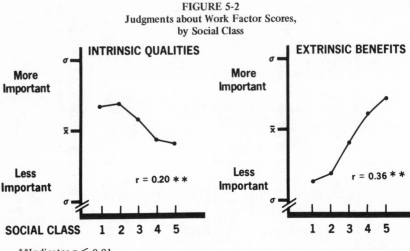

FIGURE 5-2
Judgments about Work Factor Scores,
by Social Class

**Indicates $p < 0.01$

more in determining whether men are forced to focus on the extrinsic than in determining whether they are free to focus on the intrinsic.

ORIENTATION TO SOCIETY

We expect men of higher social class position to see society as so constituted that responsible individual action is practicable; men of lower social class position will be more likely to think that following the dictates of authority is the course of wisdom. This distinction should be manifested in many ways, four of which seem especially pertinent—in how rigidly men define what is socially acceptable, in

---

[4]We limited this factor analysis to two rotations. The first factor focuses on intrinsic qualities of jobs—how much opportunity the job provides for using one's abilities ($r = 0.68$), how interesting the work is ($r = 0.64$), and how much opportunity it offers to help people ($r = 0.67$). The second factor focuses on the extrinsic benefits of the job, emphasizing hours of work ($r = -0.64$), fringe benefits ($r = -0.58$), how tiring the work is ($r = -0.58$), job security ($r = -0.57$), and not being under too much pressure ($r = -0.51$).

their definitions of appropriate moral standards, in how trustful they are of their fellowman, and in their stance toward change.

If orientations are consistent with values, men of higher social class position will be more open-minded in their views of the socially acceptable and in their tolerance of nonconformity, while men at lower class levels will hold a more authoritarian view of what is acceptable and will more rigidly reject behavior that does not conform to the acceptable. This expectation is buttressed by past investigations that have found class to be related to "authoritarianism" (cf. Christie, 1954; Hyman and Sheatsley, 1954; Srole, 1956; Lipset, 1959; Kirscht and Dillehay, 1967: 37-40) and by Stouffer's (1955) demonstration that intolerance of nonconformity is an essential ingredient of conformity.

The other aspects of social orientation that we investigated—standards of morality, trust, and stance toward change—deserve independent recognition. Self-direction implies the necessity for personally responsible moral standards; conformity requires only that one follow the letter—not necessarily the spirit—of the law. Self-direction also implies a certain degree of trust in one's fellowman, and the belief that change can be for the good; a conformist orientation is more pessimistic.

The indices that we use to investigate the relationship of class to social orientation are derived from a factor analysis of a set of 57 questions, mainly of the "agree-disagree" and "how often?" types. The derivation of the indices and the correlations of factors with component items are given in Appendix D. Here we only define the indices, and illustrate them by the principal questions from each. (Because the factors have been "orthogonally" rotated, all the indices are *empirically independent* of one another.)

1. *Authoritarian conservatism.* Men's definitions of what is socially acceptable—at one extreme, rigid conformance to the dictates of authority and intolerance of nonconformity; at the other extreme, open-mindedness.

Indexed by agreement or disagreement with such assertions as: The most important thing to teach children is absolute obedience to their parents. Young people should not be allowed to read books that are likely to confuse them. There are two kinds of people in the world: the weak and the strong. People who question the old and accepted ways of doing things usually just end up causing trouble. In this complicated world, the only way to know what to do is to rely on leaders and experts. No decent man can respect a woman who has had sex relations before marriage. Prison is too good for sex criminals; they should be publicly whipped or worse. Any good leader should be strict with people under him in order to gain their respect. It's wrong to do things differently from the way our forefathers did.

2. *Criteria of morality.* A continuum of moral positions, from opportunistic to highly responsible.

Indexed by responses to the question: Do you believe that it's all right to do whatever the law allows, or are there some things that are wrong even if they are legal? and by agreement or disagreement with such assertions as: It's all right to do anything you want as long as you stay out of trouble. If something works, it doesn't matter whether it's right or wrong. It's all right to get around the law as long as you don't actually break it.

3. *Trustfulness.* The degree to which men believe that their fellowman can be trusted.

Indexed by answers to: Do you think that most people can be trusted? and by agreement or disagreement with: If you don't watch out, people will take advantage of you. Human nature is really cooperative.

4. *Stance toward change.* Men's receptiveness or resistance to innovation and change.

Indexed by responses to the questions: Are you generally one of the first people to try out something new or do you wait until you see how it's worked out for other people? Are you the sort of person who takes life as it comes or are you working toward some definite goal? and by agreement or disagreement with: It generally works out best to keep on doing things the way they have been done before.

Class position is linearly related to all four aspects of social orientation (Figure 5-3). The strongest correlation, by a very wide margin, is with authoritarian conservatism: The lower men's social class position, the more rigidly conservative their view of man and his social institutions and the less their tolerance of nonconformity. The other aspects of social orientation are less strongly correlated with social class, but the correlations are altogether consistent with our expectations. The lower men's social class positions, the more likely they are to feel that personal morality is synonymous with obeying the letter of the law; the less trustful of their fellowman they are; and the more resistant they are to innovation and change.

SELF-CONCEPTION

Men of higher class position should see themselves as more

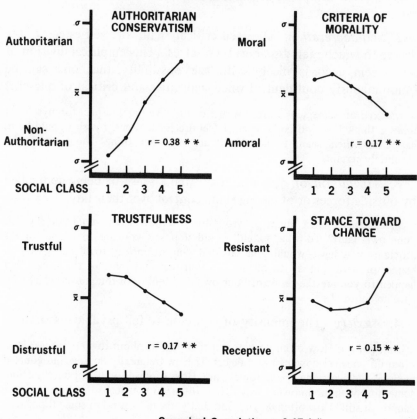

FIGURE 5-3
Social Orientation Factor Scores,
by Social Class

Canonical Correlation = 0.47 * *

**Indicates $p < 0.01$

competent, more effective, more in control of the forces that affect their lives. We investigate five aspects of self-conception: self-confidence, self-deprecation, attribution of responsibility, anxiety, and idea-conformity.

Our indices are based on the same factor analysis as those for social orientation. As before, the full description is in Appendix D; here we only define and illustrate them.

1. *Self-confidence.* The positive component of self-esteem: the degree to which men are confident of their own capacities.

Indexed by agreement or disagreement with such assertions as: I take a positive attitude toward myself. I feel that I'm a person of worth, at least on an equal plane with others. I am able to do most things as well as other people can. I generally have confidence that when I make plans I will be able to carry them out.

2. *Self-deprecation.* The self-critical half of self-esteem: the degree to which men disparage themselves. (This empirical division of self-esteem accords nicely with the possibility that one can be simultaneously confident of one's capacities and critical of oneself.)

Indexed by agreement with: I wish I could have more respect for myself. At times I think I am no good at all. I feel useless at times. I wish I could be as happy as others seem to be. There are very few things about which I'm absolutely certain.

3. *Attribution of responsibility.* Men's sense of being controlled by outside forces or of having some control over their fate.

Indexed by: When things go wrong for you, how often would you say it is your own fault? To what extent would you say you are to blame for the problems you have—would you say that you are mostly to blame, partly to blame, or hardly at all to blame? Do you feel that most of the things that happen to you are the result of your own decisions or of things over which you have no control?

4. *Anxiety.* The intensity of consciously felt psychic discomfort.

Indexed by: How often do you feel that you are about to go to pieces? How often do you feel downcast and dejected? How frequently do you find yourself anxious and worrying about something? How often do you feel uneasy about something without knowing why? How often do you feel so restless that you cannot sit still? How often do you find that you can't get rid of some thought or idea that keeps running through your mind?

5. *Idea-conformity.* The degree to which men believe their ideas mirror those of the social entities to which they belong.

Indexed by: According to your general impression, how often do your ideas and opinions about important matters differ from those of your relatives? How often do your ideas and opinions differ from those of your friends? How about from those of other people with your religious background? Those of most people in the country?

The relationship of class to self-conception is not nearly as strong as is that of class to social orientation; apparently class is less relevant for how men view themselves than for how they view the external world (Figure 5-4). But the findings are consistent with our expectations. The higher men's social class position, the more

FIGURE 5-4
Self-Conception Factor Scores,
by Social Class

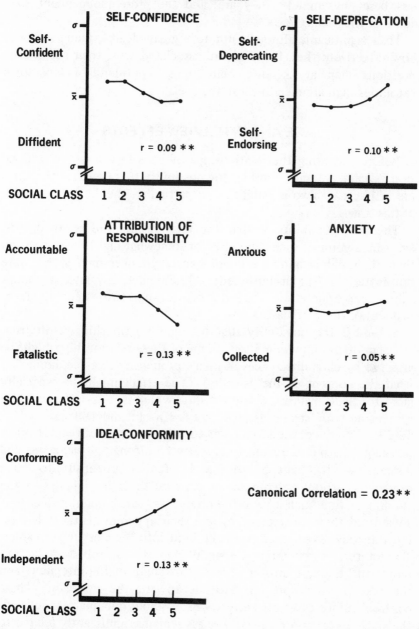

Canonical Correlation = 0.23**

**Indicates $p < 0.01$

self-confidence and the less self-deprecation they express; the greater their sense of being in control of the forces that affect their lives; the less beset by anxiety they are; and the more independent they consider their ideas to be.

To a significant, although not to a great, degree, men's views of how effectively they function are associated with their social class positions—men at the top being more confident of their own capacities than are men lower in the social hierarchy.

AGE AND INTERVIEW EFFECTS

Before accepting the relationships of class to values and orientation as valid, we must consider the possibility that these relationships are artifactual. Two possibilities, in particular, should be dealt with at this time.

The first possibility is that the relationships are really due to age—since younger men tend to be of somewhat higher class position than their elders and one might expect younger men to be more optimistic (or less disillusioned). Age, in fact, is related to men's values and orientations, but the relationships are essentially independent of those of class.

Second is the possibility that the class relationships result from artifacts of the interview itself. Some of these relationships might be affected by class differences in men's propensity to agree, no matter what the content of the assertion. (The effect might be especially great for "authoritarian conservatism," which is indexed entirely by agreement with strong assertions. Cf. Kirscht and Dillehay, 1967: 13-29.) Or, since we asked men to differentiate between *strongly* agreeing and just agreeing (and between *strongly* disagreeing and disagreeing), it might be that a differential propensity to make extreme assertions enters into the class relationships. Then, too, the amount of time men gave to the interviews (which might reflect how considered their answers were) and their apparent attitudes toward the interview experience might be built into the class relationships. To test these possibilities, we simultaneously controlled an "agree" score, an "extreme answer" score, the length of the interview, and the respondent's apparent attitude toward the interview. These controls reduce the class correlations by about one quarter, but with the single exception of anxiety, class remains significantly related to all indices of value and orientation. In fact, these controls increase the magnitude of the correlation of class to self-confidence.

The one-quarter reduction in the relationships of class to values and orientation may be an overstatement of the importance of interview effects. It may be, for example, that the propensity of men at lower class levels to agree with assertions we put to them reflects the very orientations we seek to measure; it is by no means unequivocal that explanations based on interview effects should take precedence over substantive explanations. But, even attributing the maximum possible importance to artifacts of the interview, class is pervasively related to values and orientation.

THE GENERALITY OF THE CLASS RELATIONSHIPS

Again as with parental values, we find that other social variables—principally race, region, religion, national background, and size of community—are independently related to men's values for themselves and to their orientations. Nevertheless, the relationships of class to values and orientation are essentially invariant for all major segments of American society. The magnitudes of the class relationships are little affected by taking other relevant lines of social demarcation into account. This fact is best illustrated by comparing the original class correlations with those same correlations when simultaneously controlled on race, region of the country, size of community, religious background, frequency of church attendance, national background, and men's assessments of the importance of their national backgrounds (Table 5-3). Most of the class correlations are reduced by less than one fifth. All correlations remain statistically significant.

Although the magnitudes of the class relationships are only small to moderate, class is again the most potent component of social structure. As before, we appraise the correlations of class to values and orientation by comparing them (controlled on other dimensions of social structure) to the correlations of those other dimensions (controlled on class). The class correlations are larger than those for race, or religion, or area of the country, or national background; larger, in fact, than for all of them together.

CONCLUSION

Much of the variation in men's values and orientation results from what we have to regard as idiosyncratic personal experience. Only a small proportion is attributable to the position men occupy in the

TABLE 5-3
Comparison of Class Correlations when Not Controlled and when Controlled
Simultaneously on Race, Region, Size of Community, Religion, Frequency of Church
Attendance, National Background, and Importance of National Background

	Class Correlations[a]		
	Not Controlled[b]	Controlled on All	Proportional Reduction
A. Parental values			
Self-direction/conformity	.34**	.29**	.15
B. Values for self			
Self-direction/conformity	.16**	.16**	.00
Self-direction/competence	.13**	.11**	.15
C. Judgments about work			
Importance of intrinsic qualities .	.21**	.20**	.05
Importance of extrinsic benefits..	.37**	.31**	.16
D. Social orientation			
Authoritarian conservatism	.39**	.35**	.10
Criteria of morality	.18**	.14**	.22
Trustfulness	.16**	.11**	.31
Stance toward change	.17**	.15**	.12
Canonical correlation	.49**	.43**	.12
E. Self-conception			
Self-confidence	.10**	.10**	.00
Self-deprecation	.09**	.04**	.56
Attribution of responsibility	.13**	.09**	.31
Anxiety	.06**	.05**	.17
Idea-conformity	.13**	.12**	.08
Canonical correlation	.23**	.20**	.13

* Indicates $p < 0.05$
** Indicates $p < 0.01$
[a] η (eta) or the canonical correlation for the linear component of social class.
[b] These correlations differ somewhat from those of earlier tables because some 300 respondents had to be excluded (either because of incomplete data or because of limitations in the number of cells that could be included in the design).

general social structure. Still, social structure does have pronounced and consistent effects, and, of all aspects of social structure, class is by far the most important.

The higher their social class position, the more men value self-direction and the more confident they are that self-direction is both possible and efficacious. The lower their social class position, the more men value conformity and the more certain they are that conformity is all that their own capacities and the exigencies of the world allow.

We interpret these findings to indicate that men's values, their appraisals of their own abilities, and their understanding of the world are quite consistent. Self-direction is a central value for men of higher class position, who see themselves as competent members of an essentially benign society. Conformity is a central value for men of lower class position, who see themselves as less competent members of an essentially indifferent or threatening society. Self-direction, in short, is consonant with an orientational system premised on the possibilities of accomplishing what one sets out to do; conformity, with an orientational system premised on the dangers of stepping out of line.

PART II

Values and Behavior

CHAPTER 6

Misbehavior and Punishment

Do class differences in values and orientation find expression in behavior? In this chapter, we examine an area of behavior that is directly related to values—parental responses to children's misbehavior. The strategy of analysis is to see whether class differences in parental values help explain whatever differences there may be in parents' disciplinary practices. Ordinarily, one examines the use of sanctions in order to infer values—sanctions are usually invoked in situations where values have been transgressed (cf. Williams, 1968: 285). In this analysis, we examine the use of sanctions, not to discover values, but to see whether or not actions are consonant with asserted values.

Most past research on class differences in disciplinary practices has been directed to learning whether working-class parents typically employ techniques of punishment different from those used by the middle class.[1] Bronfenbrenner (1958: 424) summarized the results of the several relevant studies as indicating that "working-class parents are consistently more likely to employ physical punishment, while middle-class families rely more on reasoning, isolation, appeals to guilt, and other methods involving the threat of loss of love." This conclusion is certainly consistent with working-class parents' greater concern about the overt act and middle-class parents' greater concern about children's internal dynamics.

For our purposes, though, the crucial question is not *which* disciplinary method parents prefer, but *when and why* they use one or another method of discipline. Past research tells us little about the when and why of discipline; most investigators have relied on

---

[1]Sometimes the question has been which class employs more *severe* techniques. This involves debatable a priori judgments of which techniques are most severe. Another major question, especially in studies of the training of infants and very young children (for example, weaning and toilet training), has been which social class is the more "permissive," which the more "rigid," in its training procedures. These terms lead to difficulty because of ambiguity about which kinds of behavior are permissive and which are rigid.

parents' generalized statements about their usual or their preferred methods of dealing with disciplinary problems, irrespective of what the particular problem might be. But not all disciplinary problems evoke the same kind of parental response. In some sense, after all, the punishment fits the crime. *Under what conditions* do parents of a given social class punish their children physically, reason with them, isolate them—or ignore their actions altogether? We shall attempt to specify the reactions of middle-class parents and of working-class parents to several concrete types of misbehavior, and from this information develop a general interpretation of the relationship of social class to the use of punishment.

The data for this analysis come primarily from the Washington study, which provides information from 339 mothers and from a subsample of 82 fathers and children on parents' responses to children's misbehavior. This study offers a numerically adequate basis for analyzing mothers' self-reports, a numerically limited basis for analyzing fathers' self-reports, and a limited but invaluable basis for analyzing the *consistency* of mothers', fathers', and children's reports on both parents' behavior. To improve the numerical basis for analyzing fathers' self-reports, we include data from the National study. These data also give us the opportunity to see whether children's age is relevant to fathers' responses to misbehavior.

MOTHERS' USE OF PUNISHMENT

In attempting to specify the conditions under which mothers punish children, we rely on their reported reactions to eight situations—when the child plays wildly, fights with brothers or sisters, fights with other children, really loses his temper, refuses to do what (you) tell him to do, swipes something from home or from other children, smokes cigarettes, or uses language (you) don't want him to use.

Mothers were questioned in detail about each of these situations. We asked, for example, whether the fifth-grade child ever really loses his temper; precisely what he does when he loses his temper; what the mother generally does when he acts this way; whether she ever finds it necessary to do anything else; if so, under what circumstances; and what else she does.

Middle- and working-class mothers were equally likely to report that their children lose their tempers, fight with others, refuse to do as they are told, swipe something, smoke, or use disapproved language. Middle-class mothers, though, were more likely[2] than were working-class mothers to tell us that their sons play wildly and fight with brothers or sisters.[3]

For most of the situations reported, middle- and working-class mothers described the children's actions similarly. Two notable exceptions are that working-class mothers tended to define sons' fights with brothers or sisters and daughters' fights with other children as physical combats, while middle-class mothers were more likely to mean arguments.

Reports on maternal responses to children's misbehavior were classified as follows:

1. Ignore: do nothing about it.

2. Scold, admonish to be good, demand that child stop, inquire into causes of behavior, scream, threaten to punish. (It has proved impossible to differentiate these several verbal reactions reliably from interview material. We could not determine, for example, whether a mother's reported attempt to discover the causes of a fight was in fact a scolding.)

3. Separate from other children or divert attention: remove the child from the situation or provide alternative activities.

4. Restrict usual activities: limit child's freedom of movement or activity short of isolation, for example, not let him play outside.

5. Isolate: confine child *alone* for a period of time, for example, send him to bed during the day.

6. Punish physically: everything from a slap to a spanking.

The last three categories—restriction of usual activities, isolation, and physical punishment—are together treated as punishment or coercion.

Most mothers—in both social classes—reported that they generally respond to all eight situations either by ignoring the children's actions altogether, or at most by admonishing them (Table 6-1). Few mothers isolate or restrict their children at this stage, and virtually

---

[2]The tests of statistical significance used in this chapter are the *t* test for the difference between two proportions and, where the number of cases is small, Fisher's exact test.

[3]This does not necessarily mean that working-class boys are actually less likely to play wildly or to fight with brothers or sisters; mothers who said that their sons do not engage in these actions are more likely than are other mothers to conceive of wild play as *aggressively* wild and of fighting as *physical* combat, and so may not report less pronounced misbehavior.

TABLE 6-1. Mothers' Reported Responses to Children's Misbehavior—under Usual Circumstances (limited to mothers who report that their children behave in the particular way)

Proportion of Mothers Who Report that They Respond by:

When child:	Ignoring		Scolding or Admonishing		Separating the Child from Others		Isolating or Restricting Activities		Punishing Physically		Number of Cases	
	Middle Class	Working Class	Middle Class	Working Class	Middle Class	Working Class	Middle Class	Working Class	Middle Class	Working Class	Middle Class	Working Class
Plays wildly												
Sons	.31	.34	.42	.45	.17	.07	.10	.12	.00	.02	(64)	(44)
Daughters	.36 *	.56	.49 *	.28	.10	.08	.05	.05	.00	.03	(42)	(39)
Fights with his brothers or sisters												
Sons	.13	.05	.54	.40	.18	.31	.13	.22	.02	.02	(65)	(55)
Daughters	.18	.10	.53	.60	.19	.08	.08	.16	.02	.06	(68)	(50)
Fights with children other than brothers or sisters												
Sons	.48	.44	.37	.36	.15	.08	.00 *	.12	.00	.00	(46)	(50)
Daughters	.35	.29	.48	.46	.17	.19	.00	.06	.00	.00	(42)	(41)
Loses his temper												
Sons	.32	.30	.49	.41	.03	.01	.11	.19	.05	.09	(81)	(74)
Daughters	.41	.32	.40	.43	.00	.00	.13	.14	.06	.11	(67)	(57)
Refuses to do what his mother tells him to do												
Sons	.14	.19	.74	.77	.00	.02	.12	.02	.00	.00	(56)	(43)
Daughters	.30 *	.09	.59	.77	.00	.00	.11	.08	.00	.06	(37)	(35)
Uses language that his mother doesn't want him to use												
Sons	.11	.03	.78	.86	.00	.00	.11	.06	.00	.05	(48)	(36)
Daughters	.04	.00	.89	.78	.00	.00	.07	.18	.00	.04	(29)	(27)
Smokes cigarettes												
Sons	.24	.27	.66	.73	.00	.00	.10	.00	.00	.00	(21)	(15)
Daughters	.64	.30	.36	.50	.00	.00	.10	.10	.00	.10	(14)	(10)
Swipes something from home or from other children												
Sons	.12	.05	.76	.90	.04	.00	.08	.05	.00	.00	(26)	(20)
Daughters	.00	.08	.67	.67	.00	.00	.11	.17	.22	.08	(9)	(12)

* Social class differences statistically significant, $p < 0.05$, using the t test for the difference between two proportions or, where the number of cases is small, Fisher's exact test.

none punishes them physically. One cannot conclude that mothers of either social class are quick to employ coercion. But when children *persist* in wild play, in fights with brothers or sisters, or in displays of temper, both middle- and working-class mothers are likely to turn to one or another form of punishment (Table 6-2).

There is no consistent difference in middle- and working-class mothers' propensity to resort to restriction or to isolation when children persist in misbehavior. There is, however, a tendency for working-class mothers to be more likely than middle-class mothers to employ physical punishment. In only 3 of 16 comparisons is the difference between the proportions of middle- and working-class mothers who use physical punishment large enough to be statistically significant—when sons persist in wild play, when they fight with brothers or sisters, and when daughters fight with other children. But in 13 of the 16 comparisons, there is some (however slight) difference in the proportions of middle- and working-class mothers who report using physical punishment, with the proportion of working-class mothers the larger.

That working-class mothers are more prone to use physical punishment in response to persistent misbehavior does not necessarily mean that they use physical punishment more frequently than do middle-class mothers; it depends on how often the situations occur. In fact, reports by both mothers and children indicate that middle-class mothers punish children physically as often as do working-class mothers (Table 6-3). It would seem, then, that the difference between middle- and working-class mothers' use of physical punishment is not in the frequency with which they use it, but in the conditions under which they use it. This is shown more pointedly by an examination of the specific conditions under which mothers of the two social classes resort to punishment, physical punishment in particular. Some actions that are intolerable to working-class mothers are not punished by middle-class mothers, and other actions, intolerable to middle-class mothers, are not punished by working-class mothers.

The Conditions under Which Working-Class Mothers Punish Sons

Working-class mothers tend to respond to their sons' misbehavior on the basis of the direct and immediate consequences of the disobedient acts. This is best illustrated by the two types of

TABLE 6-2. Mothers' Reported Use of Restriction, Isolation, and Physical Punishment—when Children Persist in Misbehavior

Proportion of Mothers Who Report that They Respond by:

	Restricting Activities		Isolating		Punishing Physically		Total of All Punishment		Number of Cases	
	Middle Class	Working Class	Middle Class	Working Class	Middle Class	Working Class	Middle Class	Working Class	Middle Class	Working Class
When child:										
Plays wildly										
Sons	.20	.18	.05	.02	.09 *	.23	.34	.43	(64)	(44)
Daughters	.17	.18	.12 *	.00	.02	.08	.31	.26	(42)	(39)
Fights with his brothers or sisters										
Sons	.06	.04	.34	.25	.17 *	.43	.57	.72	(65)	(55)
Daughters	.09	.14	.24	.26	.21	.26	.54	.66	(68)	(50)
Fights with children other than brothers or sisters										
Sons	.15	.12	.00	.06	.00	.02	.15	.20	(46)	(50)
Daughters	.14	.12	.02	.05	.00 *	.15	.16	.32	(42)	(41)
Loses his temper										
Sons	.06 *	.19	.14	.11	.20	.30	.40 *	.60	(81)	(74)
Daughters	.03	.09	.12	.12	.24	.26	.39	.47	(67)	(57)
Refuses to do what his mother tells him to do										
Sons	.18 *	.00	.04	.07	.12	.07	.34 *	.14	(56)	(43)
Daughters	.14	.06	.05	.06	.08	.23	.27	.35	(37)	(35)
Uses language that his mother doesn't want him to use										
Sons	.10 *	.00	.02	.00	.04	.11	.16	.11	(48)	(36)
Daughters	.07	.11	.03	.00	.00	.11	.10	.22	(29)	(27)
Smokes cigarettes										
Sons	.05	.00	.00	.00	.00	.00	.05	.00	(21)	(15)
Daughters	.00	.10	.00	.00	.00	.10	.00	.20	(14)	(10)
Swipes something from home or from other children										
Sons	.08	.05	.00	.00	.04	.00	.12	.05	(26)	(20)
Daughters	.00	.25	.11	.00	.12	.17	.23	.42	(9)	(12)

* Social class differences statistically significant, $p < 0.05$, using the t test for the difference between two proportions or, where the number of cases is small, Fisher's exact test.

misbehavior for which working-class mothers are significantly more likely than are middle-class mothers to punish sons physically—wild play and fighting with brothers or sisters. In either situation, the more disruptive the boys' actions, the more likely are working-class mothers to use punishment, physical punishment in particular (Table 6-4). Working-class mothers whose descriptions indicate that the wild

TABLE 6-3
Mothers' Reported Use of Physical Punishment, by Social Class and Sex of Child—
Reports by Mothers and by Children

	Proportion of Mothers Reported to Use Physical Punishment							
	Reports by Mothers				Reports by Children			
	Response to Sons		Response to Daughters		Response to Sons		Response to Daughters	
	Middle Class	Working Class	Middle Class	Working Class	Middle Class	Working Class	Middle Class	Working Class
Mother reportedly punishes child physically:								
Occasionally or frequently ..	.14	.16	.09	.16	.16	.04	.05	.09
Infrequently	.46	.44	.39	.42	.16	.12	.05	.10
Rarely or never	.40	.40	.52	.42	.68	.84	.90	.81
	1.00	1.00	1.00	1.00	1.00	1.00	1.00	1.00
Mother reportedly has punished child physically:								
Within past week	.16	.13	.13	.14	.12	.04	.00	.00
Within past month (inclusive)	.30	.28	.27	.32	.32	.08	.10	.18
Within past six months (inclusive)	.59	.55	.45	.56	.36	.28	.15	.18
Number of cases[a]	(79)	(82)	(75)	(77)	(25)	(25)	(21)	(11)

[a] These questions were not asked of the first 26 mothers interviewed.
Note: No class difference is statistically significant.

play is nothing more than boisterousness or running around are no more likely to resort to punishment than are middle-class mothers who face the same circumstances. But those whose descriptions of wild play include belligerent or destructive actions are more likely to employ punishment than are middle-class mothers. Similarly, working-class mothers are not significantly more likely than are middle-class mothers to punish sons for fights with brothers or sisters when the fights are simply arguments, but they are more likely to

TABLE 6-4

Mothers' Reported Use of Restriction, Isolation, and Physical Punishment—Controlled on Seriousness of Children's Misbehavior (sons only)

| | Proportion of Mothers Who Report that They Respond by: | | | | | | | | Number of Cases | |
| | Restricting Activities | | Isolating | | Punishing Physically | | Total of All Punishment | | | |
When son:	Middle Class	Working Class	Middle Class	Working Class	Middle Class	Working Class	Middle Class	Working Class	Middle Class	Working Class
Plays wildly										
Described as boisterousness or running around	.16	.18	.03	.04	.13	.11	.32	.33	(38)	(28)
Described as willful aggression or destruction	.26	.19	.08	.00	.04 *	.43	.38	.62 *	(26)	(16)
Fights with his brothers or sisters										
Described as argument	.10	.13	.30	.13	.10	.27 *	.50	.53 *	(30)	(15)
Described as physical encounter	.03	.00	.37	.30	.23 *	.50	.63	.80	(35)	(40)
Fights with children other than his brothers or sisters										
Described as physical encounter	.16	.12	.00	.07	.00	.02	.16	.21	(31)	(42)
Loses his temper										
Described as pouting, yelling, or sulking	.06 *	.22	.12	.06	.15 *	.26	.33 *	.54	(66)	(54)
Described as violent or aggressive outburst	.07	.10	.20	.25	.40	.40	.67	.75	(15)	(20)

*Difference statistically significant, $p < 0.05$ using the t test for the difference between two proportions or, where the number of cases is small, Fisher's exact test.

resort to punishment when the fights involve physical combat. Working-class mothers punish sons for wild play and for fights with brothers or sisters only when the consequences of the misbehavior are serious.

Apparently, extreme forms of wild play and fighting are particularly intolerable to working-class mothers. This impression is sustained by the finding that those working-class mothers who consider themselves unusually "strict" and "ready to lay down the law" are especially likely to punish sons physically for serious fights with brothers or sisters. And those working-class mothers who describe themselves as "easily angered" by their sons' actions or unwilling to "give in" to them are especially likely to use physical punishment for aggressively wild play. They cannot or will not tolerate these forms of misbehavior.

The responsiveness of working-class mothers to direct and immediate consequences is demonstrated anew by a consideration of the conditions under which they do not punish sons. There is ample evidence above that working-class mothers punish sons for certain acts of disobedience. Furthermore, they were more likely than were middle-class mothers to tell us that their last use of physical punishment was in response to disobedience. Even though working-class mothers are likely to punish boys for violating *negative* injunctions, however, they are unlikely to punish boys for refusing to do things that they are *positively* enjoined to do.

The immediate consequences of acquiescing to a son's refusal may be trivial—often nothing more than having to do a minor household chore when he will not comply. But under some conditions—specifically, when the boy is adamant about his refusal—the consequences of forcing him to do as he is told may be far from trivial. Of the working-class mothers who described their sons' refusals as prolonged delays when they had unquestionably heard the order, or as acts of outright defiance, none told us that she employed physical punishment, restriction, or isolation (Table 6-5). Working-class mothers were more likely than were middle-class mothers to tell us that they took no action at all under these circumstances. But inaction does not signify indifference. The interview reports indicate that these mothers do make an attempt to secure compliance but then back down. This is especially true of those who say they are "easily upset" by their sons' actions. They seem unable to bring themselves to take strong action but are hardly indifferent.

TABLE 6-5
Mothers' Reported Responses when Their Children
Defiantly Refuse to Do as They Are Told to Do

	Response to Sons		Response to Daughters	
	Middle Class	Working Class	Middle Class	Working Class
Proportion of mothers who report that they respond by:				
Punishing them physically	.13	.00	.09	.25
Isolating them	.02 * .00		.04	.07
Restricting their activities	.17	.00	.12	.07
Scolding, admonishing, insisting that child obey, threatening to punish .	.59	.66	.63	.57
Not doing anything about it	.09 * .34		.12	.04
	1.00	1.00	1.00	1.00
Number of cases	(46)	(32)	(33)	(28)

* Social class differences statistically significant, $p < 0.05$, using t test for the difference between two proportions.

The Conditions under Which Middle-Class Mothers Punish Sons

Middle-class mothers seem to punish or refrain from punishing, less on the basis of the *consequences* of their sons' misbehavior, and more on the basis of their interpretation of the boys' *intent*. This concern with intent is best illustrated by their differential responses to wild play and to loss of temper (Table 6-4). They are not likely to punish sons physically for wild play, however extreme it may be. Nor are they particularly likely to punish boys physically for loss of temper when it is manifested only as pouting, yelling, or sulking. But to a violent or aggressive outburst of temper, middle-class mothers are likely to respond by using physical punishment. In these circumstances, middle-class mothers are as prone as are their working-class counterparts to punish sons physically.

That middle-class mothers are likely to resort to physical punishment in response to an outburst of temper but not in response to extreme wild play, does not reflect any great difference in the boys' overt behavior. Instead, the differential response seems to reflect different interpretations of the boys' intent in acting as they do, as judged from the situational context. If, in the course of play, boys become very excited, this is not thought to be alarming—however extreme their actions. But if the actions seem to stem from the frustration of not having their own way, this is thought to be very alarming indeed. The overt behavior in the two types of situations might be, and often is, nearly identical—shouting, wrestling, slamming doors, stamping feet, running. The critical difference is whether this excited behavior is interpreted as "merely letting off steam" or as a "serious loss of control"—"a tantrum." The former is tolerable, the latter distressing.

The Conditions under Which Mothers Punish Daughters

Middle-class mothers respond to daughters' actions much as they do to sons' (Tables 6-2 and 6-5). Working-class mothers appear to be less likely to punish daughters than sons for wild play and for fighting with brothers or sisters, but this apparent difference results from boys' wild play and fighting being more disruptive. When daughters misbehave as seriously, working-class mothers are as prone to punish them.

In some situations, working-class mothers are more likely to punish daughters than sons—when the girls fight with other children, when they smoke, and when they swipe something (Table 6-2). Girls are held to more stringent definitions of appropriateness. Most dramatic of all, working-class mothers are far more likely to punish daughters than sons for defiantly refusing to do as they are told (Table 6-5). More is expected of girls than of boys: Girls must not only refrain from unacceptable behavior; they must also fulfill positive expectations.

Clearly, working-class mothers evaluate daughters' actions differently from sons', but there is no indication that children's intent is the basis of evaluation for either sex. With girls as with boys, working-class mothers tend to respond to misbehavior more in terms of direct and immediate consequences, middle-class mothers more in terms of presumed intent.[4]

---

[4]The relationships between social class and mothers' responses to children's misbehavior are not appreciably modified by controlling other relevant variables—mother's age; size of the family; ordinal position of the child in the family; length of time the family has lived in the neighborhood; the socioeconomic status of the neighborhood; whether or not the mother has a job, and if so what type of job; whether or not she has been socially mobile or feels socially mobile; her social class identification; her level of education; her religious background; whether her background is rural or urban; whether or not she reads popular literature on child rearing; and the size and type of firm, organization, or agency for which her husband works.

Hypothetical Reactions

Whenever a mother told us that a child had not performed an action about which we inquired, we asked her what she thought she would do if the situation were to occur. Middle-class mothers who said that a given situation had not occurred thought that they would probably respond in ways almost identical to those reported by middle-class mothers who said that it had. Working-class mothers, on the other hand, seem unable to envisage either the circumstances under which they would employ punishment or the circumstances under which they would not. For example, those working-class mothers who reported that their sons have engaged in aggressively wild play were likely to tell us that they punish the boys physically; but those for whom the situation is hypothetical did not think that they would use physical punishment in these circumstances. Conversely, no working-class mother who told us that her son had swiped something, smoked, or defiantly refused to carry out an order reported punishing him physically, but roughly one fifth of the working-class mothers for whom these situations were hypothetical thought that they would resort to such punishment. Apparently, working-class mothers are too closely attuned to particular situational realities to be able to predict how they would behave under hypothetical conditions.

FATHERS' USE OF PUNISHMENT

In analyzing fathers' responses to children's misbehavior, we face a problem of insufficient numbers. The 82 fathers in the Washington study are too few to make possible the control of all essential variables—social class, the child's sex, the actuality of the situation, and the seriousness of the misbehavior. The National study provides more leeway, but not enough: By our deliberate effort to cover a wide range of children's ages, we have greatly limited the number of fathers reporting on any misbehavior by children of any given age and sex. There are 1,500 fathers, but when we deal, for example, with middle-class fathers whose 7- to 9-year-old boys engage in aggressively wild play, we are down to precisely 19. We must be cautious in drawing conclusions, but some seem reasonable.

There are no appreciable class differences in the conditions under which fathers punish very young children (the 3- to 6-year-olds) or in the kinds of punishment administered. For the four types of misbehavior about which we inquired in the National study—wild play, fighting with brothers or sisters, loss of temper, and refusing to do as told—fathers of all social classes are likely to punish very young children physically.

As the children grow older and fathers become progressively less likely to use physical punishment no matter what the situation, social class begins to make a difference for fathers' responses to misbehavior. Class does not seem to make as great a difference for fathers as for mothers. Nevertheless, judging from the data of both the Washington and National studies, class differences in the conditions under which fathers resort to punishment—physical punishment in particular—are essentially the same as those for mothers: Middle-class fathers respond more to intent and working-class fathers more to consequences.

AN APPRAISAL OF THE DATA

There are several limitations in using interview data as approximations to objective reality. The most serious is that the participants in the actions—mothers, fathers, and children—may not see things as a presumably objective outsider would. Moreover, interview responses are in their nature limited: We do not learn whether parents express displeasure by grouchiness, by assuming an air of martyrdom, or simply by acting differently; and we cannot learn which parental actions are interpreted by children as a withdrawal of love. Finally, each respondent has in effect summarized a number of his own and other people's actions; we cannot tell how frequently situations of a given type have occurred, or how consistent a parent's reactions have been.

Despite these limitations, there is reason to believe that the descriptions given in these interviews are realistic. One reason for confidence is that parents are able to differentiate between what they generally do and what they do in more pressing circumstances. Another and more important reason is that where we have interviewed mother, father, and child in the same family, all three descriptions of both parents' reactions to misbehavior are in close agreement.[5] The only exceptions are that few working-class boys

---

[5]In most instances the number of cases is so small as to preclude the possibility of statistical significance.

report that their mothers punish them physically for fighting with brothers or sisters or for loss of temper. They acknowledge that their fathers do so, but say that their mothers isolate or restrict them for such actions. These minor exceptions aside, all three sources of information lead to the same conclusions. Granted that mother, father, and child could all misperceive the situation, it seems safe to treat their descriptions as fairly accurate reflections of what actually takes place.

CONCLUSION

Neither middle- nor working-class parents resort to punishment as a first recourse when children misbehave. It seems, instead, that parents of both social classes initially post limits for their children. But when children persist in misbehavior, despite parents' attempts to forestall them, parents are likely to resort to one or another form of coercion. This is true in both social classes. The principal difference between the classes is in the *specific conditions* under which parents—particularly mothers—punish children's misbehavior. Working-class parents are more likely to punish or refrain from punishing on the basis of the direct and immediate consequences of children's actions, middle-class parents on the basis of their interpretation of children's intent in acting as they do.

To say that working-class parents respond more to consequences and middle-class parents more to intent gets dangerously close to implying that while middle-class parents act on the basis of long-range goals for children, working-class parents do not. On the contrary, we believe that parents of both social classes act on the basis of long-range goals—*but that the goals are different.*[6]

The interpretive key is provided by our knowledge of class differences in parental values. Because middle- and working-class parents differ in their values, they view children's misbehavior differently; what is intolerable to parents in one social class can be taken in stride by parents in the other. In both social classes, parents punish children for transgressing important values; but, since the

---

[6]There is a stereotype, shared by many social scientists, that working-class values are "present-oriented"—in contrast to the "future-orientation" of the middle class. If there is truth to this belief, it has not been well documented and almost certainly has been exaggerated. It seems to be based largely on overgeneralization from a few tangentially relevant studies, principally Leshan, 1952; and Schneider and Lysgaard, 1953.

values are different, the transgressions are differently defined. If self-direction is valued, transgressions must be judged in terms of the reasons why the children misbehave. If conformity is valued, transgressions must be judged in terms of whether or not the actions violate externally imposed proscriptions.

It is clear that values enter into mothers' responses to children's misbehavior,[7] but our evidence is less certain for fathers. Even if the connection between values and response to misbehavior is not as strong for fathers, this need not mean that men act less in accord with their values than women do, but only that children's misbehavior is less likely to be fathers' concern. We have no direct evidence and must leave the issues unresolved. Since our interpretation is better grounded for mothers, we focus on them.

To see mothers' responses to children's misbehavior as (at least in part) a function of their values helps answer several otherwise perplexing questions.

First, why are working-class mothers more likely to punish children for fighting than for arguing with brothers or sisters, or for aggressively wild play than for boisterousness? The answer seems to be that transgressions of the value, conformity, are necessarily measured in terms of how far the misbehavior oversteps the rules. Fighting and wild play deserve punishment only when they are sufficiently serious to overstep the boundaries of the acceptable.

Second, why are working-class mothers more likely to punish daughters than sons for fighting with friends, smoking, swiping something, or defiantly refusing to do as they are told? The answer seems to lie in different conceptions of what is right and proper for boys and for girls. What may be taken as acceptable behavior (perhaps even as an assertion of manliness) in a preadolescent boy

---

[7]The thrust of our argument is that middle- and working-class mothers' differential valuation of self-direction and conformity gives us a basis for interpreting the difference in their responses to misbehavior. It is relevant (although not crucial) to this argument that in all three instances where our data permit such an analysis, we find a direct connection between a particular parental value and a propensity to punish children for behavior that transgresses that value. In both social classes, mothers who value self-control highly are more likely than are other mothers to punish children for loss of temper. Similarly, in both social classes, mothers who value consideration highly are likely to punish children for fighting. And middle-class mothers who value obedience are likely to punish both boys and girls for refusing to do as they are told; working-class mothers who value obedience punish girls. There are too few cases of children swiping something for an adequate analysis, but the limited evidence suggests that mothers' responses to this misbehavior are appropriately related to their valuation of honesty.

may be thought thoroughly unladylike in a young girl. Working-class mothers differentiate quite clearly between the qualities they regard as desirable for daughters and those they value for sons. They want daughters to be "little ladies" (a term that kept recurring in the interviews) and sons to be manly. This being the case, the criteria of disobedience are necessarily different for boys and for girls. Obedience is highly valued for both. It would appear, though, that obedience requires positive performance by a girl, while a boy need only eschew the negative. This seems to be particularly true for those working-class mothers who value obedience most highly; these mothers are especially likely to punish daughters physically for refusing to carry out parental requests and orders, while they are unlikely to take any action at all when sons refuse to do so.

Middle-class mothers make little or no distinction between what is desirable for boys and for girls—the issue for both sexes is whether or not children act in accord with internalized principles. Therefore, the conduct of both boys and girls should be judged by the same criterion: intent. The evidence—similar responses to the misbehavior of boys and girls—supports this interpretation.

Finally, why do middle-class mothers react differently to extreme wild play and to outbursts of temper? Why do they interpret these overtly similar actions as implying radically different intent? The answer is provided by the fundamental importance they attach to internal standards for governing one's relationships with other people and, ultimately, with one's self.

Wild play, however extreme, does not necessarily represent a loss of self-control (even though it may indicate that the parent has lost control over the child). It may be regarded as a childish form of emotional expression—unpleasant, but bearable, and many middle-class mothers see virtue in allowing it free expression. In fact, those middle-class mothers who value happiness most highly are the least likely to punish wild play. An outburst of temper, by contrast, may signal serious difficulty in children's efforts at self-mastery; it is the type of behavior most likely to distress parents who have tried to inculcate in children the virtue of maintaining self-control. Again, the evidence supports the interpretation: Those parents who value self-control highly are most likely to punish children for loss of temper.

If middle-class mothers are to act in accord with their values, they must take explicit account of the subjective and the emotional, including the possible effects of punishment. They give considerable evidence that they do. Of course, parents can rationalize. It is easy to believe that behavior that is at the moment infuriating ought to be punished. One gains the impression, however, that although middle-class mothers may punish when angry, they try to restrain themselves.[8] The working-class orientation, on the other hand, excludes or minimizes considerations of subjective intent and places few restraints on the impulse to punish children when their behavior is out of bounds. Instead, it provides a positive rationale for punishing in precisely those circumstances when one might most like to do so.

---

[8]It is revealing that the middle-class mothers who are most likely to report the frequent use of physical punishment are those who have little confidence in their ability to assess children's intent—that is, those who say they are "unsure of themselves" in dealing with children. The working-class mothers who are most likely to make frequent use of physical punishment are those who are most sensitive to the immediate situation—who say that they are "easily upset" by the children's actions.

CHAPTER 7

Role-Allocation

The connection between values and punishment of disvalued behavior is direct—punishment is invoked when values are transgressed. The present chapter traces some less direct but broader behavioral consequences of class differences in values and orientation. We continue to focus on the family, but enlarge that focus from specific disciplinary actions to the overall patterning of parent-child interaction.

We conceive of parent-child relationships as structured along two principal axes—"support" and "constraint." This conception is derived in part from Parsons and Bales's theoretical analysis of the structure of the family (1955, esp. p. 45) and in part from Schaefer's (1959) empirical demonstration that the findings of several past studies of parent-child relationships could be greatly clarified by arraying them along these two dimensions. We use the term "role-allocation" to mean the division between mother and father of responsibilities for support and constraint of children.

Because their values are different, middle- and working-class parents should evaluate differently the relative importance of support and constraint in child rearing. One would expect middle-class parents to feel a greater obligation to be *supportive*, if only because of their concern about children's internal dynamics. Working-class parents, because of their higher valuation of conformity to external rules, should put greater emphasis upon the obligation to impose *constraints*. We should therefore expect the ratio of support to constraint in parents' handling of their children to be higher in middle- than in working-class families. And this, according to Bronfenbrenner (1958: 425), is precisely what has been shown in those few studies that have dealt with the overall relationship of parents to child: "Over the entire . . . period studied, parent-child relationships in the middle class are consistently reported as more acceptant and equalitarian, while those in the working class are oriented toward maintaining order and obedience."

109

Within this context, the middle class has shown a shift away from emotional control toward freer expression of affection and greater tolerance of the child's impulses and desires."[1]

Whatever relative weight parents give to support and constraint, the process of child rearing requires both. These responsibilities can, however, be apportioned between mother and father in any of several ways. Mothers can specialize in providing support, fathers in imposing constraints; both parents can play both roles more or less equally; mothers can monopolize both roles, with fathers playing little part in child rearing; and there are other possible, but less likely, arrangements. Given their values, middle-class parents—mothers and fathers both—should want fathers (as well as mothers) to play an important part in providing support to the children. It would seem more appropriate to working-class values that fathers' obligations should center on the imposition of constraints.

This chapter examines the allocation, between mother and father, of responsibilities for the support and constraint of children.[2] The question here is not the absolute level of support or constraint in middle- and working-class families but, rather, the relative roles of mother and father. We begin with descriptions by mothers, fathers, and children of the actual patterns of role-allocation in middle- and working-class families. Then we shall see how these patterns are evaluated in the two social classes—for class differences in values and orientation are reflected both in characteristically different patterns of role-allocation and in characteristically different patterns of satisfaction and dissatisfaction with these allocations.

These analyses are based primarily on data of the Washington study, which provides reports by mothers and by a subsample of fathers and children. Even though the subsample of fathers and children is small, it is invaluable because it provides the perspectives

---

[1]No studies done in the decade since Bronfenbrenner's review contradict this conclusion, so far as we know.

[2]To the best of our knowledge, there had been no studies, prior to the present investigation, addressed specifically to the relationship of social class and parental role-allocation. A few studies dealt tangentially with fathers' roles, but these gave contradictory results. Two major investigations of social class and family relationships concluded, from limited evidence, that middle- and working-class fathers are equally involved in child rearing (cf. Havighurst and Davis, 1955: 441; Maccoby and Gibbs, 1954: 395). But there is some evidence that middle-class fathers play a larger part in child rearing than do working-class fathers—that they devote more time to the children (cf. Davis and Havighurst, 1946; Spinley, 1953), play a larger part in disciplining them (Anderson, 1936), and have "warmer" relationships with them (Mitchell, 1950).

of mothers, fathers, and children in the same families. The National study provides a useful supplement, for it gives us the reports of a much larger (and more representative) sample of fathers, and enables us to see whether patterns of role-allocation differ according to the age of the child.

THE SUPPORT DIMENSION IN PARENT-CHILD RELATIONSHIPS

Index of Parental Support

Since the problem is role-allocation, our index of parental support is designed to measure fathers' supportiveness as compared to mothers'. There are two intertwined aspects to measuring mothers' and fathers' relative roles in providing support to children: Which parent is the more encouraging? To which parent does the child turn for advice and reassurance? It seemed likely that both parents and children would think that children turn to the more encouraging parent. This expectation was put to empirical test by choosing two questions relevant to each aspect and determining whether answers to the set of four fall into a consistent pattern. The four questions (in the form in which they were asked of mothers) are:

1. When (the fifth-grade child) does something that pleases you, what do you usually do? What does [your husband] do when (child) does something that pleases him? (Answers were classified according to whether or not each parent encourages the child.)

2. Can you tell me whether you or your husband is quicker to praise (child) for the things he does well—or would you say that you are both equally quick to praise him, or that neither is quick to praise him?

3. Which parent is (child) more likely to feel he can talk things over with?

4. To whom does (child) turn when he's troubled, or feels unhappy—or doesn't he turn to anyone in particular?

The same questions, with appropriate changes in format, were asked of fathers and children.

These questions deliberately do not specify when and for what parents encourage children or when and for what children turn to parents. For example, the first question asks about parents' responses when pleased by children's actions, regardless of what pleases them. Middle-class parents, as we would expect from knowing their values, are more likely[3] to be pleased by children's personal accomplishments; working-class parents, by their obedience. For purposes of index construction, though certainly not for purposes of interpretation, the issue of what pleases parents was deemed irrelevant.

Few parents or children said that the father is the more encouraging parent, or that the child turns more readily to father than to mother for advice and reassurance. Therefore, we dichotomized answers to the first two questions according to whether or not the father is thought to be as encouraging as the mother, and answers to the third and fourth questions according to whether or not the child is thought to turn to his father as readily as to his mother. Considered this way, mothers', fathers', and children's answers each fall into a consistent scale pattern.[4] We use this scale as our index of supportiveness.

It must again be emphasized that the scale measures fathers' supportiveness relative to mothers'; thus, when we speak of a highly supportive father-child relationship, we use that inexact phrase as shorthand for the accurate but cumbersome expression, "a father-child relationship that is at least as supportive as the relationship of the mother to that child."

One final note: Our term, supportiveness, is an abstraction from parents' and children's reports about parental encouragement and children's turning to parents for succor. There is no direct evidence that supportiveness is an appropriate name for the dimension of parent-child interaction measured here, but there is one bit of indirect evidence: Parents' and children's scores on our scale of

---

[3]The tests of statistical significance used in this chapter are chi-squared (or its equivalent, the t test for the difference between two proportions) and, where the number of cases is small, Fisher's exact test.

[4]Reproducibility of the mothers' answers is 0.96, scalability is 0.84, and in all other relevant respects the pattern of answers is a close approximation to the model of a perfect Guttman Scale (cf. Guttman, 1950a, b; Menzel, 1953; Ford, 1950). Our samples of 82 fathers and 82 children do not meet the conventional requirement that one employ at least 100 cases in testing scale characteristics. But since the patterns of answers are quite similar to that for mothers' responses—reproducibility for fathers' responses is 0.93, for children's 0.89—it seems reasonable to treat fathers' and children's responses, too, as scales.

We are not so convinced now as when this part of the research was conducted that the Guttman scaling technique provides adequate assurance of unidimensionality (cf. Appendix D). It does, at any rate, give us assurance that the four questions are meaningfully ordered.

supportiveness are highly correlated with their answers to our further question, "To which parent would you say (child) feels closer?"

Father-Son Relationships

The reports by mothers,[5] fathers, and sons in the Washington study all attest to father-son relationships being more supportive in middle-class than in working-class families (Table 7-1). Furthermore,

TABLE 7-1
Parents' and Children's Assessments of Supportiveness
of Father-Child Relationships, by Social Class and Sex of Child

		Reports by					
		Mothers		Fathers		Children	
		Middle Class	Working Class	Middle Class	Working Class	Middle Class	Working Class
Assessments of Supportiveness (Proportions)	Scale Score						
Support of sons							
High	4	.22 } * { .11		.32 } * { .24		.48 } * { .08	
:	3	.29 }	.18	.32 }	.12	.20 }	.16
:	2	.29	.32	.16	.36	.20	.40
:	1	.15 } * { .18		.12	.20	.12 } * { .24	
Low	0	.05 }	.21	.08	.08	.00 }	.12
		1.00	1.00	1.00	1.00	1.00	1.00
Number of cases		(82)	(73)	(25)	(25)	(25)	(25)
Support of daughters							
High	4	.25	.18	.14	.00	.05	.09
:	3	.12	.10	.05	.09	.10	.09
:	2	.41	.46	.38	.64	.47	.73
:	1	.12	.21	.38	.27	.14	.09
Low	0	.10	.05	.05	.00	.24	.00
		1.00	1.00	1.00	1.00	1.00	1.00
Number of cases		(81)	(73)	(21)	(11)	(21)	(11)

* Difference statistically significant, $p < 0.05$, using the t test for the difference between two proportions.

Note: Eleven middle-class and nineteen working-class families in which mother and father were not living together at the time of the interviews have been excluded from this and all subsequent tables in this chapter.

[5]The class difference in mothers' assessments of the supportiveness of father-son relationships holds even when each of a number of relevant variables is controlled: the size

there is consensus in many middle-class families, but not in working-class families, that fathers are highly supportive of sons: In two fifths of the middle-class families where mother, father, and son were all interviewed, the three family members agreed that the father-son relationship is highly supportive; in no working-class family did mother, father, and son agree that this is the case. Where working-class parents considered the father to be supportive, the son disagreed; and where the son asserted that the father is supportive, the parents thought otherwise.

Further information is provided by the National study: Class differences in fathers' appraisals of their support of sons do not appear until the boys are about 10 years of age. Working-class fathers appear to be as supportive of younger boys as are middle-class fathers, perhaps even a little more so; but, beginning when the boys are about 10, father-son relationships seem to be more supportive in the middle than in the working class.

Father-Daughter Relationships

The reports by mothers, fathers, and daughters are consistent in indicating that there is little or no class difference in fathers' supportiveness of daughters. In both social classes, fathers are said to be less supportive of daughters than are mothers.

The data of the National study confirm the finding that father-daughter relationships are no more supportive in the middle class than in the working class. These data suggest, in fact, that working-class fathers may be more supportive of young girls (younger than 10) than are middle-class fathers. By the time the girls are 10, this difference disappears.

The National study provides one more relevant fact about paternal supportiveness: Whatever their social class position, the higher

---

of the family; the age, religion, rural or urban background, and social mobility of each parent; family income; the socioeconomic status of the neighborhood in which the family lives; the size and type of enterprise in which the father is employed; the mother's education; whether or not she has a job outside the home and, if so, what type of job; her social class identification; and whether or not she reads popular literature on child rearing. (There are too few fathers and sons in the sample for comparable analyses of their assessments.)

fathers' valuation of self-direction, the more supportive of their sons and daughters they claim to be.

THE CONSTRAINT DIMENSION

Index of Constraint

Our measure of constraint is an index of the relative roles played by mothers and fathers in setting limits upon children's freedom of movement or activity. We asked each parent: Can you tell me whether you or your husband (wife) is *stricter* toward (the fifth-grade child)—or would you say that you are both equally strict, or that neither is strict? In three later questions we substituted for stricter the expressions, more likely to lay down the law when (child) misbehaves, more likely to dominate (child), and more likely to restrict (child's) freedom. (The children were asked much the same questions.) Each of these questions was scored 0 if the mother was said to exceed the father, 1 if the parents were said to be equal, and 2 if the father was said to exceed the mother. Answers to the set of four questions could thus be scored from 0 (mother predominates in setting limits for the child) to 8 (father predominates).

This index is not a unidimensional scale; its justification is its serviceability as an approximate measure of the role played by each parent in setting limits for the specific child.

Mothers' and Fathers' Roles in Imposing Constraints

The reports by mothers, fathers, sons, and daughters (in the Washington study) all lead to the conclusion that there is little or no difference between middle- and working-class families with respect to which parent predominates in setting limits either for sons or for daughters (Table 7-2). In most families, both parents play some part in limit-setting, with as many mothers as fathers playing the larger part.

Reports by fathers (in the National study) confirm these findings and add that the pattern is essentially the same, no matter what the child's age.

TABLE 7-2
Mothers' Assessments of Limit-Setting, by Social Class and Sex of Child

Assessments of Limit-Setting (Proportions)	Scale Score	Vis-à-vis Boys		Vis-à-vis Girls	
		Middle Class	Working Class	Middle Class	Working Class
Mother predominates	0	.13	.08	.11	.08
:	1	.07	.10	.13	.10
:	2	.16	.18	.16	.14
:	3	.15	.08	.07	.12
:	4	.04	.12	.15	.16
:	5	.11	.20	.11	.10
:	6	.16	.11	.16	.12
:	7	.07	.03	.06	.09
Father predominates	8	.11	.10	.05	.09
		1.00	1.00	1.00	1.00
Number of cases..		(82)	(73)	(81)	(73)

Note: There are no statistically significant class differences.

THE RELEVANCE OF CONSTRAINT IN APPRAISALS OF THE SUPPORTIVENESS OF FATHER-SON RELATIONSHIPS

The constraint axis does not, in itself, differentiate middle- from working-class families. But, although fathers' roles in setting limits are much the same in the two social classes, the "same" limit-setting role is differently evaluated. As many middle-class mothers see it, limit-setting is antithetical to supportiveness.[6] From the perspective of many working-class mothers, however, it is difficult if not impossible for fathers to be supportive of sons unless they play a major part in imposing constraints (Table 7-3).

There thus appears to be a critical difference in middle- and working-class mothers' conceptions of what is required of a father if his son is to turn to him for advice and reassurance. Some middle-class mothers feel that fathers' playing a major part in limit-setting interferes with such a relationship, others, that fathers' limit-setting role is irrelevant; but few middle-class mothers, it would seem, see limit-setting as facilitative of a supportive relationship. In

---

[6]The negative relationship between assessments of fathers' supportiveness and their playing a major part in limit-setting is strongest for the least experienced and least self-assured middle-class mothers—the younger mothers, those for whom the boy in question is their first-born, those who seek advice on child rearing from the popular literature, and those who say they are less sure of themselves in dealing with the boys than are their husbands. For more experienced and more self-assured middle-class mothers, fathers' role in limit-setting is, at most, only slightly related to judgments of how supportive they are.

TABLE 7-3
Mothers' Assessments of Supportiveness and Limit-Setting,
by Social Class and Sex of Child

Assessments of Supportiveness (Proportions)	Middle Class			Working Class		
	Limits Set Primarily by					
	Father[a]	Both Equally	Mother	Father	Both Equally	Mother
Support of sons						
High[b]	.50	.50	.53	.35	.33	.19
Intermediate	.18	.29	.40	.36	.34	.31
Low	.32	.21	.07	.29	.33	.50
	1.00	1.00	1.00	1.00	1.00	1.00
Number of cases	(28)	(24)	(30)	(17)	(30)	(26)
Support of daughters						
High	.18	.48	.41	.10	.32	.38
Intermediate	.37	.45	.40	.57	.36	.50
Low	.45	.07	.19	.33	.32	.12
	1.00	1.00	1.00	1.00	1.00	1.00
Number of cases	(22)	(27)	(32)	(21)	(28)	(24)

[a] Scores on the index of limit-setting have been trichotomized as follows: 0-2 = mother predominates, 3-5 = parents play approximately equal parts in setting limits, 6-8 = father predominates.

[b] Scores on the index of supportiveness have been trichotomized as follows: 0-1 = low, 2 = intermediate, 3-4 high.

the middle-class conception, emotional support is crucial; constraint interferes or is at best irrelevant. For many working-class mothers, however, limit-setting is seen as a necessary condition if the father-son relationship is to be deemed supportive.

One might wonder if working-class mothers see limit-setting as facilitative of supportiveness only because their husbands are so unlikely to take any part in child rearing that even a constraining role is seen as more supportive than no role at all. Plausible though it seems, this explanation does not stand up to empirical test. It is true that working-class fathers tend to participate less in child care and in leisure-time activities with the children than do middle-class fathers. But the extent of participation is unrelated to working-class mothers' assessments of fathers' supportiveness.[7] Fathers' role in setting limits

[7]To middle-class mothers, fathers' not participating in activities with the children would almost preclude considering the relationship to be supportive. Only five middle-class mothers said that their husbands do not engage in a variety of leisure-time activities with the children, but these five included three of the four who judged their husbands to be not at all supportive (Scale Type 0).

for sons is of critical import for their wives' appraisals, not because the setting of limits is the only way they are likely to take part in child rearing, but because working-class values assign high strategic importance to limit-setting.

Fathers' role in setting limits provides the key to understanding why working-class parents and sons assess the supportiveness of father-son relationships so very differently. Of the 25 working-class families in which we interviewed mother, father, and son, there were 5 in which the parents considered the father-son relationship to be highly supportive but the sons did not. In four of these five, the fathers indicated that they play a major part in limit-setting. In another five families, the sons considered the relationship to be highly supportive but the parents disputed this. In four of these five, the fathers indicated that they do not play much part in limit-setting. Even though the number of cases is small, the implication is clear: Working-class *parents* consider fathers supportive only if they play a major part in limit-setting; working-class *sons* consider fathers supportive only if they do not play a major part in limit-setting.

Limit-setting, however, is not all that is required for working-class

TABLE 7-4
Mothers' Assessments of Supportiveness of Sons, by Their Assessments
of Limit-Setting and of Fathers' Affection

Assessments of Supportiveness (Proportions)	Mother Says that Father "Displays Affection"		Mother Says that Father Is "Reserved"	
	Limits Set Primarily by[a]			
	Father	Mother	Father	Mother
Middle class				
High	.52	.59	.33	.54
Intermediate	.20	.38	.27	.31
Low	.28	* .03	.40	.15
	1.00	1.00	1.00	1.00
Number of cases	(25)	(29)	(15)	(13)
Working class				
High	.50	* .16	.15	.14
Intermediate	.29	.48	.23	.15
Low	.21	.36	.62	.71
	1.00	1.00	1.00	1.00
Number of cases	(28)	(25)	(13)	(7)

* Difference statistically significant, $p < 0.05$, t test for the difference between two proportions or, where the number of cases is small, Fisher's exact test.

[a] Scores on the index of limit-setting have been dichotomized as follows: 0-3 = mother predominates, 4-8 = father predominates.

parents to consider fathers supportive of sons. In the working-class conception, it is the *combination of limit-setting and affection* that makes for supportiveness (Table 7-4). Affection alone is insufficient, as is limit-setting alone. Only when a working-class father tempers authority with affection does his wife see him as supportive.[8] Since a substantial majority of working-class mothers believe that their husbands either do not play a major part in limit-setting, or are not affectionate to the sons, or both, few think that the father-son relationship is particularly supportive.

PATTERNS OF ROLE-ALLOCATION

Even though middle- and working-class parents have rather different conceptions of what constitutes a supportive father-child relationship, these conceptions have enough in common that we can use them as an approximate basis for comparing patterns of role-allocation (Table 7-5). The middle-class pattern is for both

TABLE 7-5
Mothers' Descriptions of Patterns of Role-Allocation,
by Social Class and Sex of Child

Mothers' Assessments (Proportions)	Middle Class		Working Class	
	Sons	Daughters	Sons	Daughters
A. Mother is predominant limit-setter				
Father not supportive	.03	.08	.18	.04
Intermediate	.15	.16	.11	.16
Father supportive	.19	.16	.07	.12
B. Both parents play active part in limit-setting				
Father not supportive	.06	.02	.14	.12
Intermediate	.08	.15	.13	.14
Father supportive	.15	.16	.14	.12
C. Father is predominant limit-setter				
Father not supportive	.11	.12	.07	.10
Intermediate	.06	.10	.08	.16
Father supportive	.17	.05	.08	.04
	1.00	1.00	1.00	1.00
Number of cases	(82)	(81)	(73)	(73)

[8]So far as can be ascertained from relatively few cases, limit-setting is relatively less important, affection relatively more important, for Catholic than for Protestant working-class mothers' assessments of supportiveness. This appears to be especially the case for Catholic sons who attend parochial schools. We suspect that these mothers see less necessity for fathers to set limits, because parochial schools assume some of this responsibility.

mothers and fathers to play an active part, not only in the imposition of constraints but also in the provision of support. Insofar as there is any division of labor, it is primarily a matter of each parent taking greater responsibility for being supportive of children of the parent's own sex. The working-class pattern of role-allocation is for mothers to play the predominant part in providing support, especially for sons. If fathers play a major part in child rearing, it is likely to be in the imposition of constraints.[9]

The question then arises: How are these patterns of role-allocation evaluated by family members?

CONCEPTIONS OF MOTHERS' AND FATHERS' PROPER ROLES

Vis-à-vis Sons

Both middle- and working-class mothers feel strongly that fathers should be at least moderately supportive of sons; those mothers who judged the father-son relationship to be not even moderately supportive were likely to make spontaneous comments, during the interview, that were critical of their husbands' performance as fathers (Table 7-6).

If fathers are highly supportive, middle-class mothers are unlikely to be critical of them, no matter what role they play in setting limits. But no matter how supportive fathers are, working-class mothers are critical of them unless they play a major part in limit-setting. Middle-class mothers value a supportive father-son relationship; working-class mothers seem to value a "directive" relationship, in which fathers, by an admixture of encouragement and constraint, guide sons. The actual patterns of role-allocation being what they are, middle-class mothers are more likely than are working-class mothers to be satisfied with their husbands' performance as fathers.

Despite their wives' dissatisfaction, most working-class fathers are satisfied with the present allocation of responsibilities vis-à-vis sons. We asked each parent, Are there any ways you'd rather act differently toward (the fifth-grade child) from the way you do? and

---

[9]Fragmentary data suggest sharp class differences in the husband-wife relationship that complement the differences in the division of parental responsibilities discussed in the text. For example, virtually no working-class wife reported that she and her husband ever go out on an evening or weekend (without the children). And few working-class fathers do much to relieve their wives of the full-time burden of caring for the children. By and large, working-class fathers seem to lead a largely separate social life from that of their wives; wives have full-time responsibility for the children, while husbands are free to go their own way.

TABLE 7-6
Mothers' Criticisms of Husbands' Performance, by Social Class,
Sex of Child, and Mothers' Assessments of Limit-Setting and Supportiveness

	Proportion Who Made Critical Comments about Husbands' Performance			
	Middle Class		Working Class	
	Limits Set Primarily by			
	Father[a]	Mother	Father	Mother
Mothers' assessments of fathers' supportiveness of sons				
High	.06 (18)[b]	.08 (24)	.19 (16)	.40 (5)
Intermediate	.11 (9)	.33 (15)	.09 (11)	.31 (13)
Low	.38 (13)	—[c] (3)	.57 (14)	.57 (14)
Mothers' assessments of fathers' supportiveness of daughters				
High	.08 (13)	.06 (17)	.11 (9)	.27 (11)
Intermediate	.22 (18)	.20 (15)	.06 (18)	.38 (16)
Low	.42 (12)	.33 (6)	.31 (13)	.33 (6)

[a] Scores on the index of limit-setting have been dichotomized as follows: 0-3 = mother predominates, 4-8 = father predominates.

[b] Numbers in parentheses represent the number of cases on which proportions are based.

[c] Proportion not shown because N is only 3. Two of these three mothers were critical of their husbands.

Are there any ways you'd rather your wife (or husband) acted differently . . .? Working-class fathers were notably unlikely to say that there were any ways in which they would prefer to act differently or to have their wives act differently toward the sons. Middle-class fathers were likely to prefer that both parents be more understanding, patient, and attentive.

Vis-à-vis Daughters

Working-class mothers are less likely to be critical of husbands who are not supportive of daughters than of husbands who are not supportive of sons. They deem it nearly as important for daughters as for sons, however, that fathers play a major part in limit-setting. Unfortunately, we have interviewed too few working-class fathers of girls to learn much about these fathers' conceptions of their proper role. We do know that working-class fathers are no more likely to want to act differently or to have their wives act differently toward daughters than toward sons. It would seem that working-class fathers assume little responsibility toward daughters, feeling, for daughters as for sons, that child rearing is mothers' domain.

As for father-daughter relationships in the middle class: Mothers' conceptions of fathers' responsibilities toward daughters are similar to their conceptions of fathers' responsibilities toward sons—with one notable difference, illustrated by those extreme cases where mothers believe that fathers do not play much part in limit-setting, and yet are not very supportive. In the case of sons, such mothers were likely to say that they wish their husbands were more understanding, patient, and attentive; in the case of daughters, such mothers wanted their husbands to be more the disciplinarian. Fathers have a somewhat greater responsibility to be supportive of sons and to set limits for daughters. Still, they do have a responsibility to be supportive of daughters, and middle-class mothers tend to be critical of husbands who do not fulfill this responsibility.

From all the evidence at our disposal, it seems that, although some middle-class mothers are critical of their husbands, the general pattern is for middle-class parents, both fathers and mothers, to be reasonably well satisfied with the patterns of role-allocation in their families. But many working-class fathers do not play the roles their wives would have them play; nor do they see any reason why they should. Rather, it would seem, these men see child rearing as more completely their wives' responsibility.[10] Working-class wives decry this attitude (many of them saying that their husbands shirk responsibility) and want their husbands to play a more active part. Toward sons, this means a directive role—a combination of encouragement and limit-setting; toward daughters, it means primarily limit-setting.

CONCLUSION

In both the middle class and the working class, mothers would

---

[10]When asked what they find most difficult about being a father, working-class fathers were likely to talk of the problems of meeting the family's financial needs, while middle-class fathers talked about the physical and emotional strain entailed in raising children. (It is noteworthy that the wives of those middle-class fathers who emphasized the strain of child rearing were even more likely than were other middle-class mothers to consider their husbands highly supportive.)

have their husbands play a role that facilitates children's development of valued characteristics. To middle-class mothers, it is
important that children be able to decide for themselves how to act,
and that they have the personal resources to act on these decisions.
In this conception, fathers' responsibility for imposing constraints is
secondary to their responsibility for being supportive; in the minds
of some middle-class mothers, for fathers to take a major part in
imposing constraints interferes with their ability to be supportive. To
working-class mothers, on the other hand, it is more important that
children conform to externally imposed rules. In this conception,
fathers' primary responsibility is to guide and direct the children.
Constraint is accorded far greater value than it has in the middle
class.

Mothers of both social classes believe that fathers have somewhat
different responsibilities toward sons from those they have toward
daughters. In the middle class, fathers' primary responsibility toward
sons is to be sufficiently supportive that the boys are able to turn to
father for advice and reassurance. Fathers should be supportive of
daughters, too, but their responsibility for support is a little less, and
for limit-setting a little more toward daughters than toward sons.
Most middle-class fathers seem to share their wives' views of fathers'
responsibilities toward sons and act accordingly. They accept less
responsibility for being supportive of daughters—apparently feeling
that this is more properly mothers' role.

From the point of view of working-class mothers, fathers' primary
responsibility to sons is to play a major part in setting limits and yet
to be sufficiently assuring that the sons can accept these limits as
guidelines for their behavior, not just as arbitrary authority.
Working-class mothers would have their husbands play a more active
part in setting limits for daughters, too. (But, whereas the setting of
limits is thought to be conducive to a son's turning to his father, for
a daughter it means relying more heavily on her mother for advice
and reassurance.) Many working-class fathers do not accept the
obligations their wives would have them assume, either toward sons
or toward daughters.

One can readily understand why mothers would have their
husbands share responsibility for what they conceive to be crucial
aspects of child rearing. One can also understand why fathers act as
they do. Given middle-class parents' high valuation of self-direction,
fathers would feel an obligation for being supportive, especially of

sons. Sons must be able to turn to and rely upon their fathers if they are to develop self-assurance as boys and as men-to-be; daughters can rely more heavily on their mothers. Given working-class parents' higher valuation of conformity, what is there to impel fathers to assume the responsibilities for child rearing that their wives would have them assume? These men do not see the constraining role as any less important than their wives do, but many of them see no reason why fathers should have to shoulder this responsibility. From their point of view, the important thing is that children be taught what limits they must not transgress. It does not particularly matter who does the teaching, and since mothers have primary responsibility for child care, the job should be theirs. Of course, there will be occasions when fathers have to backstop their wives. But there is no ideological imperative that makes it fathers' responsibility to play a larger part in child rearing.

The Allocation of Parental Responsibilities

Theories of personality development, up to and including Parsons and Bales's (1955) sociological reinterpretation of the classical Freudian developmental sequence,[11] have generally been based on the model of a family in which the mothers' and fathers' intra-family roles are necessarily differentiated, with mothers specializing in support and fathers in constraint (cf. Bronfenbrenner, 1960). However useful a first approximation this may be, both middle- and working-class variations on this general theme are sufficiently great to compel a more precise formulation.

Our data are partly consistent with the mother-supportive, father-constraining formulation, for even in middle-class families almost no one reports that fathers are more supportive than mothers. Yet, in a sizeable proportion of middle-class families, mothers take primary responsibility for imposing constraints on sons, and fathers are at least as supportive as mothers. And, although middle-class

---

[11]Parsons and Bales (1955: 45) talk of fathers' role as being relatively high on "instrumentality," low on "expressiveness," mothers' role as being complementary to that. We interpret this to mean that fathers specialize in imposing constraints, and mothers in being supportive; this makes sense in the context of their general argument, and some of their specific statements indicate this to be their intention (for example, see page 80). It must be noted, however, that for Parsons and Bales the instrumental role refers not only to fathers' role within the family, but also to their role in mediating between the family and the outside world.

fathers are not likely to be as supportive of daughters as their wives are, it cannot be said that fathers typically specialize in constraint, even with daughters.

It would be a gross exaggeration to say that middle-class fathers have abandoned the prerogatives and responsibilities of authority in favor of being friend and confidant to their sons. Yet, the historical drift is probably from primary emphasis on imposing constraints to primary emphasis on support (cf. Bronson, *et al.,* 1959; Bronfenbrenner, 1961a). In any event, mothers' and fathers' roles are not sharply differentiated in most middle-class families; both parents tend to be supportive. Such division of labor as exists is chiefly a matter of each parent taking special responsibility for being supportive of children of the parent's own sex.

Mothers' and fathers' roles are more sharply differentiated in working-class families, with mothers almost always being the more supportive. Yet, despite the high valuation put on the constraining function, fathers do not necessarily specialize in setting limits, even for sons. In some working-class families, mothers specialize in support, fathers in constraint; in many others, the division of responsibilities is for mothers to raise the children, fathers to provide the wherewithal. This pattern of role-allocation probably is and has been far more prevalent in American society than the formal theories of personality development have recognized.

It may well be that the trend once was from authoritarian to nonparticipant fathers but is now from nonparticipant to supportive fathers.

Consequences for the Personality Development of Children

By age 10 or 11, the age of the children in the Washington study, boys would be expected to identify with their fathers, girls with their mothers. From what we know of the different patterns of role-allocation in middle- and working-class families, we should expect the problems of identification to be different for children in the two social classes.

Few working-class boys feel that their fathers are very supportive. Even those who do are in an anomalous situation, for their mothers do not think the fathers are setting a good example of how fathers should act and may be quite dissatisfied with the fathers' behavior. Other working-class boys are in the unsatisfying situation of having fathers who usually ignore them, or whose interest—so far as the boys can tell—is, for the most part, confined to the imposition of constraints. We take it as symptomatic of working-class boys' difficulties in identifying with their fathers that almost no working-class parents told us that the sons "try to act like" their fathers.[12]

Middle-class boys are far more likely to feel that they can turn to their fathers, and are said to be more likely to try to act like their fathers. Presumably, they find it easier to identify with their fathers. But we know little about the effects on children of growing up in families where mothers and fathers may play almost indistinguishable roles, or where mothers play more of a constraining role than do fathers.[13] Nor do we know much about the processes by which both middle- and working-class girls identify with their mothers. We can, however, say with certainty that the processes are not adequately described by our formal theories of personality development, for they are based on a too-simple model of family structure.

-----

[12]In a study of New York State high school students, Rosenberg (1965: 39-48) found that middle-class boys have higher self-esteem than have working-class boys, but that there is little or no class difference in girls' self-esteem. He interpreted these findings as stemming from the class difference we had found in the supportiveness of father-son, but not of father-daughter, relationships. To test this interpretation, he first confirmed our essential findings for his (older) sample, then showed that the supportiveness of father-child relationships is related to children's self-esteem. Finally, he standardized the comparison of middle- and working-class boys' levels of self-esteem on the supportiveness of the father-son relationship, finding that the class difference in boys' levels of self-esteem was reduced by about half. This suggests that the class difference we have found in the supportiveness of father-son relationships has an important bearing on the self-esteem of the sons.

[13]Bronfenbrenner (1961b: 267) suggests that "boys thrive in a patriarchal context, girls in a matriarchal..." and that "the most dependent and least dependable adolescents [describe their own families as] neither patriarchal nor matriarchal, but equalitarian." (See also Bronfenbrenner, 1961a.)

PART III

An Interpretation

CHAPTER 8

Class, Its Components, and Its Attendant Conditions

Why is class consistently related to values and orientation? This chapter lays the groundwork for an interpretation of the class relationships, by specifying the nature of these relationships. Precisely how is class related to values and orientation—are the relationships continuous or discontinuous? Class is multidimensional; which dimensions of class are most important in accounting for its relationships to values and orientation? Finally, men's present class positions are highly correlated with the social class of their parental families; is it present class position or class of origin that is more important for explaining the relationships?

The data for these analyses are provided by the National study, whose large, representative sample makes possible the types of analysis required to answer these questions.

DISCRETE CLASSES OR A CONTINUOUS HIERARCHY?

If one conceives of social classes as arbitrary divisions of what in social reality is a hierarchically organized continuum of social positions, one would predict essentially linear relationships of class to values and orientation. If, on the other hand, one conceives of relatively discrete social classes, then one would predict some discontinuities in the relationships—the discontinuities occurring at the points of maximum class cleavage. There might, for example, be relatively sharp distinctions between the working class and the middle class, between a stable working class and a lower class beneath them, and between the middle class and an elite above them. Such an arrangement of relatively discrete classes might in some instances be reflected in curvilinear relationships of class to values and orientation; in some respects, the elite and lower classes might be closer to each other than to the vast majority of people in between.

The data give no evidence of discontinuities in the stratification hierarchy. The relationships of class to values and orientation are preponderantly linear (Table 8-1), with virtually no significant curvilinear or higher order relationships, no sharp breaks,[1] no departures from pattern. If we use finer gradations than Hollingshead's 5 social class levels (for example, the 67 levels on which the index is based), the essentially linear nature of the relationships is illustrated even more sharply. From the point of view of describing

TABLE 8-1
Values and Orientation, by Social Class—Linear Component
of Class Compared to Total of All Components

	Class Correlations[a]	
	Linear Component	All Components
A. Parental values		
Self-direction/conformity	.34**	.34**
B. Values for self		
Self-direction/conformity	.17**	.19**
Self-direction/competence	.14**	.15**
C. Judgments about work		
Importance of intrinsic qualities	.20**	.21**
Importance of extrinsic benefits	.36**	.36**
D. Social orientation		
Authoritarian conservatism	.38**	.38**
Criteria of morality	.17**	.18**
Trustfulness	.17**	.17**
Stance toward change	.15**	.21**
Canonical correlation	.47**	.48**
E. Self-conception		
Self-confidence	.09**	.10**
Self-deprecation	.10**	.11**
Attribution of responsibility	.13**	.14**
Anxiety	.05**	.06**
Idea-conformity	.13**	.13**
Canonical correlation	.23**	.24**

* Indicates $p < 0.05$
** Indicates $p < 0.01$
[a] η (eta) or the canonical correlation.
Note: $N > 2985$, except for parental values, where $N = 1499$.

---

[1]This is apparent from an examination of the means presented in Tables 4-1, 5-1, and 5-2, and in Figures 4-1, 5-1, 5-2, 5-3, and 5-4. Moreover, statistical tests of the relationships of class to values and orientation show that the strongest linear relationship is produced when the "distances" between classes are assumed to be equal—that is, when the metric "1-2-3-4-5" is used. Metrics that assume discontinuity between classes (for example, a sharper break between the middle and working classes, as in the metric "1-2-3-5-6") produce weaker linear relationships.

and explaining the relationships of class to values and orientation, it is profitable to think of a continuous hierarchy of positions, not of discrete social classes.

The implication of these findings is that interpretations of the relationship of class to values and orientation must look to conditions of life that are continuously related to class position; interpretations based on conditions that impinge on only a portion of the hierarchy or that divide the population into only two or three discrete groups are not sufficient.

DIMENSIONS OF SOCIAL CLASS

Our use of the Hollingshead Index as the measure of social class has been based on the beliefs that class is multidimensional and that, of all relevant dimensions, occupational position and education are the most important in contemporary American society. The social-psychological data of our investigations can neither confirm nor refute these beliefs, which concern the organization of society rather than the relationship of social organization to men's values and orientation. Our data can, however, tell us whether the facets of social class that we believe to be pivotal are in fact the most pertinent for explaining the relationships of class to values and orientation. We should expect both education and occupational position to contribute to the class relationships and such other aspects of stratification as income and subjective class identification to add relatively little.

Education and Occupational Position

Do both components of our index of social class—education and occupational position—contribute independently to the relationships we have credited to class? It might be that one component is solely responsible for the class relationships. Or it might be that these relationships result from particular combinations of education and occupational position—that education matters only for people at certain occupational levels; or that some relationships are principally due to "discrepancies" between education and occupational position, as implied by theories of "status inconsistency."[2]

---

[2]For relevant discussions of "status inconsistency," see: Lenski, 1954; Goffman, 1957; Parker and Kleiner, 1966; Blalock, 1967. A most useful review and clarification is provided by Kasl, 1967.

In fact, education and occupational position are each related, independently of the other, to almost all aspects of values and orientation that we have measured (Table 8-2). Education is the more potent of the two dimensions, being more strongly related to parental values, to self-values, to judgments about the extrinsic features of jobs, and—most strongly of all—to authoritarian conservatism.[3] Occupational position is more strongly related than is

TABLE 8-2
Values and Orientation, by Education and Occupational Position[a]

	Education (Linear) Controlled on Occupational Position	Occupational Position (Linear) Controlled on Education	Interaction of Education and Occupational Position
A. Parental values			
Self-direction/conformity	.22**	.10**	.01
B. Values for self			
Self-direction/conformity	.10**	.02	.03
Self-direction/competence	.14**	.01	.00
C. Judgments about work			
Importance of intrinsic qualities . . .	.04*	.14**	.02
Importance of extrinsic benefits . . .	.21**	.16**	.04*
D. Social orientation			
Authoritarian conservatism	.32**	.05*	.04*
Criteria of morality	.09**	.10**	.03
Trustfulness	.09**	.09**	.03
Stance toward change	.10**	.09**	.07**
Canonical correlation . . .	.38**	.18**	.09**
E. Self-conception			
Self-confidence	.04*	.04*	.00
Self-deprecation	.05**	.05**	.02
Attribution of responsibility	.05**	.08**	.00
Anxiety	.04*	.09**	.02
Idea-conformity	.09**	.03	.03
Canonical correlation . . .	.13**	.14**	.04

* Indicates $p < 0.05$
** Indicates $p < 0.01$
[a] Entries are partial correlations, either, η (eta) or the canonical correlation.
Note: $N > 2690$, except for parental values, where $N = 1424$.

---

[3]In a critique of Lipset's (1959) analysis of "working-class authoritarianism," Lipsitz (1965) argued that the correlation of class with authoritarianism is almost entirely attributable to education. Our data with respect to "authoritarian conservatism" (a closely linked concept) show that education is decidedly more important than is occupational position in accounting for the class relationship, but that occupational position is significantly (albeit weakly) related to authoritarian conservatism even when education is controlled.

education to an emphasis on the intrinsic features of jobs, and it is as strongly related to most measures of self-conception and social orientation. Overall, education is the more powerful variable, but occupational position contributes importantly to the class relationships.

The relationships of occupational position to values and orientation are essentially the same at all levels of education, and the relationships of education to values and orientation are essentially the same regardless of occupational position.[4]

Thus, the class relationships result primarily from the *additive* effects of education and occupational position.

Income and Subjective Class Identification

Two aspects of class—income and subjective class identification—are often treated as central and are sometimes used as indices. We have thus far excluded them from our analyses, judging them not to be basic to the concept, class, but rather concomitants of class. What might income and subjective class identification add to our conception (and possibly, index) of class?

For the analysis of income, we use total family income rather than men's incomes from their own primary occupations, because family income seems the more appropriate measure of family status. (An analysis based on job income yields almost identical results, in any case.) We lack data on nearly one tenth of the respondents, questions on income having been the one type of question that any significant number of people refused to answer in these interviews. For the other nine tenths of the sample, class as measured by education and occupational position (or by either of them, alone) is generally more important than income in its relationship to values and orientation (Table 8-3). The one aspect of values or orientation for which income seems to be as important as education and occupational position is self-conception—in particular, self-confidence, self-deprecation, and anxiety. But for values, for judgments about work, and for social orientation, class as measured by education and occupational position is two or three times as important as is income.

---

[4]Limitations of space preclude our presenting the mean scores. Some of the evidence for our conclusion is given by the statistical significance and size of the interaction effects produced in the analysis of variance. Most of the interaction effects shown in Table 8-2 are statistically nonsignificant and, even where significant, comparatively small.

TABLE 8-3
Values and Orientation, by Social Class and Family Income[a]

	Class (Linear) Controlled on Family Income	Family Income (Linear) Controlled on Class	Interaction of Class and Income
A. Parental values			
Self-direction/conformity	.25**	.11**	.01
B. Values for self			
Self-direction/conformity	.12**	.06**	.01
Self-direction/competence	.11**	.02	.04*
C. Judgments about work			
Importance of intrinsic qualities . . .	.17**	.01	.00
Importance of extrinsic benefits . . .	.31**	.05**	.05*
D. Social orientation			
Authoritarian conservatism	.31**	.09**	.04*
Criteria of morality	.13**	.06**	.03
Trustfulness	.15**	.04*	.00
Stance toward change	.09**	.11**	.02
Canonical correlation . . .	.40**	.17**	.05
E. Self-conception			
Self-confidence	.05**	.07**	.05*
Self-deprecation	.05*	.09**	.03
Attribution of responsibility	.10**	.05*	.00
Anxiety	.02	.06**	.02
Idea-conformity	.09**	.03	.03
Canonical correlation . . .	.15**	.14**	.07*

* Indicates $p < 0.05$
** Indicates $p < 0.01$
[a] Entries are partial correlations, either η (eta) or the canonical correlation.
Note: $N > 2585$, except for parental values, where $N = 1364$.

In fact, controlling income produces only a small reduction in the correlations of class with these several aspects of values and orientation.

In general, the interaction effects of class and income are small and statistically nonsignificant; thus, we find no evidence in support of theories that would look to disparities between education, occupational level, and income as an important source of variation in values and orientation. Taking this information altogether, we conclude that the relationships we have been attributing to class are not to be explained in terms of income or of discrepancies between income and other dimensions of stratification—except that income does matter for self-conception.

The question of the possible importance of subjective class identification, as contrasted to the importance of objective class position, is readily dealt with. Subjective class identification is more strongly related to self-confidence than is objective class position; but with that single exception, objective class position is far more important. Furthermore, interaction effects are negligible, and the correlations of objective class position with values and orientation are only slightly reduced by controlling subjective class identification. The class relationships result from objective position, not subjective identification.

There is one other relevant question: Would the class relationships be appreciably stronger if income and class identification were added to our index of class? The answer is unequivocally, "no." Only one class correlation—the correlation with self-confidence—would be increased by more than a trivial amount if we were to include these other aspects of stratification. There is no empirical power to be gained by adding income and class identification.

We conclude that the relationships of class to values and orientation result from the additive impact of education and occupational position with, at most, minor contributions from income and subjective class identification. This certainly does not mean that all class relationships can be explained primarily in terms of education and occupational position. It may be, for example, that the relationship of class to political party preference can be best understood in terms of subjective class identification. And it may be that the relationship of class to rates of ill health results primarily from class differences in income levels. We cannot say. However, we do have evidence that the relationships of class to values and orientation are essentially a result of the additive impact of education and occupational position. Thus, in interpreting why social class is related to values and orientation, we must look to the conditions of life attendant on men's occupational and educational circumstances, not to such other aspects of social stratification as income and subjective class identification.

CLASS ORIGINS AND SOCIAL MOBILITY

Are the class relationships to be explained by the conditions of life associated with men's present, achieved class positions or by those associated with the class positions of the families in which they were raised? We find (Table 8-4) that present class position is substantially more important for values and orientation than are class origins.[5]

We do not have data on the educational attainments of the respondents' grandfathers, but we do have data about their occupations. If we use these occupational data as an approximate index of

TABLE 8-4
Values and Orientation, by Present Class Position and Class Origins[a]

	Present Class Position Controlled on Class Origins	Class Origins Controlled on Present Class Position
A. Parental values		
Self-direction/conformity	.27**	.10**
B. Values for self		
Self-direction/conformity	.13**	.09**
Self-direction/competence	.08**	.07**
C. Judgments about work		
Importance of intrinsic qualities	.19**	.01
Importance of extrinsic benefits	.30**	.12**
D. Social orientation		
Authoritarian conservatism	.32**	.11**
Criteria of morality	.14**	.07**
Trustfulness	.15**	.02
Stance toward change	.11**	.06*
Canonical correlation	.41**	.13**
E. Self-conception		
Self-confidence	.08**	.03
Self-deprecation	.07**	.03
Attribution of responsibility	.09**	.05*
Anxiety	.06**	.05*
Idea-conformity	.10**	.04
Canonical correlation	.18**	.08*

* Indicates $p < 0.05$
** Indicates $p < 0.01$
[a] Entries are partial correlations, either η (eta) or the canonical correlation.
Note: $N > 2270$, except for parental values, where $N = 1199$.

---

[5]The Hollingshead Index is not quite appropriate for measuring class origins, because the occupational and educational composition of the country has changed so greatly over the many decades our data cover that its weighting of the two variables would not be valid. Rather than develop a new index (or series of indices) to reflect the proper weightings, we have simply used the respondent's father's (or father-surrogate's) education and occupational position as covariates in an analysis of variance. This, in effect, maximizes their additive impact. The defect of this procedure is that we have no measure of the interaction of present class position and class origins. But separate analyses, one based on the respondent's father's education and the other on his occupational position, suggest that interaction effects would be small.

class origins, we can consider not only men's own class origins, but those of their parents as well. This analysis reaffirms our prior finding: Present class position is more important than are class origins. We cannot overlook the obvious and critical fact that class origins play a major part in determining present class position (cf. Blau and Duncan, 1967). To that extent, class origins surely are important. But when men move into class positions different from those of their parents (and their grandparents), their values and orientation come to agree with those of their achieved class positions.

It is possible, of course, that the distance men have come from their families' class positions may matter less for values and orientation than how their achievements, or lack of achievement, compare to those of other members of the family. To deal with this issue, we have computed the average occupational level of all brothers who survived to adulthood. This score, we find, is almost irrelevant to men's values and orientation, when class is controlled.

Present class position bears the same relationship to men's values and orientation, no matter what their class origins and no matter how their occupational achievements compare to those of their brothers. We should look to the conditions of life associated with men's present social class positions rather than to class origins or to social mobility for most of the explanation of the class relationships.

CONCLUSION

The logical first step toward an explanation of why class is related to values and orientation is to examine class itself, its components, and related aspects of stratification. This analysis yields four principal findings. The first is that the class relationships are preponderantly linear, with virtually no indication of discontinuity in the relationships. Second, the two components of our index of class—education and occupational position—are each independently related to values and orientation, and these relationships are essentially additive. Third, such other aspects of stratification as income and subjective class identification bear only a small relationship to values and orientation, when social class (as we have indexed it) is controlled. On the other hand, class is nearly as strongly related to values and orientation when income and subjective class identification are controlled as when they are not. Finally, present social class position matters more for values and orientation than do class origins.

These four findings make it possible to formulate the problem—why class is related to values and orientation—more precisely. The class relationships must be interpreted in terms of conditions of life that vary continuously with present class position, specifically with education and with occupational position.

CHAPTER 9

Occupational Self-Direction and Parental Values

Interpreting the relationships of social class to values and orientation requires that we determine which of the many conditions of life associated with class position actually contribute to explaining these relationships. We have already shown that many class-correlated conditions of life are not relevant for these explanatory purposes. We have further narrowed the range of possibilities by finding that only those conditions that vary continuously with education and with occupational position can be relevant. But there remains still a multitude of possibly relevant conditions.

In this chapter, we investigate the relevance of one set of conditions—the *occupational*[1] conditions that are conducive to or restrictive of the exercise of self-direction in work—for explaining the relationship of social class to parental valuation of self-direction or conformity. These conditions have great a priori appeal for explaining why social class is related to parental values (and to values and orientation in general). Few other conditions of life are so closely bound up with education and with occupational position as are those that determine how much opportunity (even necessity) men will have for exercising self-direction in their work. Moreover, there is an appealing simplicity to the supposition that the experience of occupational self-direction is conducive to valuing self-direction, off as well as on the job, and to seeing the possibilities for self-direction not only in work but also in other realms of life.

OCCUPATIONAL SELF-DIRECTION

Definition and Specification

By "occupational self-direction" we mean the use of initiative,

---

[1] Since social scientists have become accustomed to thinking of occupation in terms of only *one* of its dimensions—status—it must be stressed that we mean occupational

thought, and independent judgment in work. Although many conditions of work are either conducive to or deterrent of the exercise of occupational self-direction, three in particular are critical.

First, a limiting condition: Men cannot exercise occupational self-direction if they are closely supervised. Not being closely supervised, however, does not necessarily mean that men are required—or even free—to use initiative, thought, and independent judgment; it depends on how complex and demanding is their work.

A second and far more important condition for occupational self-direction is that the work, in its very substance, requires initiative, thought, and independent judgment. Work with data or with people is more likely to require initiative, thought, and judgment than is work with things. Complex work with data or with people—synthesizing or coordinating data, teaching or negotiating with people—is especially likely to require initiative, thought, and judgment. Thus, occupational self-direction is most probable when men spend some substantial amount of their working time doing complex work with data or with people.

The third condition for occupational self-direction is that the work allow a variety of approaches; otherwise the possibilities for exercising initiative, thought, and judgment are seriously limited. The organization of the work must be complex; it must involve a variety of tasks that are in themselves complexly structured.

No one of these conditions is definitional of occupational self-direction. Even though most work with things, for example, does not require a great deal of self-direction, some work with things is highly self-directed—consider the sculptor. And work with data may not be self-directed—consider routine office jobs. Nevertheless, each of these three occupational conditions tends to be conducive to the exercise of occupational self-direction, and the combination of the three both enables and requires it. Insofar as men are free of close supervision, do complex work with data or with people, and work at complexly organized tasks, their work is necessarily self-directed. Insofar as men are subject to close supervision, work with things, and work at simply organized tasks, their work does not permit self-direction.[2]

---

conditions *other than,* although necessarily correlated with, status—for example, closeness of supervision or the amount of time spent working with things.

[2]Perrow (1967: 195-196), in his analysis of organizational structures, focuses on some of the same components of occupation by emphasizing "the number of exceptional cases encountered in the work" and "the nature of the search process that is undertaken by the individual when exceptions occur." *(Footnote Continues.)*

Occupational Self-Direction and Valuing Self-Direction for Children

At higher social class levels, occupations typically allow and even require a great deal of self-direction; at lower class levels, occupations typically limit and even preclude the exercise of self-direction. Thus, there is at least congruence among social class, occupational requirements, and parental values. Moreover, it is a reasonable supposition, even if not a necessary conclusion, that middle- and working-class parents have differing values for children because of these differences in occupational circumstances.[3] This supposition does not necessarily assume that parents consciously train children to meet future occupational requirements; it may simply be that occupational experiences affect people's conceptions of the desirable.

We think that these differences in occupational circumstances are of central importance for the relationship that we have found between social class and parental values. But we do not think that occupational self-direction alone will sufficiently explain the class relationship. For a sufficient explanation of the relationship of class to values, it is necessary to take into account other class differences in conditions of life that reinforce these differences in occupational circumstances.

Education, above and beyond its importance as a determinant of occupational self-direction, probably contributes independently to class differences in parental values. Middle-class parents' greater interest in children's internal dynamics is facilitated by their learned ability to deal with the subjective and the ideational. Differences in levels and stability of income also may contribute to class differences in parental values. Higher levels of income and greater stability of income may enable middle-class parents to take for granted much that is problematic for working-class parents. Middle-class parents

---

Blauner's (1964) incisive analysis of the occupational conditions that are conducive to "alienation" overlaps our analysis of the conditions that are involved in self-direction. Since he, however, worked entirely with manual occupations, he did not deal with our central concept of the complexity of work with data, with things, and with people. Moreover, alienation is so encompassing a concept that his systematic spelling out of all relevant occupational conditions results in a list that is too large and diverse for our purposes.

Any analysis of how the conditions of occupational life affect the psyche, values, and spirit of men is indebted, ultimately, to the insights of Marx and Weber.

[3]For thoughtful discussions of the influence of occupational role on parental values, see Aberle and Naegele, 1952; Miller and Swanson, 1958; McKinley, 1964.

can afford to concentrate on motives and feelings—which, in the circumstances of their lives, are more important.

In all probability, then, the relationship of social class to parental values derives from the entire complex of life conditions characteristic of the various social classes. Our hypothesis is that the most important of these many conditions are the occupational conditions that foster or inhibit the exercise of self-direction in work.

LOGIC OF THE INQUIRY

The analyses of this chapter are based on data from the Turin and the National studies, both of which provide information about fathers' experiences of occupational self-direction. The opportunity to do parallel analyses of these two sets of data enables us to see whether men's experience of occupational self-direction bears the same relationship to parental values in the dissimilar cultural contexts of Italy and of the United States. Moreover, the two studies complement each other. The National study provides better indices than does the Turin study; and the Turin study, with its sample of mothers as well as fathers, gives us a valuable opportunity to see whether men's occupational conditions are related not only to their own values but also to those of their wives.

We use different statistical methods for analyzing the data of the Turin and National studies, but the logic of our inquiry is precisely the same. (1) We determine whether or not a given occupational condition is significantly related both to social class and, independently of its relationship to class, to parental valuation of self-direction or conformity. In addition to the technical requirement that the occupational condition be related to parental values when class is not controlled,[4] we impose the more restrictive requirement that the condition be significantly related to parental values *even when class is controlled.*[5] We do this to avoid the danger of

---

[4]This requirement is imposed by arithmetic; no "third" variable can affect the relationship of any two variables—say, social class and parental values—unless it is related to *both* of them (cf. Rosenberg, 1968: 259-271).

[5]It need hardly be stressed that *statistical* controls are not fully equivalent to *experimental* matching—not all the variance attributable to the control variables is actually controlled, particularly when the control variables have few categories. This poses no serious problem, provided we recognize that variables other than those with which we explicitly deal may implicitly be intertwined in the analysis. The way to cope with this possibility is to transform the implicit into the explicit, by testing alternative interpretations of the relationships.

explaining the relationship of class to values in terms of phenomena that can themselves be explained as functions of class. (2) Then, for occupational conditions that prove to be related to parental values (independently of their relationship to social class), we ask: Does controlling the occupational condition appreciably reduce the correlation of class to parental values? If so, this provides prima facie evidence that the occupational condition is pertinent for explaining the relationship of class to parental values.

EVIDENCE FROM TURIN

Indices Used in Turin

The Turin study was designed and carried out before we had fully formulated our conception of which occupational conditions are most critical for self-direction. Thus, the indices of the relevant occupational conditions are incomplete—they are limited to an index of closeness of supervision and one based on information about whether men work principally with data, with things, or with people. These indices provide a reasonably adequate basis for assessing the possibilities for exercising self-direction in work, but not for assessing whether or not self-direction is actually required. To infer the requirement for self-direction in work, we use men's subjective appraisals of "the need for self-reliance" in their jobs.

Since the Turin study does not provide a composite index of parental valuation of self-direction or conformity, we borrow from the analysis of Italian fathers' valuation of self-control and obedience (in Chapter 3) and use the *differential* valuation of these two characteristics (cf. Table 3-3) as our index. Thus, we treat fathers' statement that self-control is important to indicate that they value self-direction, and their statements that obedience is important and self-control is not, to indicate that they value conformity.

Closeness of Supervision

Even though no single condition is a sufficient determinant of occupational self-direction, it is analytically useful to deal with the relevant occupational conditions one at a time, and only afterwards treat them all together. We begin with the limiting condition, closeness of supervision. The expectation is that, since close supervision precludes the opportunity for exercising self-direction in work, men who are closely supervised will value conformity for their children.

Closeness of supervision is here indexed by a scale[6] based on the following questions: (1) How much control does your direct supervisor exercise over your work? (2) [Do you feel that you] have the power to make decisions about the things that have true importance to [your] work? (3) Do you have much influence on the way things go at your work?

Only for the working class is the relationship between closeness of supervision and parental values sufficiently pronounced to be statistically significant;[7] the tendency, however, is the same in both social classes: The more closely supervised men are, the more likely they are to value conformity for their children (Table 9-1).

TABLE 9-1
Fathers' Valuation of Self-Direction and Conformity,
by Social Class and Closeness of Supervision

		Middle Class			Working Class		
	Self-Employed	Loose Supervision	Intermediate	Close Supervision	Loose Supervision	Intermediate	Close Supervision
Proportion of fathers who:							
Value self-direction ...	.51	.49	.52	.40	.39	.38	.26
(Intermediate)	.26	.30	.24	.10	.31	.25	.19
Value conformity	.23	.21	.24	.50	.30	.37	.55
Total	1.00	1.00	1.00	1.00	1.00	1.00	1.00
Number of cases ...	(77)	(57)	(17)	(10)	(62)	(48)	(38)

χ^2 (linear regression)= 1.3, 1 $d.f.$ $p < 0.30$ χ^2 (linear regression)= 4.0, 1 $d.f.$ $p < 0.05$

The Substance of Work with Data, Things, and People

The Turin study provides no information about the complexity of

---

[6]Reproducibility = 0.95, Scalability = 0.83, and the pattern of errors is essentially random, using Ford's (1950) criteria.

[7]The statistical tests employed in the analyses of data from the Turin study are chi-squared, with appropriate correction for continuity; Fisher's exact test; and Cochran's test for a linear regression of p—which is based on chi-squared (cf. Cochran, 1954: 434-436; Maxwell, 1961: 63-72). In the analyses of data from the National study, we employ the F ratio.

All findings presented in this chapter are the same whether or not the sex of the child (and, for the National study, the age of the child) is controlled.

men's work with data, with things, and with people, nor precise information about the amount of time men spend at each of these activities. It does provide, as an approximate indication of the substance of men's work, their answers to this question: In almost all occupations, it is necessary to work with things, with people, and with ideas, but various occupations differ in the extent to which they require these three types of activities. Considering now your typical day's work . . .which of these three is most important in your work? The qualitative evidence in the interview reports indicates that almost all respondents gave realistic appraisals.

The correspondence between social class and whether one works primarily with data, with people, or with things is close, but fortunately for analytic purposes, there are some middle-class men who deal principally with things and some working-class men who deal principally with people or with data. Those middle-class men who say that *things* are most important to their work are concentrated in technical and engineering fields but also include a few managers and sales people whose work is directly related to the manufacture or distribution of hard goods. The majority of working-class men who say that they work primarily with *people* are in service occupations; the remainder are foremen. Working-class men who indicate that *data* are most important to their work are concentrated in highly skilled jobs. They are differentiated from other skilled workers in that their jobs seem to require more independence of judgment—as in the case of mechanics who specialize in diagnosis, or testers in the Fiat automobile factory.

Since work with things typically is least self-directed and work with data typically is most self-directed, we should expect men who work mainly with things to be the most likely to value conformity for children, and men who work mainly with data to be the most likely to value self-direction. These expectations are confirmed (Table 9-2) for both social classes.

The Requirement of Self-Reliance in Work

The supervision to which men are subject and the type of work they do determine the degree of self-direction their jobs permit. Within the limits of the permissible, some jobs in fact require that men make independent judgments and take responsibility, while others do not. This is the last aspect of self-direction we can index with the Turin data—the degree to which jobs require self-reliance.

TABLE 9-2
Fathers' Valuation of Self-Direction and Conformity,
by Social Class and the Substance of the Work

	Middle Class			Working Class		
	Things	People	Data	Things	People	Data
Proportion of fathers who:						
Value self-direction	.27	.51	.64	.23	.45	.62
(Intermediate)	.45	.26	.21	.29	.16	.27
Value conformity	.28	.23	.15	.48	.39	.11
Total	1.00	1.00	1.00	1.00	1.00	1.00
Number of cases .	(22)	(73)	(58)	(96)	(31)	(26)
	$\chi^2 = 9.2$, 4 $d.f.$ $p < 0.06$			$\chi^2 = 18.7$, 4 $d.f.$ $p < 0.01$		

In the interview, men were given a list of 17 qualities and asked to indicate the rank order of the three that are most important for doing well in their jobs. They were then asked to classify the others as important or unimportant. Four of these items have been used to index self-reliance. They are: to understand oneself, to be intelligent, to have trust in oneself, and to have a sense of responsibility. Each of these four items was scored four if it was ranked first in importance, three if it was ranked second, two if it was ranked third, and one if it was considered important but not ranked among the top three. These scores were then added. Essentially, the higher a man's score, the more he thinks that his work requires self-reliance.[8]

In both social classes, there is a consistent relationship between men's appraisals of job requirements and their values for their children (Table 9-3). The greater the requirement for self-reliance in men's work, the higher is the probability that they will value self-direction for their children and the lower the probability that they will value conformity.

The Independence of the Three Aspects of Occupational Self-Direction

Although closeness of supervision, the substance of men's work,

---

[8]The four items taken three at a time and dichotomized on the basis of whether or not the characteristic is considered important form satisfactory Guttman scales. But the cutting-points are too close together for all four items to be used in one scale, and the requirement that we score each item dichotomously (for independence) unduly restricts the power of the index. A simple additive scoring of the four items provides a more useful index.

TABLE 9-3
Fathers' Valuation of Self-Direction and Conformity,
by Social Class and Degree of Self-Reliance Required in Work

	Middle Class				Working Class			
	Least Self-Reliance	(Next Least)	(Next Greatest)	Greatest Self-Reliance	Least Self-Reliance	(Next Least)	(Next Greatest)	Greatest Self-Reliance
Proportion of fathers who:								
Value self-direction ...	.05	.46	.57	.83	.14	.37	.41	.65
(Intermediate)	.58	.26	.24	.00	.33	.28	.21	.21
Value conformity	.37	.28	.19	.17	.53	.35	.38	.14
Total	1.00	1.00	1.00	1.00	1.00	1.00	1.00	1.00
Number of cases ...	(19)	(50)	(70)	(24)	(36)	(64)	(42)	(14)

χ^2 (linear regression) = 16.4,
1 $d.f.$ $p < 0.01$ χ^2 (linear regression) = 9.7,
1 $d.f.$ $p < 0.01$

and the requirement of self-reliance in work are conceptually distinct, they are empirically closely related. (It could not be otherwise or occupations would not have structural integrity.) Accordingly, it is useful to examine their interrelationships, to be certain that each is related to parental values independently of the others. For example, does the need for self-reliance in work affect fathers' valuation of self-direction and conformity, regardless of the substance of their work? The answer is "yes." In both social classes, whether men work primarily with things, with people, or with data, those men whose jobs require greater self-reliance are likely to value self-direction for their children and those men whose jobs require less self-reliance are likely to value conformity. Similarly, the association between parental values and working with things, with people, or with data holds both for men whose jobs require a great deal of self-reliance and for men whose jobs require little. Although there is considerable correspondence between working with things, with people, or with data and the degree of self-reliance the job requires, the relationships of these two aspects of occupation to parental values are independent and reinforcing. Men who work primarily with things, on jobs that require little self-reliance, are most likely to value conformity; at the other extreme, men who work primarily with data, on jobs that require much self-reliance, are most likely to value self-direction.

Comparable analyses show that the relationship of closeness of supervision to parental values is independent of the relationships of the other two aspects of occupation.

The Relevance of Occupational Self-Direction to the Relationship between Class and Fathers' Values

We have established that the occupational conditions determinative of self-direction are related to parental values, and that these relationships are not simply a function of class. Now we reverse the procedure, to ask whether the relationship of class to parental values can be explained as resulting from class differences in the conditions that make for occupational self-direction.

It must be emphasized that in dealing with these occupational conditions we are concerned, not with distinctions that *cut across* social class, but with experiences *constitutive of* class. The objective is to learn whether these constituent experiences are pertinent for explaining the class relationship. To achieve this objective, we control occupational dimensions that have proved to be independently related to values and orientation, to determine whether this reduces the correlation between class and fathers' valuation of self-direction or conformity for children. The procedure is altogether hypothetical, for it imagines an unreal social situation—social classes that do not differ from one another in the occupational conditions experienced by their members. But it is analytically appropriate to use such hypothetical procedures, for it helps us differentiate those occupational conditions that are pertinent for explaining the relationship of class to parental values from those that are not.

The method of statistical control that we use in analyzing the Turin data is Rosenberg's (1962b) technique of test factor standardization.[9] This technique is an extension of the method used by demographers when they "standardize" populations of differing age

---

[9]Since the index of parental values derived from the Turin data cannot be treated as an interval scale, analyses of variance and of covariance would not be appropriate here. Test factor standardization accomplishes the same analytic goal, uses essentially the same logic, and does not require that the dependent variable be treated as an interval scale.

With small numbers of cases, the procedure of standardization is somewhat arbitrary; because few, if any, men have certain atypical combinations of occupational characteristics, categories must be grouped. We have tried to be conservative, to combine categories in ways that go counter to our hypothesis.

distributions on a common population base; in our case, we standardize the occupational characteristics of the middle- and working-class samples, using as our standard the average of the two. The effect is to overweight the value-choices of those men who have occupational characteristics atypical of their social class and to underweight the value-choices of those men who have occupational characteristics typical of their class.

The original class difference of 17 percent in the proportion of fathers who value self-direction is reduced to zero when occupational self-direction is standardized (Table 9-4). Thus, middle- and working-

TABLE 9-4
Fathers' Valuation of Self-Direction and Conformity,
by Social Class—Original and Standardized Comparisons

	Original Comparison[a]		Standardized Comparison	
	Middle Class	Working Class	Middle Class	Working Class
Proportion of fathers who:				
Value self-direction	.52	.35	.41	.41
(Intermediate)	.26	.25	.34	.24
Value conformity	.22	.40	.25	.35
Total	1.00	1.00	1.00	1.00
Number of cases	(144)	(141)	(144)	(141)

[a] The original comparison differs slightly from Table 3-3, for it excludes those fathers who could not be classified on all three dimensions of occupation.

class fathers' differential valuation of self-direction appears to be entirely attributable to their differential occupational experiences. At the other extreme, the original class difference of 18 percent in the proportion of fathers who value conformity is reduced to 10 percent by standardization. Other aspects of class must still contribute substantially to the greater likelihood of working-class fathers valuing conformity.

The Relevance of Men's Occupational Experiences for Their Wives' Values

Our proposed interpretation of the relationship of social class to parental values is directly applicable to fathers, but makes no provision for the fact that many mothers (especially in Italy) do not work at jobs outside the home. In all probability, though, these women are exposed to the occupational realities that their husbands experience. A partial test of this expectation is to examine the relationship of men's occupational circumstances to their wives' values.

Women Analyses directly comparable to those shown in Tables 9-1, 9-2, and 9-3 reveal that the closeness of supervision to which men are subject, the substance of their work with things, with people, or with data, and the degree of self-reliance required in their jobs are each related to their wives' values, although not to the same extent as to their own. These relationships appear to be stronger for the middle than for the working class.

To estimate the effect of occupational self-direction on the relationship of social class to mothers' values, we again use the technique of standardization. The effect of standardizing middle- and working-class mothers' values on their husbands' occupational conditions is to reduce the original class difference in mothers' values, but not by as much as is the case for fathers (Table 9-5).

TABLE 9-5
Mothers' Valuation of Self-Direction and Conformity,
by Social Class—Original and Standardized Comparisons

	Original Comparison[a]		Standardized Comparison	
	Middle Class	Working Class	Middle Class	Working Class
Proportion of mothers who:				
Value self-direction	.49	.31	.41	.35
(Intermediate)	.28	.27	.34	.25
Value conformity	.23	.42	.25	.40
Total	1.00	1.00	1.00	1.00
Number of cases.	(131)	(131)	(131)	(131)

[a] This analysis is limited to those mothers whose husbands were interviewed, for we have no data about the occupational circumstances of the others' husbands.

Specifically, the original difference of 18 percent between the proportion of middle- and of working-class mothers who value self-direction is reduced to 6 percent; the original difference of 19 percent in the proportion valuing conformity is reduced to 15 percent. It would appear that their husbands' occupational circumstances have substantial importance for mothers' valuation of self-direction, but have little importance for their valuation of conformity. Although both middle- and working-class mothers' valuation of self-direction seems to be affected by their husbands' occupational conditions, the effect is stronger for middle-class mothers.

These data say nothing about the mechanisms by which men's occupational conditions affect their wives' values—it may be that men's occupational conditions affect their own values and that men influence their wives; it may be that men communicate something of their occupational experiences to their wives and that this knowledge affects the wives' value-choices; or it may be any of several other possibilities. The communication linkage is especially likely because of evidence that better husband-wife communication exists in the middle class, and that middle-class parents' valuation of self-direction is more affected by occupational conditions than is working-class parents'. Whatever the intervening process, middle- and working-class mothers' differential valuation of self-direction for children is substantially attributable to their husbands' occupational conditions.

Provisional Conclusion

Men who work under occupational conditions that facilitate the exercise of self-direction are likely to value self-direction for their children; men who work under occupational conditions that inhibit or preclude the exercise of self-direction are likely to value conformity. This is true for both the middle and the working class. Moreover, the class difference in fathers' values for children is, in large measure, statistically attributable to the experience of occupational self-direction. Even some substantial part of the class difference in mothers' values is statistically attributable to their husbands' differential experiences of occupational self-direction.

To say that a large part of the relationship of social class to parental values is *statistically attributable* to occupational self-direction is not to say that we have demonstrated causality. There are several unresolved problems to be faced before we can conclude that the experiences of occupational self-direction are, in fact, instrumental in producing the class relationship. For the moment, we defer consideration of these problems because they can be treated more effectively when some alternative possibilities have been considered. We conclude simply that the Turin data indicate that the relationship of social class to parental values is largely attributable to class differences in men's experience of occupational self-direction. Since this conclusion is based on a limited analysis of Turinese families, we turn to the National study for verification—to see if the findings can be replicated in an analysis that utilizes a sample representative of American men.

EVIDENCE FROM THE NATIONAL STUDY

The National study provides that luxury rare in field research—the opportunity to repeat an analysis in a different cultural context with better indices, with a larger and more representative sample, and with more precise statistical tools. The same question is before us: To what degree is the relationship between social class and parental values attributable to the occupational conditions determinative of the exercise of self-direction in work?

The logic of the inquiry is also the same. We test to be certain that each condition of work is correlated with fathers' valuation of self-direction or conformity, independently of its relationship to social class. (It is unimportant that the partial correlations—controlled on social class—will necessarily be small; all that matters is that there be *some* statistically significant, independent association between a given occupational condition and fathers' valuation of self-direction.) Then, for conditions of work that prove to be independently associated with fathers' values, we ask the hypothetical question: How much would the relationship of social class to parental values be reduced if there were no class differences in these conditions of work?

For this part of the inquiry, we have indices of the precise conditions that we earlier specified as definitional of occupational self-direction: closeness of supervision; the substance of men's work with data, with people, and with things; and the complexity of organization of the work. Moreover, we can once again use the composite index of fathers' valuation of self-direction or conformity that was developed from the factor analysis of parental values presented in Chapter 4.

Closeness of Supervision

The index of closeness of supervision used here is a scale[10] based on five questions about how much latitude men's supervisors allow them and how supervisory control is exercised:

1. How closely does (the man who has the most control over what you do on the job) supervise you—does he decide what you do and how you do it; does he decide what you do but let *you* decide how you do it; do you have some freedom in deciding both what you do and how you do it; or are you your own boss so long as you stay within the general policies of the firm (organization, department)?

2. When he wants you to do something, does he usually just tell you to do it, does he usually discuss it with you, or is it about half and half?

3. How free do you feel to disagree with him—completely free, largely but not completely, moderately, not particularly, or not at all free?

4. Is the speed at which you work controlled mostly by you, your boss, your work group, the speed of machinery with which you work, or what? (The relevant aspect here is whether or not the supervisor controls the speed at which the man works.)

5. [How important is it for doing your job well that you] do what you're told?

The more closely supervised men are, the higher is their valuation of conformity for their children (Table 9-6).

The Substance of Work with Data, Things, and People

The indices of the "substance of the work" are based on detailed inquiry about precisely what men do and how much time they spend working with data, with things, and with people. Early in the interview—immediately after learning the title of the man's principal occupation and its institutional locus—the interviewer asked these questions:

One thing we'd like to be able to pin down particularly accurately is how much of your working time is spent reading and writing, how much working with your hands, and how much dealing with people.

---

[10]Reproducibility = 0.93; the pattern of errors seems essentially random (using Ford's criteria).

TABLE 9-6
Parental Valuation of Self-Direction/Conformity, by Closeness of Supervision
(controlled on social class)

	Mean Valuation of Self-Direction/Conformity[a] (Adjusted for Social Class)	Number of Cases
Closeness of supervision		
Owners	-0.15	(253)
Least closely supervised employees	-0.26	(222)
:	0.03	(266)
:	-0.08	(307)
:	0.08	(238)
:	0.13	(155)
Most closely supervised employees	0.16	(58)
		(1499)

Degree of association η (eta) with valuation of self-direction/conformity
Closeness of supervision (linear), controlled on social class—
Employees only: 0.07*
Owners treated as if equivalent to the least closely supervised employees:..   0.06*

* Indicates $p < 0.05$
** Indicates $p < 0.01$
[a] High valuation of self-direction is indicated by a negative score, of conformity by a positive score.

We realize, of course, that you can be doing two or even all three of these at the same time.

1. First—reading or writing. Here we should like to include any type of written materials—letters, files, memos, books, or blueprints. About how many hours a week do you spend reading, writing, dictating, or dealing with any kind of written materials on your job?
   (If any time at all)
   a.   What do you do?
   b.   What are they about?

2. Second—working with your hands, using tools, using or repairing machines. We should like to include everything that involves working with your hands—operating a lathe or a dentist's drill, moving furniture, playing the piano. About how many hours a week do you spend working with your hands on your job?
   (If any time at all)
   a.   What do you do? (*Probe*: What operations do you perform?)

    b.   What materials do you work on?

    c.   What tools or equipment do you use?

    d.   *(If relevant)* What do you do to set up and maintain your equipment?

3. Third—dealing with people. Here we do *not* mean to include passing the time of day, but only conversations necessary for the job; for example, talking to your boss, teaching, supervising, selling, advising clients. About how many hours a week does your job require you to spend dealing with people?

(If any time at all)

What kinds of things do you do—do you teach students, supervise subordinates, receive instructions from the boss, sell to customers, advise clients, discuss the work with co-workers, or what? (Be sure to ascertain *what* he does and to *whom.*)

(If more than one such activity)

At which one of these do you spend the most time?

From men's answers to these questions, we rated the degree of *complexity* of their work with data, with things, and with people;[11] the amount of *time* they spend working at each of these three types of activity; and the *overall complexity* of their jobs (cf. Appendix E). These seven indices comprise our measurements of the substance of the work.

Men's work with data, with things, and with people are all related to their valuation of self-direction or conformity for their children, even when social class is controlled. But the relative importance of time and complexity vary for the three types of work. In work with people (Table 9-7), only the complexity of the work matters; the amount of time men spend dealing with people is of little or no relevance for their values. In work with data (Table 9-8), both the

---

[11]The classifications of the complexity of work with data, with things, and with people are based on those used in the third edition of the *Dictionary of Occupational Titles* (U.S. Department of Labor, 1965). The *Dictionary's* ratings, based on *in situ* observations by trained occupational analysts, provide objective appraisals of typical job requirements for all major occupations. These appraisals are keyed to the average conditions for entire occupations; any plumber, for example, will be rated in the fourth-highest of eight categories of complexity of work with data, the lowest of nine categories of complexity of work with people, and the second-highest of nine categories of complexity of work with things. Our ratings for particular jobs prove to be highly consistent with the *Dictionary's* ratings for entire occupations, even though we have deliberately chosen to depart from their apparent rating procedures in a few instances (cf. Appendix E).

TABLE 9-7
Parental Valuation of Self-Direction/Conformity, by Complexity of Work with People
(controlled on social class)

	Mean Valuation of Self-Direction/Conformity[a] (Adjusted for Social Class)	Number of Cases
Complexity of work with people		
Mentoring	-0.29	(37)
Negotiating	-0.19	(117)
Instructing	-0.14	(83)
Supervising	-0.04	(304)
Diverting/persuading	-0.06	(203)
Speaking-signalling	0.05	(462)
Serving/receives orders or instructions	0.21	(194)
Does not work with people	0.07	(99)
		(1499)

Degree of association η (eta) with valuation of self-direction/conformity— controlled on social class	
Complexity of work with people (as above):	0.08**
Complexity of work with people, controlled on time spent working with people:	0.08**
Time spent working with people:	0.03
Time spent working with people, controlled on complexity of work with people:	0.02
Time + complexity of work with people:	0.09**

  * Indicates $p < 0.05$
 ** Indicates $p < 0.01$
[a]High valuation of self-direction is indicated by a negative score, of conformity by a positive score.

complexity of the work and the amount of time spent at that work
are relevant for values. And in work with things (Table 9-9), time is
of predominant importance; the complexity of that work does not
bear any independent relationship to values.[12]

The specifics of men's work with data, with things, and with

---

[12]These conclusions are based on our ratings of the "usual" level of complexity of men's
work with data, with things, and with people. We have also rated the highest and lowest
levels at which men ever work. In work with data, what matters most for men's values is the
highest level of complexity at which they ever work; the usual level is of lesser importance
and the lowest level is irrelevant. It thus seems that the most relevant aspect of work with
data is not how humdrum is the most routine task men ever perform, nor even the level at
which they usually work, but how far men have to stretch themselves in dealing with the
most complex problems they ever meet.
    In work with things, all three ratings of complexity yield the same conclusion: It is not
the complexity of the work with things but the amount of time spent working with things
that counts.
    In work with people, it is the usual level of complexity that is most closely related to
values.

TABLE 9-8
Parental Valuation of Self-Direction/Conformity, by Complexity of Work with Data
(controlled on social class)

	Mean Valuation of Self-Direction/Conformity[a] (Adjusted for Social Class)	Number of Cases
Complexity of work with data		
Synthesizing	-0.54	(62)
Coordinating	-0.07	(187)
Analyzing	-0.00	(156)
Compiling	0.03	(326)
Computing	0.04	(43)
Copying	0.03	(305)
Comparing	-0.30	(42)
Reading instructions	-0.05	(129)
Does not work with data.................	0.19	(249)
		(1499)
Degree of association η (eta) with valuation of self-direction/conformity— controlled on social class		
Complexity of work with data (as above):		0.06*
Complexity of work with data, controlled on time spent working with data:		0.02
Time spent working with data:		0.09**
Time spent working with data, controlled on complexity of work with data:		0.04
Time + complexity of work with data:		0.09**

* Indicates $p < 0.05$
** Indicates $p < 0.01$
[a]High valuation of self-direction is indicated by a negative score, of conformity by a positive score.

people—the types of data with which they work, the tools they use, the nature of their relationships with the people with whom they interact—are relatively unimportant for their values as fathers. [13]

---

[13]The effects of working with *data* are somewhat enhanced if the data are principally memoranda or technical reports rather than blueprints, general instructions, structured forms, literary materials, or numerical materials. In general, though, it is the fact of working with data, not the subject matter or form of the data, that matters.

In work with *things*, such facets of the work as the tools used and responsibility for their maintenance, the heaviness of the work, the physical and atmospheric conditions under which the work is done, all prove to be unrelated to men's values when the amount of time spent working with things is taken into account.

In work with *people*, it does not seem to matter for men's values whether the principal activity is teaching, learning, supervising, giving or receiving instructions, selling, buying, advising, or discussing. The interpersonal context of the job does not seem to be important either. No substantial effects depend upon what proportion of time men work alone, or in the company of several other people; on whether or not they work on teams and, if so, how many people are on the team and who they are. Value patterns are not even related to whether they regard their co-workers as competitors.   *(Footnote Continues.)*

TABLE 9-9
Parental Valuation of Self-Direction/Conformity, by Complexity of Work with Things
(controlled on social class)

	Mean Valuation of Self-Direction/Conformity[a] (Adjusted for Social Class)	Number of Cases
Complexity of work with things		
Setting up	0.03	(59)
Precision working	0.10	(88)
Operating-controlling	-0.17	(102)
Driving-operating	0.13	(291)
Manipulating	0.01	(533)
Tending	0.15	(64)
Feeding-offbearing	0.11	(26)
Handling	0.02	(114)
Does not work with things	-0.22	(222)
		(1499)
Degree of association η (eta) with valuation of self-direction/conformity – controlled on social class		
Complexity of work with things (as above):		0.05*
Complexity of work with things, controlled on time spent working with things:		0.00
Time spent working with things:		0.10**
Time spent working with things, controlled on complexity of work with things:		0.04
Time + complexity of work with things:		0.10**

* Indicates $p < 0.05$
** Indicates $p < 0.01$
[a]High valuation of self-direction is indicated by a negative score, of conformity by a positive score.

What does matter for fathers' values is the complexity of work with data and with people, the time spent working with data and with things, and the overall complexity of the job. Each of these is independently relevant, and their multiple correlation with men's valuation of self-direction or conformity is a bit greater than the correlation of any one of them.

The Complexity of Organization of Work

Some jobs are endlessly repetitive, others offer a variety of different tasks or at least variety in the ways that essentially similar

---

Although closeness of supervision and complexity of work with people are inextricably intertwined, they do more than measure the same thing. Each of them continues to be correlated with values even when the other is controlled, and their combined correlation with values is greater than that of either alone.

tasks can be performed. In some jobs, the "units" of which the stream of work is composed are nearly identical; in others, the units are complex entities—each with a structural integrity of its own—or the work is so highly diversified that it cannot meaningfully be split into units. Again the essence of the matter is complexity, but now from the perspective of the organization of the work. Simply organized jobs cannot allow much self-direction; complexly organized jobs require it.

Although we prefer objective indices of occupation, we have to rely on subjective appraisals for this part of the inquiry. To measure the first component of the complexity of organization of work—the *repetitiveness* or *variety* of tasks—we asked: Does your work involve doing the same thing in the same way repeatedly, the same kind of thing in a number of different ways, or a number of different kinds of things? We find that men whose work is repetitive tend to value conformity for their children; men whose work is varied tend to value self-direction.[14]

To measure the second component of organization of work—the complexity of the structure of the basic job units—we used the following line of questioning:

What it takes to do a complete job varies a great deal from occupation to occupation. To a worker on an assembly line a complete job may be to tighten two or three bolts; to an auto mechanic a complete job is to repair a car; to a coal miner, a complete job may be to load 18 tons.
   a.   What do you ordinarily think of as a complete job in your occupation? (*Probe:* What do you have to do in order to feel that you've finished a piece of work? *Second Probe:* Do you ever feel that you've finished? At what point?)

---

[14]The issue of *repetitiveness* necessarily raises questions about *predictability,* because men who repeatedly do the same thing can predict with certainty what the next task will be. One way to separate the two is to focus attention on men who do a variety of different tasks. We asked those men: When you begin your day's work, can you predict what kinds of things are going to happen on the job that day, or is it a job in which you can't tell what may come up? Their replies show that predictability of task is related to the positive valuing not of conformity but of self-direction. In fact, the job circumstances that are likely to result in valuing conformity are either a completely routine *or* a highly varied and altogether unpredictable job; the circumstances that are likely to result in valuing self-direction are a varied job in which one can predict quite well what one will be doing. The reason may be simple: Either of the former circumstances indicates that men have little control over what they do at work; the latter circumstances, the opposite.

b.   How long does it take you to do a complete job? (*If it varies:* What is the range of variation?)

The internal structure of the job unit is related to men's valuation of self-direction or conformity for children independently of the repetitiveness or variety of the work. Those men who see "a complete job" as the amount of work that can be done in a given amount of time—an hour, a day, a week, a semester, or a season—are most likely to value conformity; they are followed closely by those who define a job in terms of a given quantity of product—3 pounds, 6 feet, or 16 tons. At the other extreme, the men who value

TABLE 9-10
Parental Valuation of Self-Direction/Conformity, by
the Complexity of Organization of the Work
(controlled on social class)

	Mean Valuation of Self-Direction/Conformity[a] (Adjusted for Social Class)		
	Work Involves Doing:		
	The Same Thing in the Same Way Repeatedly	The Same Kind of Thing in Different Ways	Different Kinds of Things
"A complete job" is defined in terms of:			
The amount of work that can be done in a given unit of time..........	0.12 (100)[b]	0.13 (50)	-0.01 (52)
A given quantity of work..........	0.11 (164)	0.01 (171)	0.02 (244)
A completed unit where something intrinsic to the job determines what is a unit	0.15 (80)	-0.06 (170)	-0.05 (295)
No unit; work flow is indivisible	-0.13 (30)	-0.08 (44)	-0.30 (65)

Degree of association η (eta) with valuation of self-direction/conformity— controlled on social class	
Repetitiveness of the work:	0.06
Structural complexity of job unit:	0.08*
Complexity of organization (repetitiveness of work + structural complexity of job unit):	0.10*

* Indicates $p < 0.05$
** Indicates $p < 0.01$
[a] High valuation of self-direction is indicated by a negative score, of conformity by a positive score.
[b] Numbers in parentheses represent the number of cases on which means are based.

self-direction most highly are those who cannot divide their work into units—work seems to be an indivisible flow, one operation inseparable from the next—followed by those who define a job in terms of its intrinsic properties—a solution to a particular problem or the production of some object.[15]

The two components of how the work is organized are additive in their effects (Table 9-10). Thus, self-direction is highly valued both by men who see their work as an indivisible flow and by men who work on varied jobs; it is most valued by men who see their work as an indivisible flow of highly varied tasks. Conformity is most valued by men whose work consists of repetitive and simply structured tasks. In sum, the more diverse and complexly structured is men's work, the higher is their valuation of self-direction; the more routine and simply structured, the higher is their valuation of conformity.

Occupational Self-Direction and Fathers' Values

Each of the three conditions that make for occupational self-direction—the absence of close supervision; doing complex work with data or with people, and not working with things; and working at complexly organized tasks—is significantly related to fathers' valuation of self-direction for their children. Moreover, each occupational condition is *independently* related to fathers' valuation of self-

TABLE 9-11
Parental Valuation of Self-Direction/Conformity, by
the Conditions Determinative of Occupational Self-Direction
(controlled on social class)

	Correlation[a]
Closeness of supervision	0.06*
Substance of the work with data, with people, and with things	0.12**
Complexity of organization of the work	0.10**
Total of all three components of occupational self-direction	0.15**
(N = 1450)	

  * Indicates $p < 0.05$
  ** Indicates $p < 0.01$
  [a] η (eta) for the linear components of the relevant occupational conditions.

---

[15]Coders found it difficult to distinguish between units defined in terms of a given quantity of work and those defined in terms of the intrinsic nature of the job. Therefore, coding reliability was only 64 percent (absolute agreement, on a blind test), considerably below our usual standard (cf. Appendix C).

direction; that is, each continues to be related even when the other two are controlled. The multiple correlation of the three is greater than the correlation of any one of them (Table 9-11).

In sum, all three conditions of occupational self-direction are related to fathers' valuation of self-direction, independently of social class and independently of each other. The substance of the work with data, with people, and with things matters most of all, but closeness of supervision and the complexity of organization of work add to that impact.

The Relevance of Occupational Self-Direction to the Relationship between Class and Parental Values

We return to the central question: Is occupational self-direction pertinent for explaining the relationship of social class to fathers'

TABLE 9-12
Comparison of the Correlation of Class to Parental Valuation
of Self-Direction/Conformity When Not Controlled and When Controlled
on the Conditions Determinative of Occupational Self-Direction

	Correlation of Class to Parental Valuation of Self-Direction/ Conformity[a]	Proportional Reduction in the Class Correlation
Class, uncontrolled	0.34**	
Class, controlled on closeness of supervision	0.28**	.18
Class, controlled on the substance of the work with data, with people, and with things	0.14**	.59
Class, controlled on the complexity of organization of the work	0.28**	.18
Class, controlled on all three determinants of occupational self-direction .... (N = 1450)	0.12**	.65

* Indicates $p < 0.05$
** Indicates $p < 0.01$
[a] η (eta) for the linear component of social class.

valuation of self-direction or conformity for their children? As we did with the Turin data, we deal with the question by the hypothetical procedure of controlling the relevant occupational conditions, to see if this reduces the class correlation. (This time, though, we use analysis of variance and of covariance as our statistical procedures.)

The results of this analysis are altogether consistent with those of the Turin data:[16] Controlling the conditions that make for occupational self-direction reduces the correlation of class to fathers' valuation of self-direction or conformity by nearly two thirds (Table 9-12). The lion's share of the reduction is attributable to the substance of men's work with data, with things, and with people, but the other occupational conditions are relevant, too.

In short, the relationship of social class to fathers' valuation of self-direction or conformity for their children is, in large measure, attributable to class-correlated variations in the degree to which jobs allow and require self-direction.

CONCLUSION

The Turin study and the National study lead to precisely the same conclusion: The relationship of social class to parents' valuation of self-direction or conformity for children is largely attributable to class-correlated variations in men's exercise of self-direction in work. That the two studies are in such complete agreement indicates that the interrelationship of class, occupational self-direction, and parental values is not limited to the specific circumstances of either Italian or American life but is a more general phenomenon, built into the structure of industrial society.

Because the relationship between exercising self-direction on the job and valuing self-direction for children is so direct, one might conclude that parents are simply preparing children for occupational life to come. We believe, rather, that parents come to value self-direction or conformity as virtues in their own right, not simply as means to occupational goals. One important piece of evidence buttresses this impression: Both studies show that the relationship between men's occupational experiences and their values is the same for daughters as for sons, yet it is hardly likely (especially in Italy) that most fathers think daughters will have occupational careers

---

[16]For closer comparability, we developed a set of indices for the National study that are equivalent to those used in Turin—indices of closeness of supervision; men's assessments of the relative importance of their work with data, with things, and with people; and their assessments of the need for self-reliance in their work. Each of these is related to men's valuation of self-direction, class controlled. Controlling these variables, in turn, reduces the correlation of class to parental values by *precisely* the same amount as does controlling the conditions of occupational self-direction as indexed in the National study.

comparable to those of sons. Occupational experience helps structure men's view not only of the occupational world, but of social reality in general. This belief will be tested in the next chapter. There we ask: Is occupational self-direction as important for all the relationships of class to values and orientation as it has proved to be for the relationship of class to parental values?

To conclude that the relationship of social class to parental values is largely attributable to the experiences of occupational self-direction is something less than to conclude that these occupational conditions do, in fact, enter into the processes by which class affects values. There are alternative interpretations to consider. In particular, there are many other aspects of occupation that are correlated with social class and that we might expect to be related to one or more aspects of values and orientation; do any of these occupational conditions provide alternative (or supplementary) explanations of the class relationships? More generally: What else, in addition to occupational self-direction, is relevant for explaining the relationships of social class to values and orientation?

CHAPTER 10

Class, Occupation, and Orientation

We have seen that the experience of occupational self-direction is important for explaining the relationship of social class to men's valuing self-direction or conformity for their children. Is occupational self-direction—as we hypothesize—also important for explaining the relationships of social class to men's values and orientation in general?

Are there any aspects of occupation other than those involved in self-direction that are important for explaining the relationships of class to values and orientation? Take one possibility—bureaucracy. Men of higher social class position tend disproportionately to work in bureaucratic organizations. Might this finding be pertinent for explaining the class relationships? Bureaucracy is but one of many class-correlated aspects of occupation that must be considered.

To answer these questions, we follow the same two-step model used in Chapter 9: first, an examination of the relationships of various occupational conditions to values and orientation, controlling always on social class; second, an examination of the effects on the class correlations of controlling those occupational variables that prove to be independently related to values and orientation.

The data for these analyses come from the National study, which provides information about a wide range of occupational variables and about all the aspects of values and orientation with which our investigations have dealt.

THE RELATIONSHIP OF OCCUPATIONAL SELF-DIRECTION TO VALUES AND ORIENTATION

The conditions that are determinative of the exercise of occupational self-direction are related (independently of their relationship to social class) to virtually all aspects of values and orientation that we have studied (Table 10-1). Specifically:

Closeness of supervision is associated with a constricted orientation. Closely supervised men tend not only to value conformity for their children, but also to emphasize extrinsic benefits that jobs provide rather than opportunities for intrinsic accomplishment, to have standards of morality keyed to the letter rather than the spirit of the law, to be distrustful, to be resistant to innovation and change, to lack self-confidence, and to be anxious. These relationships exist, no matter how many levels of formal authority intervene between men and the supervisors who actually exert the most control over them.

The substance of the work—that is, the complexity of work with data, with things, and with people and the amount of time spent at

TABLE 10-1
Values and Orientation by the Conditions Determinative of Occupational Self-Direction[a]

	Closeness of Supervision	Substance of the Work: Data, Things, and People	Organization of the Work: Repetitiveness and Structural Complexity	Total of All Three Components of Occupational Self-Direction
A. Parental values				
Self-direction/conformity	.06*	.12**	.10*	.15**
B. Values for self				
Self-direction/conformity	.02	.08*	.04	.08
Self-direction/competence	.01	.05	.05	.07
C. Judgments about work				
Importance of intrinsic qualities .	.11**	.14**	.10**	.18**
Importance of extrinsic benefits .	.07**	.15**	.15**	.18**
D. Social orientation				
Authoritarian conservatism	.03	.10**	.11**	.14**
Criteria of morality	.12**	.13**	.11**	.18**
Trustfulness	.04*	.09**	.05	.10**
Stance toward change	.06**	.13**	.07*	.15**
Canonical correlation .	.14**	.21**	.18**	.26**
E. Self-conception				
Self-confidence	.08**	.09**	.04	.12**
Self-deprecation	.02	.07*	.07*	.10**
Attribution of responsibility	.02	.06	.05	.08
Anxiety	.07**	.04	.04	.09*
Idea-conformity	.03	.07*	.06	.09*
Canonical correlation .	.11**	.13**	.08	.16**

* Indicates $p < 0.05$
** Indicates $p < 0.01$

[a]Entries are partial correlations, either η (eta) or the canonical correlation, always controlled on social class. Closeness of supervision and the seven component indices of the substance of the work have been tested linearly, the organization of the work has been tested *in toto*.

Note: $N > 2900$, except for parental values, where $N = 1450$.

each—is related to almost all aspects of values and orientation. Doing complex work with data or with people is consistently associated with valuing self-direction (for oneself as well as for one's children) and holding a consonant orientation; working with things is consistently associated with having conformist values and orientation.[1]

The complexity of organization of work also is associated with the self-directedness of men's orientations. Specifically, men who work at complexly organized jobs,[2] in addition to valuing self-direction for children, tend to emphasize intrinsic aspects of the job, to be open-minded and tolerant of nonconformity, to have moral standards that demand more than conformity to the letter of the law, to be receptive to change, and not to be self-deprecatory.

In sum, each of the three conditions that are determinative of occupational self-direction—closeness of supervision; the substance of work with data, with things, and with people; and the complexity of organization of work—is consistently related to values and orientation, hence might help explain the class relationships. Moreover, each is significantly related to values and orientation independently of the other two. The substance of work with data, with people, and with things is the most important of the three components of occupational self-direction; but closeness of supervision and the complexity of organization of work add to the total impact. Thus, occupational self-direction, independently of its close association with social class, is significantly related to almost all aspects of values and orientation that we have investigated.[3]

OTHER FACETS OF OCCUPATION

Previous theoretical and empirical studies suggest many other class-correlated occupational conditions that might be related to

---

[1]The relative importance of time and complexity in work with people is somewhat different for orientation to self and to society from what we found it to be for parental values. For parental values, only the complexity of work with people matters; for orientation, time matters too.

[2]The index, as before, is based on the variety of tasks done and the complexity of structure of the units of work. We now find, in addition, that men whose work is comprised of units that (regardless of their structural complexity) take a long time to perform are especially likely to value self-direction, to emphasize the intrinsic aspects of work, to be open-minded, and to have personally demanding standards of morality.

[3]One other occupational condition clearly implicated in the issue of self-direction (even though not built into our indices) is related to values and orientation: Men who are required to assume some given posture for long periods of time without being free to shift—

values and orientation and therefore might help explain the class relationships. These studies indicate that ownership, bureaucracy, time-pressure, interpersonal relations, and job satisfaction are particularly worthy of investigation.

Ownership, Job Rights, and Job Security

If only to acknowledge its historical importance, we should consider the possibility that ownership of the means of production (in Marx's term) and of the means of administration, of inquiry, and of violence (in Weber's expanded conception) is really the issue in the relationship of class to values and orientation. Dahrendorf's analysis (1959:136) suggests, though, that the separation of legal ownership from factual control has greatly diminished the usefulness of ownership for contemporary analyses of class.

Ownership,[4] independently of class as we have measured it, is related to some aspects of values and orientation; it is associated with emphasizing intrinsic aspects of work, believing that morality requires more than obeying the letter of the law, not being self-deprecatory, and not being anxious (Table 10-2). Ownership is also related (and somewhat more strongly) to authoritarian conservatism: There is a disproportionate tendency for owners to hold authoritarian conservative beliefs. But this tendency cannot help explain the relationship of class to authoritarian conservatism, for owners tend to be of higher class position than nonowners, and the higher classes tend to have less authoritarian, more open-minded beliefs. (Were it not that owners tend to hold authoritarian beliefs, the negative correlation of class with authoritarian conservatism would be stronger than it is.) Thus, ownership per se can be of only limited importance for explaining the relationships that we have credited to class.

It has been suggested that, in an economy of large-scale public and private organizations, the modern equivalent to ownership is the "right to one's job" (cf. Porter, 1954). Perhaps this facet of economic position, rather than ownership as such, is pivotal for

---

particularly men who have to *sit* for long periods of time without being free to get up and move about—are likely to have conformist values and orientation.

[4]Ownership status has been classified along a continuum (full ownership, majority ownership, half ownership, minority ownership, and nonownership). The results are essentially the same if we dichotomize: ownership—nonownership.

TABLE 10-2
Values and Orientation, by Ownership, Competition,
and Likelihood of Loss of Job or Business[a]

	Degree of Ownership	Amount of Competition	Likelihood of Loss of Job or Business
A. Parental values			
Self-direction/conformity	.01	.05*	.03
B. Values for self			
Self-direction/conformity	.02	.04*	.00
Self-direction/competence	.01	.01	.01
C. Judgments about work			
Importance of intrinsic qualities . . .	.04*	.04*	.00
Importance of extrinsic benefits . . .	.02	.03	.02
D. Social orientation			
Authoritarian conservatism	.08**	.05*	.05*
Criteria of morality	.05*	.02	.01
Trustfulness	.00	.01	.06**
Stance toward change	.00	.07**	.02
Canonical correlation . . .	.09**	.08**	.08**
E. Self-conception			
Self-confidence	.01	.03	.03
Self-deprecation	.04*	.02	.08**
Attribution of responsibility	.01	.03	.04
Anxiety	.05**	.02	.05**
Idea-conformity	.01	.07**	.04*
Canonical correlation . . .	.07*	.09**	.11**

* Indicates $p < 0.05$
** Indicates $p < 0.01$
[a] Entries are partial correlations, either η (eta) or the canonical correlation, always controlled on social class.
Note: $N > 2830$, except for parental values, where $N > 1470$.

men's values and orientation. But the job rights and job protections about which we inquired—union contracts, seniority, and established grievance procedures; tenure, civil service job protection, and like guarantees of job security; and lesser job protections—prove to be unrelated to values and orientation.

Closely connected to the question of job rights are issues of job security and insecurity, particularly those insecurities attendant on competition and on the vagaries of impersonal economic forces. As for competition: Having no objective criteria by which to assess actual situations, we rely on men's judgments of how much competition they face. Men of higher class position (employees as well as entrepreneurs) claim to face greater competition; competition, in turn, is related to several aspects of values and orientation in a direction consistent with the class relationships. But, like owner-ship, competition is positively associated with authoritarian conserva-tism. Thus, competition may be relevant for explaining some of the class relationships, but not that of class to authoritarian conserva-tism.

Competition does not necessarily mean serious job insecurity. To pursue the issue of job security, we asked entrepreneurs to estimate the likelihood of business failure and employees to estimate the likelihood of a cutback in the work force that would result in temporary or permanent loss of job. These job insecurities, which are greater at lower class levels, are associated with apprehensiveness. That is, men who think that they face considerable risk of losing their jobs or businesses tend to be somewhat more authoritarian, distrustful, self-deprecating, anxious, and conformist in their ideas than are other men of comparable class position. Whether job insecurity is conducive to being apprehensive or apprehensiveness leads men to overestimate job insecurity we cannot tell. Since our intent is to discover all job conditions whose possible relevance for explaining the class relationships can be contrasted to that of occupational self-direction, we shall act as though we had demon-strated that job insecurity leads to apprehensiveness.

Considered together, ownership, competition, and serious job insecurity are related (independently of class) to many aspects of values and orientation, and thus might prove relevant for explaining some of the class relationships. Even at this point of the analysis, though, it is clear that ownership and competition cannot help explain the relationship of class to authoritarian conservatism, for their influence contravenes that of class.

Bureaucracy

By "bureaucracy" we mean a form of organizational structure characterized by large size and multiple levels of supervision.[5] Critics

---

[5]The classic analysis of bureaucracy is Weber's (cf. Gerth and Mills, 1946: 196-244). Merton (1952:362) has summarized the main points of Weber's characterization of bureaucratic structure as follows: "[B]ureaucracy involves a clear-cut division of integrated activities which are regarded as duties inherent in the office. A system of differentiated controls and sanctions is stated in the regulations. The assignment of roles occurs on the basis of technical qualifications which are ascertained through formalized, impersonal procedures (for example, examinations). Within the structure of hierarchically arranged authority, the activities of 'trained and salaried experts' are governed by general, abstract, clearly defined rules which preclude the necessity for the issuance of specific instructions for each specific case."

of bureaucracy emphasize its propensity to reward, and thereby to foster, conformity. Miller and Swanson (1958) address such criticism specifically to the effects that bureaucratization of American economic enterprise has purportedly had on parents' goals and methods of child rearing. Their thesis is that in the day of small business enterprises it was considered appropriate to raise children to be self-reliant, to exercise great self-control, and to assume an active, manipulative stance toward the environment. Parents whose perspective has been conditioned by the bureaucratic way of life will consider self-reliance and self-control less appropriate as goals of child rearing and will encourage their children, instead, to be accommodating.

These criticisms of bureaucracy may misinterpret the conditions of life faced by the inhabitants both of the entrepreneurial and of the bureaucratic worlds. We often fail to recognize just how little the small- or medium-sized entrepreneur controls the conditions of his own existence and just how much he is subject to the authority of customers, sources of credit and capital, insurance companies, and officialdom. And we often fail to recognize that monolithic-seeming bureaucracies allow free play for—in fact, may require—initiative of new sorts: in the creation of ideas, in the building of empires, and in the competition for advancement.

Contrary to what the critics have charged, employment in bureaucracies is associated with having self-directed values and orientation (Table 10-3). The larger the organization[6] in which men work and the more levels of supervision[7] it has, the more likely men are to value self-direction, to emphasize intrinsic and to de-emphasize extrinsic aspects of jobs, to hold nonauthoritarian beliefs, to be receptive to innovation and change, not to be self-deprecatory, and to think that their ideas are independent of the social entities to which they belong. These relationships exist no matter whether men

---

[6]To estimate the size of the firm or organization, we asked one of three questions, as appropriate: Altogether, about how many people work for the . . . (1) entire firm? [asked of the self-employed and of employees of profit-making firms], or . . . (2) entire organization? [asked of employees of nonprofit organizations], or . . . (3) entire department or agency? [asked of government employees].

[7]For firms or organizations having fewer than 10 employees, we assumed that there is one level of supervision; for those having 500 or more employees, we assumed that there must be at least two intermediate levels of supervision between the people at the bottom and those at the top. Where there are 10 or more but fewer than 500 employees, we asked: Is this a firm (organization, department) where everyone is supervised directly by the same man, where there is one level of supervision between the people at the bottom and the top, or where there are two or more levels of supervision between the people at the bottom and the top?

TABLE 10-3
Values and Orientation, by Size and Supervisory Structure of the Organization,
Closeness of Supervision, and Hierarchical Position[a]

	Size and Supervisory Structure of the Organization	Hierarchical Position (Number of Subordinates)	Size and Supervisory Structure of the Organization, Controlled on Closeness of Supervision	Closeness of Supervision, Controlled on Size and Supervisory Structure
A. Parental values				
Self-direction/conformity	.05	.02	.08**	.09**
B. Values for self				
Self-direction/conformity	.06**	.01	.07**	.03
Self-direction/competence	.06*	.03	.05*	.01
C. Judgments about work				
Importance of intrinsic qualities .	.05*	.07**	.01	.10**
Importance of extrinsic benefits .	.07**	.05*	.05	.05*
D. Social orientation				
Authoritarian conservatism	.08**	.00	.08**	.00
Criteria of morality	.03	.00	.08**	.14**
Trustfulness	.02	.03	.03	.04*
Stance toward change	.06**	.08**	.09**	.08**
Canonical correlation .	.11**	.09**	.16**	.17**
E. Self-conception				
Self-confidence	.03	.05**	.06**	.09**
Self-deprecation	.06**	.02	.07**	.05**
Attribution of responsibility	.03	.01	.04	.03
Anxiety....................	.03	.01	.03	.08**
Idea-conformity	.05*	.00	.05*	.03
Canonical correlation .	.07**	.06	.10**	.14**

* Indicates $p < 0.05$
** Indicates $p < 0.01$
[a] Entries are partial correlations, either η (eta) or the canonical correlation, always controlled on social class.
Note: $N > 2815$, except for parental values, where $N > 1470$.

work in government, in profit-making firms, or in nonprofit organizations[8] and regardless of their positions in the supervisory hierarchy. (Higher position in the supervisory hierarchy[9] is itself

---

[8]There is little difference in values and orientation between the employees of government, profit-making firms, and nonprofit organizations. Moreover, among men who are employed by government, it does not matter whether they work for national government, state government, or local government, or what is the function of the particular department in which they are employed.

[9]The index of position in the supervisory hierarchy is the number of subordinates, both those directly supervised and those lower in that supervisory hierarchy.

related, independently of the size and structure of the organization, to a decided interest in the intrinsic aspects of work, a positive stance toward change, and self-confidence.)

The consistent association between employment in a bureaucracy and having self-directed values and orientation is especially noteworthy because employees of bureaucratic organizations tend to be more closely supervised than are other men of their class position, and—as we have seen—closeness of supervision is associated with conformist values and orientation. Closeness of supervision and bureaucracy pull in opposite directions; each of them, controlled on the other, proves to have more general and more sizeable relationships to values and orientation than had been apparent. Consider, for example, the relationships of closeness of supervision and of size of organization to fathers' valuing self-direction or conformity for their children (Table 10-4). Self-direction is most valued by the least closely supervised employees of large organizations; conformity is

TABLE 10-4
Parental Valuation of Self-Direction/Conformity, by
Size of Firm or Organization and Closeness of Supervision
(controlled on social class)

| | Mean Valuation of Self-Direction/Conformity[a] (Adjusted for Social Class) | | | |
| | Size of Firm (Number of Employees) | | | |
	1000+	100-999	10-99	1-9
Closeness of supervision				
Least closely supervised	-0.17 (87)[b]	-0.31 (51)	-0.14 (89)	0.04 (244)
Intermediate	-0.05 (289)	-0.01 (127)	-0.04 (100)	0.05 (54)
Most closely supervised	0.02 (205)	0.16 (96)	0.23 (104)	0.26 (41)

Degree of association η (eta) with valuation of self-direction/conformity—
controlled on social class

Size of firm or organization, not controlled on closeness of supervision: . . .	0.05
Size of firm or organization, controlled on closeness of supervision:	0.07**
Closeness of supervision, not controlled on size of firm or organization: .	0.06*
Closeness of supervision, controlled on size of firm or organization:	0.09**

  * Indicates $p < 0.05$
  ** Indicates $p < 0.01$
  [a] High valuation of self-direction is indicated by a negative score, of conformity by a positive score.
  [b] Numbers in parentheses represent the number of cases on which means are based.

most valued by closely supervised employees of small organizations. Similarly for other aspects of values and orientation (Table 10-3): The importance of both closeness of supervision and bureaucracy is enhanced by controlling the other.

Clearly, employment in a bureaucracy, far from being conducive to conformity, is associated with self-directed values and orientation.

The Use and Organization of Time

We have seen that one class-correlated aspect of how time is used on the job—namely, its allocation to work with data, with things, and with people—is highly relevant to values and orientation. There are many other ways in which class position is related to the use of time on the job, some of which also may be relevant for values and orientation. Of particular interest are time-pressure, its determinants, and its consequences. Blauner (1964:21) argued that, "The pace of work is probably the most insistent, the most basic, aspect of a job and retaining control in this area is a kind of affirmation of human dignity." Our data confirm that control over the pace of work is indeed relevant for self-conception, and add that the sheer fact of working under time-pressure has even more general relevance for values and orientation.

Some men control the pace at which they work[10] —in contrast to those whose pace of work is determined by the speed of machinery, or by boss or co-workers, or by the total volume of work to be done. Men who control their pace of work are likely to be self-confident, not to be self-deprecatory, and to feel that they have some control over their fate; this is true no matter how much time-pressure they face. Control over the pace of one's work does matter for human dignity.

Even more important for values and orientation than control over the pace of work is the fact of working under time-pressure. Men of higher class position are likely to work under greater time-pressure. Regardless of class position, men who work under greater pressure of time tend to value self-direction for both self and children, and to

---

[10]The questions used to index time-pressure, its determinants, and its consequences are: How often do you have to work under pressure of time? Is the speed at which you work controlled mostly by you, your boss, your work group, the speed of machinery with which you work, or what? When you're working under time-pressure, does this involve working longer hours, heavier physical work, faster physical movements, or faster thinking?

hold a generally consonant orientation–de-emphasizing the extrinsic aspects of work, holding nonauthoritarian beliefs, being trustful, favoring innovation and change, being self-confident, and believing that one's ideas are independent of the social entities to which one belongs (Table 10-5). There is a single exception to a pattern that is otherwise consistently parallel to that associated with higher class position, predictable but no less interesting for that: Time-pressured men are likely to be anxious.

The relationship of time-pressure to values and orientation is remarkably stable, no matter who or what determines the pace at which work is done. Moreover, time-pressure bears a similar

TABLE 10-5
Values and Orientation, by Time-Pressure and Amount of Overtime[a]

	Frequency of Time-Pressure	Frequency-of Time-Pressure, Controlling Determinants	Frequency + Consequences of Time-Pressure	Amount of Overtime
A. Parental values				
Self-direction/conformity	.13**	.13**	.15**	.01
B. Values for self				
Self-direction/conformity	.04*	.03	.06*	.04*
Self-direction/competence	.03	.04	.04	.02
C. Judgments about work				
Importance of intrinsic qualities .	.02	.02	.09**	.08**
Importance of extrinsic benefits .	.05**	.06**	.09**	.08**
D. Social orientation				
Authoritarian conservatism	.10**	.09**	.11**	.07**
Criteria of morality	.02	.02	.06*	.00
Trustfulness	.04*	.05*	.05	.00
Stance toward change	.13**	.14**	.16**	.11**
Canonical correlation .	.18**	.18**	.21**	.13**
E. Self-conception				
Self-confidence	.05**	.05**	.09**	.04*
Self-deprecation	.01	.01	.02	.04*
Attribution of responsibility	.01	.00	.02	.03
Anxiety..................	.13**	.13**	.14**	.05**
Idea-conformity	.05**	.05**	.07**	.01
Canonical correlation .	.15**	.15**	.17**	.08**

  * Indicates $p < 0.05$
  ** Indicates $p < 0.01$

[a] Entries are partial correlations, either η (eta) or the canonical correlation, always controlled on social class.

Note: $N > 2735$, except for parental values, where $N > 1425$.

relationship to values and orientation no matter what its consequences—whether it forces men to think faster, to move faster, or to
work longer hours. Time-pressure matters most, though, when it
forces men to *think* faster; it matters least (but still, it matters) when
it requires men to *move* faster. Thus, the combined influence of
time-pressure and its consequences is greater than the influence of
time-pressure alone. Men are most likely to have self-directed values
and orientation when they not only work under considerable
pressure of time, but when that pressure forces them to think faster.

Time-pressure, especially when it results in having to think (rather
than move) faster, may reflect occupational self-direction. We
nevertheless treat time-pressure and its consequences as part of the
growing battery of occupational conditions whose importance for
explaining the class relationships will be contrasted to that of the
conditions previously defined as determinative of occupational
self-direction.

Clearly, then, the use and organization of time on the job is
relevant for values and orientation. On the other hand, aspects of
time that define the *boundaries of the job* rather then the *internal
structure of work* generally seem to have little relevance for values
and orientation. It is essentially irrelevant how work time is
separated from nonwork time—whether men work days, nights, or on
varying shifts; how regular and how predictable is their schedule of
work and nonwork hours; the length of their ordinary workdays; and
when in the week their nonwork days occur. There is one exception:
Working a great deal of overtime (paid or unpaid) is associated with
valuing self-direction and holding a generally consonant orientation.
It is of course possible that working overtime simply reflects
self-directed values and orientation. Even so, we treat overtime as if
it were an externally imposed occupational condition.

Thus, two aspects of time—time-pressure (together with its
consequences) and the total amount of overtime—may well prove
pertinent for explaining many of the class relationships.

Interpersonal Relations

Another possible explanation of the class relationships could be
based on class differences in the interpersonal networks in which jobs
are embedded. A large research literature documents the importance
of interpersonal relations and interpersonal contexts for job per-

formance and for job satisfaction (cf. Whyte, 1961). We want to know whether the interpersonal relations of the job are also important for extra-occupational values and orientation. Earlier analyses have shown that two aspects of interpersonal relations implicated in occupational self-direction—closeness of supervision and complexity of work with people—are each related, independently of class, to values and orientation. The question is whether interpersonal relations more broadly conceived are pertinent for values and orientation or whether interpersonal relations matter only insofar as they bear on occupational self-direction.

It is not possible to answer this question definitively in research that samples men from a multitude of firms and organizations, because a thorough analysis would have to consider all the interpenetrating networks of individual firms and organizations. We do, however, get an overview of the interpersonal circumstances in which men work from their answers to some generally applicable questions. We asked all men how much of their working time they spend alone and how much in the company of others; whether they work as part of a team and, if so, how large the team is and of whom it is constituted; whose evaluation of their work performance matters most to them, and in how good a position these people are to judge their work performance; what, precisely, they do in their dealings with other people—inform or learn, supervise or receive instructions, sell or buy, advise or receive advice, cooperate or compete, aid or receive assistance; whether they think that they are in competition with their co-workers; how many people they supervise *directly* (as distinguished from how many people are beneath them in the supervisory hierarchy); and even the extent of their participation in union activities and in the activities of other work-related groups.[11]

None of these aspects of interpersonal relations has general relevance for values and orientation, when social class is controlled.

Although this examination has not been exhaustive, it seems reasonable to conclude that what is important for values and orientation is not the nature and extent of men's interrelatedness with other people with whom they deal at work, but specifically, the

---

[11]Union membership, per se, is not related to values and orientation; similarly for membership in other occupationally connected groups. Perhaps a more detailed analysis than has been possible here would yield a contrary conclusion, but we see in these data no evidence that the influence of such occupational groups on the values and beliefs of their members extends into areas beyond their specific concerns.

degree to which interpersonal aspects of the job facilitate or inhibit occupational self-direction.

Job Satisfaction, Occupational Commitment, and Subjective Reactions to the Job

Our investigation has focused, as far as possible, on objective job conditions—the realities of occupational life that determine what requirements men must meet and what possibilities their jobs afford. It could be, though, that values and orientation are molded less by objective job conditions and more by men's subjective reactions to their jobs—their occupational satisfactions, dissatisfactions, and commitments. Alternatively, it could be that subjective reactions are the mediating mechanism through which objective job conditions

TABLE 10-6
Values and Orientation, by Job Satisfaction and Occupational Commitment[a]

	Job Satisfaction	Occupational Commitment
A. Parental values		
Self-direction/conformity	.09**	.07**
B. Values for self		
Self-direction/conformity	.04*	.04*
Self-direction/competence	.07**	.06**
C. Judgments about work		
Importance of intrinsic qualities	.13**	.18**
Importance of extrinsic benefits	.02	.01
D. Social orientation		
Authoritarian conservatism	.09**	.15**
Criteria of morality	.01	.04*
Trustfulness	.05**	.05**
Stance toward change	.03	.04*
Canonical correlation	.11**	.16**
E. Self-conception		
Self-confidence	.12**	.08**
Self-deprecation	.09**	.06**
Attribution of responsibility	.06**	.01
Anxiety	.19**	.10**
Idea-conformity	.06**	.04*
Canonical correlation	.25**	.15**

* Indicates $p < 0.05$
** Indicates $p < 0.01$
[a] Entries are partial correlations, either η (eta) or the canonical correlation, always controlled on social class.
Note: $N > 2850$, except for parental values, where $N > 1480$.

come to be reflected in values and orientation. McKinley (1964) has argued, for example, that men at the lower socioeconomic levels are oppressed by job frustrations that manifest themselves both in the direct expression of hostility and in efforts to secure compensatory rewards from nonoccupational activities; therein lie the wellsprings of much lower-class behavior. Although this picture seems over-drawn, it certainly is both plausible and consistent with much available data.

Consider, first, job satisfaction and dissatisfaction. We find, as have many predecessors (cf. Blauner, 1966), that there is a direct (albeit weak) relationship between social class and overall job satisfaction: The higher men's social class, the more satisfied they are with their jobs. But, contrary to what those who attribute working-class values to job dissatisfaction would predict, job dis-satisfaction is associated with valuing *self-direction,* both for self and for children (Table 10-6). Working-class men value conformity not because of, but despite, their generally greater job dissatisfaction. This one finding casts doubt on any interpretation that would attribute working-class values to occupational frustration.

To put the matter more generally, job satisfaction seems (not surprisingly) to be associated with acceptance of the status quo, job dissatisfaction with a more questioning stance—independent, yet not without self-doubt.[12] The associations cut across those of social class, indicating that satisfaction or dissatisfaction with the job as a whole cannot be the key to explaining the set of class relationships.

It could still be that some *specific* job dissatisfactions are important for explaining the class relationships. To investigate this possibility, we tried to ascertain how satisfied men are with each of those attributes of jobs that they consider to be important (cf. Chapter 5). Seven sources of job dissatisfaction are related to men's values and orientation: insufficient pay, inadequate fringe benefits, uninteresting work, discontent with the supervisor, job insecurity, too much pressure, and too limited a chance to use one's abilities. Even though the range of dissatisfactions is great, dissatisfaction with

---

[12]In particular (Table 10-6), job satisfaction is associated not only with valuing conformity for children and for self, holding authoritarian conservative beliefs, and believing that one's ideas mirror those of other people in the social groupings of which one is a member, but also with judging the intrinsic aspects of jobs to be important, being trustful of others, being self-confident and not being self-deprecatory, believing that one has some control over the forces that affect one's life, and not being anxious.

any specific aspect of the job bears the same relationship to values and orientation as does dissatisfaction with the job as a whole: Job satisfactions of every sort are associated with favoring the status quo, dissatisfactions with questioning and doubt.

Thus, job dissatisfactions, individually and collectively, cannot be relevant for explaining the set of class relationships; some of the principal class relationships—notably, the relationships to valuation of conformity and to authoritarian conservatism—would be even stronger were it not for the job dissatisfactions of the lower classes and the job satisfactions of the higher classes.

Job satisfaction or dissatisfaction is but a limited, and not necessarily the most important, aspect of men's subjective reactions to their occupations. For a larger perspective on how men view their occupations, we investigated "occupational commitment," as measured by a scale[13] based on the following questions:

1. Some people are so attached to their occupation that they cannot imagine wanting to do anything else, while others would be only too glad to change to some other occupation. How about you?
2. If you were to inherit a million dollars, would you continue doing the work you do now, shift to something else, or retire?
3. Do you think it is a real accomplishment to be a good (*respondent's occupation*)?
4. How much good do you think your work does for mankind—a great deal, some, a little, it doesn't help but doesn't hurt, or does it hurt?

Strong occupational commitment (independently of job satisfaction) is associated with a generally favorable orientation to the status quo. It is not so much that the occupationally committed are conformist—in fact, both the highly committed and the uncommitted tend to value self-direction; it is the people in the middle who value conformity most highly. Rather, the occupationally committed seem to find everything to their satisfaction: They tend to hold authoritarian beliefs, yet to trust others; they tend to think that their ideas mirror those of the social groupings to which they belong, yet to have confidence in their own capacities; they are favorably oriented to things as they are, yet are receptive to change. This is not

---

[13]Reproducibility = 0.92; the pattern of errors seems essentially random (using Ford's criteria).

the stuff of which the class relationships are made. Occupational commitment could conceivably be relevant for explaining why people at higher class levels (who are generally the more committed) are more confident of their own capacities, but it could not be relevant for explaining the relationship of class to such pivotal issues as valuing self-direction and being tolerant of nonconformity.[14]

What is true for job satisfaction and for occupational commitment is true, too, for men's subjective reactions to the firms, organizations, or agencies in which they work—men who are more favorable toward the firm or organization tend to be of higher class position, but in important respects to have values and orientations inconsistent with that position. Orientation to trade unions[15] is quite different. The men who are most favorable to unions tend to be moderately anxious and to have moral standards that demand more than conformity to the letter of the law—interesting in itself, but hardly a basis for explaining the set of class relationships.

The relationships between men's subjective reactions to their jobs (and to the social entities that encompass those jobs) and their orientation to realities outside the domain of work are intriguing in themselves but tangential to the main thrust of our analysis. In fact, the principal class relationships would be even stronger were it not that men at higher class levels tend to be both occupationally satisfied and occupationally committed.

Occupational Contexts

Although we have reviewed the possible relevance for values and orientation of many class-correlated aspects of occupation, we must acknowledge that much has escaped us. There are aspects of occupation that we have not been able to measure and other ways of indexing and analyzing those that we have measured. Moreover, even though we have examined many interrelationships—that between bureaucracy and closeness of supervision, to cite one important

---

[14]We also investigated men's appraisals of how much *prestige* is accorded their occupations. The intent here was to see whether discrepancies between these judgments and the prestige actually accorded those occupations by society at large (as reflected in our index of class) are related to values and orientation. We find that such discrepancies in appraisals of occupational prestige are related to men's appraisals of self, but to little else.

[15]The index here is based on a series of questions addressed to union members about the conditions of their membership and to nonmembers (excepting only the self-employed) about their prospects for and possibilities of joining a union.

example—we have not been able to examine fully the patterns of interrelationship that make up concrete occupations—doctor, plumber, or any other occupation. Finally, and most important, we have failed to do justice to various types of occupational *context*. We could not examine men's occupational characteristics in context of those of their co-workers;[16] we could not take adequate account of the location of the job in the context of a particular industry or of a particular level and type of technology;[17] and we could not evaluate the conditions attendant on any given job in context of the conditions of an entire career.[18]

These limitations notwithstanding, we have been able to study a wide range of class-correlated occupational conditions, and have found several of them to be related to values and orientation, independently of their correlation with class. This lays sufficient groundwork for assessing whether or not the conditions that make for occupational self-direction are *especially* pertinent for explaining the class relationships.

THE RELEVANCE OF OCCUPATIONAL CONDITIONS FOR EXPLAINING THE CLASS RELATIONSHIPS

We have seen that not only the conditions determinative of occupational self-direction but also several other class-correlated occupational conditions are significantly related, independently of their relationship to social class, to values and orientation. (The latter conditions are: ownership status, amount of competition, likelihood of loss of job or business, size and supervisory structure of the firm or organization, position in the supervisory hierarchy, time-pressure and the consequences of time-pressure, and amount of overtime.)

---

[16]Cf. Blau (1960) for a discussion of the possible consequences of having characteristics different from those of the occupational group of which one is a member.

[17]Such analysis as we have been able to do of industrial and technological contexts suggests that they are not particularly relevant to values but may be relevant to social orientation. Many studies suggest that a more thorough analysis would be productive. (Cf. Cottrell, 1940; Walker and Guest, 1952; Chinoy, 1955; Walker, 1957; Whyte, 1961; Blauner, 1964.)

[18]Men's appraisals of how well they have done in their careers (as compared to other men who started out in the same line of work at about the same time) are not related to values and orientation when social class is controlled. Optimism about *future* career prospects is related (independently of class and of age) to valuing self-direction, to holding nonauthoritarian beliefs, and to evaluating one's capacities favorably. The interpretive problems are obvious; it is safer to treat optimism about career prospects as a reflection of men's orientation than as a valid indicator of their actual career prospects.

Now we can test our principal hypothesis: that the conditions determinative of *occupational self-direction* are highly relevant for explaining the relationships of class to values and orientation, and that *other occupational conditions* (even though they are related to values and orientation) are of little relevance for explaining these relationships. To test this hypothesis, we once again use the method of controlling occupational conditions, to see how much the class correlations are thereby reduced.

Controlling the conditions determinative of occupational self-direction greatly reduces the correlations of class to values and orientation[19] —in almost all instances by half and in several by two thirds or more (Table 10-7). Controlling the other occupational conditions has much weaker effects—in general, reducing the class correlations by less than one third.[20] Controlling both sets of conditions reduces the correlations of class to values and orientation by no more than does controlling the conditions of occupational self-direction alone.[21] Thus, the relationships of class to values and orientation are in large measure attributable to those conditions that are determinative of occupational self-direction.

THE RELEVANCE OF OCCUPATIONAL SELF-DIRECTION TO THE COMPONENTS OF SOCIAL CLASS

The relationships of social class to values and orientation result from the additive effects of education and occupational position (cf. Chapter 8). Are the conditions determinative of occupational self-direction pertinent primarily for explaining the relationships of *education* to values and orientation, primarily for explaining the relationships of *occupational position* to values and orientation, or equally for explaining both sets of relationships?

The conditions determinative of occupational self-direction are far

---

[19]More detailed analysis shows that controlling the substance of work with data, with things, and with people has greater effects on the class relationships than does controlling closeness of supervision or the complexity of organization of the work. But all these conditions bear independently on the class relationships.

[20]No single occupational condition (of those that are not directly involved in occupational self-direction) has a substantial effect on any of the class relationships. Even time-pressure and bureaucratic structure prove to have only limited relevance for the class relationships—less than that of any of the three components of occupational self-direction.

[21]It is not possible to further reduce the class correlations by adding to the set of occupational conditions that is controlled; in fact, if we add such variables as job satisfaction and occupational commitment to the set of controls, the total effect on the class relationships is reduced.

TABLE 10-7

Effects on the Class Correlations of Controlling Sets of Occupational Variables

	Initial Correlation with Social Class[a]	Proportional Reduction in the Magnitude of the Correlation When Controlling:		
		Occupational Self-Direction[b]	Other Occupational Conditions[c]	All Significant Occupational Conditions
A. Parental values				
Self-direction/conformity	.33**	.65	.33	.67
B. Values for self				
Self-direction/conformity	.16**	.56	.23	.54
Self-direction/competence	.15**	.49	.25	.50
C. Judgments about work				
Importance of intrinsic qualities	.19**	.94	.36	.94
Importance of extrinsic benefits	.35**	.57	.21	.58
D. Social orientation				
Authoritarian conservatism	.38**	.50	.21	.50
Criteria of morality	.18**	.87	.32	.87
Trustfulness	.17**	.61	.22	.61
Stance toward change	.15**	.95	.58	.99
Canonical correlation.	.48**	.56	.22	.56
E. Self-conception				
Self-confidence	.09**	.99	.64	.96
Self-deprecation	.09**	.87	.23	.86
Attribution of responsibility ...	.12**	.45	.30	.49
Anxiety	.06**	.35	.10	.38
Idea-conformity	.13**	.57	.30	.60
Canonical correlation	.22**	.57	.31	.60

* Indicates $p < 0.05$

** Indicates $p < 0.01$

[a] η (eta) or the canonical correlation. These figures differ slightly from those of preceding Tables because respondents for whom data were not complete are dropped. $N > 2600$, except for parental values where $N > 1285$.

[b] Substance of the work with data, things, and people + closeness of supervision + complexity of organization of the work.

[c] Size and supervisory structure of the organization + time-pressure and its consequences + position in supervisory hierarchy + amount of competition + likelihood of loss of job or business + ownership status + amount of overtime.

more important for explaining why occupational position[22] is related to most aspects of values and orientation than for explaining

[22] Since the object of this analysis is to see how controlling occupational self-direction affects the specifically occupational position component of the class relationships, education is also controlled. Similarly, when we examine how controlling occupational self-direction affects the relationships of education to values and orientation, occupational position is controlled.

why education is related to them (Table 10-8). For example, when these conditions are controlled, the canonical correlation of occupational position with social orientation is reduced by more than three fifths, but the canonical correlation of education with social orientation is reduced by less than one fifth. There is one domain of orientation—self-conception—whose correlations with education and with occupational position are equally affected by controlling the conditions of occupational self-direction. But controlling these conditions reduces the correlations of occupational position with all

TABLE 10-8
Effects on the Educational and on the Occupational Position
Correlations of Controlling Occupational Self-Direction

	Education (linear) Controlled on Occupational Position		Occupational Position (linear) Controlled on Education	
	Initial Correlation[a]	Proportional Reduction[b]	Initial Correlation[a]	Proportional Reduction[b]
A. Parental values				
Self-direction/conformity	.23**	.18	.09**	.83
B. Values for self				
Self-direction/conformity	.12**	.12	.05*	1.00
Self-direction/competence	.13**	.11	.02	—
C. Judgments about work				
Importance of intrinsic qualities	.04*	—[c]	.14**	.86
Importance of extrinsic benefits	.20**	.18	.15**	.70
D. Social orientation				
Authoritarian conservatism . . .	.32**	.13	.05**	.98
Criteria of morality	.08**	.44	.08**	.87
Trustfulness	.09**	.27	.08**	.70
Stance toward change	.06**	.58	.05*	.00
Canonical correlation	.36**	.15	.14**	.62
E. Self-conception				
Self-confidence	.05*	.31	.05*	.37
Self-deprecation	.03	—	.03	—
Attribution of responsibility . .	.03	—	.05**	.43
Anxiety	.04*	—	.09**	.19
Idea-conformity	.08**	.19	.02	—
Canonical correlation	.11**	.24	.12**	.24

* Indicates $p < 0.05$
** Indicates $p < 0.01$

[a] These figures differ slightly from those of Table 8-2 because the respondents for whom occupational data are incomplete have been excluded.

[b] When controlling occupational self-direction.

[c] Proportional reduction not computed where the initial correlation is less than 0.05.

Note: $N > 2625$, except for parental values, where $N = 1366$.

other aspects of values and orientation much more than it reduces the correlations of education.

One implication is that occupational position would cease to be relevant for most aspects of values and orientation if higher occupational position did not mean greater occupational self-direction. It would seem that occupational position matters not for its own sake, but because higher positions provide greater opportunities for self-direction.

A second implication is that, although the magnitude of the correlations would be reduced, education would still be relevant for almost all aspects of values and orientation even if educated men were not so disproportionately situated in self-directed jobs. Why, then, is education pertinent? Our original hypothesis, to which we still adhere, was that educational level is pertinent to values and orientation insofar as education provides the intellectual flexibility and breadth of perspective that are essential for self-directed values and orientation; lack of education must seriously interfere with men's ability to be self-directed.

We do not have the data to test this hypothesis directly. We can, however, show that intellectual flexibility is involved in the relationship of education to values and orientation. As an approximate measure of intellectual flexibility we rely on scores based on a single factor comprising several indices of how well men dealt with problems they encountered in the interview.[23] These indices are disparate in form and apparent content—some are based on problems that are abstractly intellectual in content (a seemingly simple but highly revealing problem in business economics; another question designed to ascertain whether men see both sides of a controversial public issue), some are perceptual (a test of men's ability to

---

[23]The components of this factor (together with the factor loadings) are: (1) A rating of the adequacy of men's answers to the question, Suppose you wanted to open a hamburger stand and there were two locations available. What questions would you consider, in deciding which of the two locations offers a better business opportunity? ($r = 0.37$). (2) A rating of their answers to: What are all the arguments you can think of for and against allowing cigarette commercials on TV? First, can you think of arguments *for* allowing cigarette commercials on TV? And can you think of arguments *against* allowing cigarette commercials on TV? ($r = 0.41$). (3) A measure of the frequency with which men agreed when asked agree-disagree questions ($r = 0.52$). (4) Their summary scores on a portion of the Embedded Figures Test (cf. Witkin, 1962), which was given at the end of the interview ($r = 0.67$). (5) The interviewers' appraisals of their intelligence ($r = 0.60$). (6) Witkin's (1962) summary score for the Draw-A-Man test (administered at the end of the interview) ($r = 0.75$). (7) The Goodenough estimate of intelligence (cf. Witkin, 1962), also based on the Draw-A-Man test ($r = 0.78$).

differentiate figure from ground in complex color designs), and some are motoric (the ability to draw a functionally adequate—even if aesthetically deficient—male figure).

Scores on this measure of intellectual flexibility are correlated with education, hence with class, and are independently associated with most aspects of values and orientation. Controlling intellectual flexibility reduces many of the class correlations, notably the correlations with social orientation.[24]

Most important, the reductions in the class correlations are *specific* to the educational component of class; for example, controlling intellectual flexibility reduces the canonical correlation of education with social orientation by two fifths, but it reduces the correlation of occupational position with social orientation by less than one tenth. Although this finding is hardly definitive, it does strengthen the supposition that much of the importance of education for the class relationships lies in its contribution to the intellectual flexibility that we believe to be essential for self-directed values and orientation.

CONCLUSION

The conditions determinative of occupational self-direction (closeness of supervision; the substance of work with data, with things, and with people; and the complexity of organization of the work) are significantly related to virtually all aspects of values and orientation, independently of their relationship with social class. Several other occupational conditions (notably, ownership, competition, serious job insecurity, bureaucracy, position in the supervisory hierarchy, time-pressure and its consequences, and the amount of overtime) are also related, independently of class, to values and orientation.

Only those aspects of occupation involved in occupational self-direction prove to be of any great importance for explaining the relationship of class to values and orientation. The impact of such conditions as time-pressure and employment in a bureaucratic

---

[24]Most class correlations are reduced by one quarter to one half when intellectual flexibility is controlled. All correlations except that with self-deprecation remain significant. These findings provide a powerful argument against interpreting the class relationships as a simple reflection of higher levels of intelligence at higher class levels. It is not just that class is related to men's capacities to perceive and to judge, but that class shapes the reality that is there to be seen and to be judged.

organization is essentially independent of and irrelevant to that of class. What do matter for the class relationships are the three job conditions that are directly implicated in occupational self-direction.

More specifically, the job conditions determinative of occupational self-direction are of great importance for explaining the *occupational position* component of the class relationships, but are decidedly less important for explaining the *educational* component of these relationships. Occupational position seems to matter for values and orientation because it determines the conditions of self-direction that jobs provide or preclude; the critical facet of occupational position is that it is determinative of occupational self-direction. Education, on the other hand, seems to matter for values and orientation chiefly because it can be so very important for intellectual flexibility and breadth of perspective. Thus, the class relationships are built on the cumulative effects of educational training and occupational experience. The former is pertinent insofar as it provides or fails to provide the capability for self-direction, the latter insofar as it provides or fails to provide the experience of exercising self-direction in so consequential a realm of life as work.

Again we must acknowledge that there is a difference between demonstrating that class relationships are statistically attributable to occupational conditions and demonstrating that these occupational conditions do, in fact, enter into the processes by which class affects values and orientation. This issue is a major focus of the next chapter, which discusses the broader social implications of our findings.

CHAPTER 11

Class and Conformity:
An Interpretation

Our thesis—the central conclusion of our studies—is that social class is significant for human behavior because it embodies systematically-differentiated conditions of life that profoundly affect men's views of social reality.

The essence of higher class position is the expectation that one's decisions and actions can be consequential; the essence of lower class position is the belief that one is at the mercy of forces and people beyond one's control, often, beyond one's understanding. Self-direction—acting on the basis of one's own judgment, attending to internal dynamics as well as to external consequences, being open-minded, being trustful of others, holding personally responsible moral standards—this is possible only if the actual conditions of life allow some freedom of action, some reason to feel in control of fate. Conformity—following the dictates of authority, focusing on external consequences to the exclusion of internal processes, being intolerant of nonconformity and dissent, being distrustful of others, having moral standards that strongly emphasize obedience to the letter of the law—this is the inevitable result of conditions of life that allow little freedom of action, little reason to feel in control of fate.

Self-direction, in short, requires opportunities and experiences that are much more available to people who are more favorably situated in the hierarchical order of society; conformity is the natural consequence of inadequate opportunity to be self-directed.

In interpreting the consistent relationships of class to values and orientation, it is useful to recall the many conditions that our analyses have shown to have little or no explanatory relevance. The relationship of class to parental values is not a function of parental aspirations, family structure, or—insofar as we have been able to measure them—family dynamics. The relationships of class to values and orientation in general are clearly not a function of such class-correlated dimensions of social structure as race, religion, or national background. Nor are they to be explained in terms of such facets of stratification as income and subjective class identification, or of conditions that impinge on only part of the class hierarchy, or of class origins or social mobility. Finally, the class relationships do not stem from such important (but from our point of view, tangential) aspects of occupation as the bureaucratic or entrepreneurial setting of jobs, time-pressure, job dissatisfaction, or a host of other variables. Any of these might be important for explaining the relationship of class to other social phenomena; none of them is important for explaining why class is consistently related to values and orientation.[1]

By contrast, we have substantial evidence that any interpretation of the relationships of class to values and orientation must take into account the cumulative impact of education and occupational position and must recognize that occupational self-direction is importantly implicated in these relationships.

 Our interpretation of these facts is that the conformist values and orientation held by people in the lower segments of the class hierarchy are a product of the limited education and constricting job conditions to which they are subject. Education is important because self-direction requires more intellectual flexibility and breadth of perspective than does conformity; tolerance of nonconformity, in particular, requires a degree of analytic ability that is difficult to achieve without formal education. But education is not all that is involved. The conformity of people at lower social class levels is in large measure a carry-over from the limitations of their occupational experiences. Men of higher class position, who have the opportunity to be self-directed in their work, want to be self-directed off the job, too, and come to think self-direction possible. Men of lower class position, who do not have the opportunity for self-direction in work, come to regard it a matter of necessity to conform to authority, both on and off the job. The job does mold the man—it can either enlarge his horizons or narrow them. The conformity of the lower social classes is only partly a result of their lack of education; it results also from the restrictive conditions of their jobs.

---

[1] It could be argued that the class relationships stem not from currently applicable structural conditions, but from historically derived cultural traditions. "Working-class culture," in this view, is derived from the historical tradition of the working class, rather than stemming from the realistic conditions of today's working class. But explanations of class culture based either on accidental origins or on past structural conditions that no longer hold sway seem to us to be insufficient. We want to know: Why does a historically derived class culture persist under present conditions?

The Efficacy of Education

Self-directed values and orientation require that one look beyond externals, think for oneself. Education does not insure the development of these capacities, but lack of education must seriously impede their development. For most people, self-directed values and orientation require formal educational experience.

The effects of education on values and orientation are not immutable—men who are subject to occupational conditions different from those normally experienced at their educational level are likely to have somewhat different values and orientation from those of their educational peers. Nevertheless, the relationship of education to values and orientation is not greatly affected by occupational experience or by any other experiences that we have examined. The importance of education for men's values and orientation—at least under the conditions of life in the United States in the mid-1960's—is great, no matter what conditions men subsequently encounter.

Implicit in this interpretation is the assumption that the predominant direction of effect is *from* education *to* values and orientation, rather than the reverse. We do not argue that men's values have no effect on their educational attainment. Quite the contrary: It is probable that self-directed values and orientation are a powerful impetus for educational attainment. In the actual circumstances of most people's lives, though, values and orientation probably have less effect upon educational attainment than educational attainment has upon values and orientation. This is in part because critical, often irreversible, decisions about education are made in behalf of children and adolescents by parents and other adults (and thus reflect the adults' values). In larger part, it is because of the inequitable distribution of social resources. Educational opportunities—good schools, stimulating teachers—and the economic resources to take advantage of such opportunities are not equally distributed, nor are children of varying class backgrounds always treated equally even within the same school. This issue is so much at the forefront of informed public attention that it need hardly be pursued further here.

Values and orientation undoubtedly influence educational attainment, but for most people education is primarily a determinant, rather than a consequence, of self-directed values and orientation.[2]

---

[2]The point is well illustrated by Rosenberg's (1957) study of changes in students' values during their college years.

Occupational Position and Occupational Self-Direction

In industrial society, where occupation is central to men's lives, occupational experiences that facilitate or deter the exercise of self-direction come to permeate men's views, not only of work and of their role in work, but of the world and of self. The conditions of occupational life at higher social class levels facilitate interest in the intrinsic qualities of the job, foster a view of self and society that is conducive to believing in the possibilities of rational action toward purposive goals, and promote the valuation of self-direction. The conditions of occupational life at lower social class levels limit men's view of the job primarily to the extrinsic benefits it provides, foster a narrowly circumscribed conception of self and society, and promote the positive valuation of conformity to authority. Conditions of work that foster thought and initiative tend to enlarge men's conceptions of reality, conditions of constraint tend to narrow them.

The processes by which men come to generalize from occupational to nonoccupational realities need not be altogether or even mainly rational; all that we mean to assert is that occupation markedly affects men, not that men rationally decide on values and orientations to fit the facts of their occupational experiences.[3] The essential point was made more than a third of a century ago by Waller (1932:375-376) in his classic study of teachers and teaching:

> What does any occupation do to the human being who follows it? ... We know that some occupations markedly distort the personalities of those who practice them, that there are occupational patterns to which one conforms his personality as to a Procrustean bed by lopping off superfluous members. Teaching is by no means the only occupation which whittles its followers to convenient size and seasons them to suit its taste. The lawyer and the chorus girl soon come to be recognizable social types. One can tell a politician when one meets him on the street. Henry Adams has expanded upon the unfitness of senators for being anything but senators; occupational molding, then, affects the statesman as much as lesser men. The doctor is always the doctor, and never quite can quit his role. The salesman lives in a world of selling configurations. And what preaching most accomplishes is upon the preacher himself. Perhaps no occupation that is followed long fails to leave its stamp upon the person.

As with education, there is a question of direction of effect.[4] We

---

[3]Cf. Breer and Locke, 1965, for experimental evidence on how "task experience" affects values and beliefs.

[4]We intend, in our further research, to try to differentiate the effects of "occupational self-selection" from those of occupational experience. This analysis will have to take account of men's entering and leaving occupations.

have assumed—as did Waller—that the job does affect the man, that the relationship between occupational self-direction and values does not simply reflect the propensity of self-directed men to gravitate into self-directed jobs. We recognize the tendency for self-directed men to search out opportunities for occupational self-direction. Nevertheless, there are stringent limitations to men's deciding for themselves how much self-direction they will exercise in their work.

The most important limitation is that occupational choice is dependent on educational qualifications—which are greatly affected by the accidents of family background, economic circumstances, and available social resources. At any educational level, most occupational choice is among jobs of about the same degree of self-direction—men of limited educational background may perhaps choose between factory work and construction work, but neither offers much opportunity for self-direction, and jobs that do are not open to them.

Moreover, the possibilities for enlarging the sphere of self-direction by shifting to other occupations are seriously limited. Most job changes are not radical. Having completed their educations and embarked on their first jobs, few men have the chance to make any substantial change in these occupational conditions.

Furthermore, there are limits to how much men actually can mold their jobs. It is true that men placed in similar occupational positions will play their roles differently, some utilizing every opportunity for self-direction, some being altogether dependent on external direction. But there are structural limitations upon the leeway that jobs provide, and the limits are most severe at the lowest levels.

The reinforcing processes by which jobs affect values and orientation, and values and orientation reflect back on jobs, are undoubtedly more complex than we have represented. The thrust of our discussion is not that all influence is in one direction, but rather that the occupational conditions attendant on men's class positions are important in shaping their values and orientation.

Historical Trends

If our interpretation that education and occupational self-direction underlie class differences in values and orientation is valid, it suggests that a major historical trend probably has been—and will continue to be—toward an increasingly self-directed populace.[5] It is

---

[5]Moreover, the industrialization of non-Western countries is probably having much the

well known that educational levels have long been rising and are continuing to do so. What is not so well recognized is that levels of occupational self-direction have also been rising, and almost certainly will continue to rise.

Despite the widely held belief that the industrial revolution substituted a multitude of unskilled operations for an earlier pattern of skilled artisanship, industrialization probably has increased the general level of occupational self-direction (cf. Blauner, 1966:484). Men have thought otherwise because their images of past and present treated as typical of the times the craftsman of preindustrial days and the assembly line worker of today. The facts, though, are that most men in preindustrial times were agricultural laborers, not craftsmen, and that the degradation of work on the assembly line is far from typical of industrial occupations today. Even in automobile plants, most men do not work on the line (cf. Walker and Guest, 1952; Chinoy, 1955). What is more important, the assembly line has never become the dominant type of industrial organization (cf. Blauner, 1964) and is clearly not the model for present and future industrial development.

The industrial model for the future, automation, far from extending the assembly-line practice of dividing skilled jobs into a series of unskilled jobs, gives mindless tasks to the machines and substitutes for mere drudgery, newly created thinking tasks (cf. Blauner, 1964; Walker, 1957). Automation builds on the rising levels of education of the population and markedly increases the opportunities and requirements for occupational self-direction. The introduction of automation comes at high social cost—ever-shrinking employment opportunities for the less educated and the untrained. The long range prospect, though, is for a better educated society of men whose jobs require substantially more judgment, thought, and initiative than did those of any past era.

The United States and Other Industrialized Nations

Is our interpretation as applicable to other industrialized societies

same effect today. There is growing evidence from Inkeles's (1966) research on underdeveloped countries that everywhere the movement of peasants into industrial occupations results in changes in attitudes, values, and beliefs (changes which Inkeles calls "modernization") that are altogether consonant with the effects we attribute to occupational self-direction. Inkeles sees education and occupational experience as independently contributing to these effects.

as to the United States? It has been said, for example, that the family is a weak institution in the United States, easily penetrated by the occupational system. Perhaps occupational experiences are less relevant, and family more, in other countries. Perhaps occupational self-direction is a less critical aspect of life in societies that have a less activist ethos. Or perhaps class identification matters more and objective occupational conditions less in societies where class ideologies are more pronounced. Unfortunately, there are only limited data with which to examine these possibilities.

The most important data are those compiled by Inkeles in "Industrial Man: the Relation of Status to Experience, Perception, and Value" (1960). His thesis is that industrialization has everywhere produced comparable effects on man, manifested especially in similar relationships of class to perceptions, attitudes, and values in all industrialized countries. In support of this thesis, he has gathered evidence from a great diversity of sources and countries. For example, in the United States, Italy, West Germany, Norway, the Soviet Union, and Sweden, occupational position is consistently related to job satisfaction, with highly placed men always more satisfied. In the United States, Italy, West Germany, Norway, England, France, Australia, Mexico, and the Netherlands, there are fairly consistent relationships between class position and feelings of happiness or psychic well-being: The "better off" are in all instances happier. In 8 of 11 countries for which data on parental values exist, the lowest class (of those studied) is the most likely to value obedience. And in some seven countries, class position is positively related to men's belief in the possibility of change in human nature—which Inkeles takes as an indication of confidence that man can master his environment.

There are additional data in Inkeles's storehouse, but these are sufficient to demonstrate the validity of his assertion that class has similar effects in all industrial societies. What is lacking, as he explicitly states, is evidence that class has similar effects for the same reasons in all these countries.

To our knowledge, the only directly pertinent data are those we have reported from Turin. These data show, not only that class is related to parental values in northern Italy as in the United States, but also that occupational self-direction is as important for explaining the relationship of class to values in northern Italy as in the United States. Occupation penetrates the family in Italy, too.

Valuable as the Turin findings are, they speak only of parental values, not of values and orientation in general. Moreover, although it is invaluable to know that occupational self-direction plays as important a role in the relationship of class to parental values in Italy as in the United States, the same may not be true for non-Western societies, for non-capitalist societies, or even for these same societies under changed economic or social circumstances. Still, we have one critical bit of information (Turin), many pertinent supplementary data (primarily those provided by Inkeles), and considerable tangential evidence (the corpus of studies of social stratification in other societies)—all of which are consistent with the inference that what we have said of the United States is true for industrial societies generally.

Our best guess is that, as more is learned, we shall come to conclude that the American situation represents a perhaps extreme instance of a very general pattern. There may be minor variations on this pattern; class identification, for example, may be of greater importance in societies where class divisions are more recognized and more ideologically relevant. But we doubt that there are any sizeable industrial societies—Western or non-Western, capitalist, socialist, or communist—in which the relationship of class to conformity is much different, or in which occupational self-direction does not play a major part in this relationship.

VALUES AND BEHAVIOR

Class differences in values and orientation have far-ranging effects on behavior. That men of higher class position are more self-directed in their views of social reality and men of lower class position more conformist, means that they see—and respond to—decidedly different realities.

Granted, men do not simply act out their preconceptions: Behavior is almost always responsive to situational and institutional constraints and, even in areas of high emotional involvement, may be greatly affected by these constraints.[6] Still, there is always some (and often great) latitude for differential perception of the elements of a given situation, differential evaluation of these elements,

---

[6]The evidence comes principally from one arena—race relations—but the lessons are equally applicable to other behavior. (Cf. LaPiere, 1934; Mannheim, 1941; Lohman and Reitzes, 1952; Kohn and Williams, 1956.)

differential choice, and differential action. The crux of the matter is elegantly summarized in W. I. Thomas's dictum, "If men define situations as real, they are real in their consequences" (Thomas and Thomas, 1928:572). Class profoundly affects men's definitions of reality and their evaluations of reality so conceived.

Our findings about parental responses to children's misbehavior are especially pertinent in illustrating how class differences in definitions of reality affect behavior. If only the external consequences of children's actions are thought to be real, parents will attend only to external consequences. If parents are oriented to children's internal dynamics, they will try to be attentive to and will respond to what they understand to be the children's motives and feelings. Neither middle- nor working-class parents necessarily follow the rationally appropriate course of action for accomplishing their goals. Nevertheless, class differences in responses to children's misbehavior can best be understood when one realizes how class differences in parental values and orientation affect parents' perceptions and evaluations of children's actions.

Since social scientists understand (and largely share) middle-class values, we find middle-class parental behavior self-evidently reasonable. But, because many of us have not had an adequate grasp of working-class values, it has been less apparent that working-class parental behavior is also reasonable. Some have asserted, for example, that working-class parents are oriented only to the present and give little thought to the effects of their actions on their children's futures. We contend, instead, that working-class parents are as concerned as are middle-class parents about their children's futures, but that social scientists have not sufficiently understood working-class goals. Parental actions that seem, from the middle-class perspective, to be oblivious to the children's needs are, from the working-class perspective, altogether appropriate to parental goals in child rearing.

Similarly, from the point of view of middle-class values, fathers who are not supportive of sons shirk an important responsibility. From the point of view of working-class values, there is no such paternal responsibility.

Even though the evidence in this book deals with only a limited segment of human behavior, this evidence demonstrates that values and orientation provide an important mechanism by which social structure is translated into individual actions. Admittedly, values and orientation are not the only intervening mechanism from class to behavior; in all probability, a variety of other processes reinforce the ones on which we focus. If we over-emphasize the set of processes that leads from class-determined conditions of life, to values and orientation, to behavior, it is because we deem these processes central, our data support this supposition, and previous interpretations have for the most part failed to recognize their importance.

The power of this interpretation lies in its ability to help us understand why class is important for many diverse facets of human behavior. The implications of this one fundamental class difference in values and orientation—the higher valuation of self-direction at higher class levels and of conformity at lower class levels—extend to such varied social problems as schizophrenia, the perpetuation of inequality, and political illiberalism.

In discussing these problems, we focus on the negative consequences of conformity. We do this not because we fail to see the virtue of some measure of social order or the dangers of unconstrained individualism, but because we are convinced that conformity poses far more serious problems in the United States (and throughout the industrial world). A creative, democratic society needs more self-direction—and could do with less conformity—than is evident.

Schizophrenia

Class differences in values and orientation may help clarify the problem that originally motivated this research—the relationship of class to schizophrenia. As earlier formulated, the problem revolved around the complex interrelationship of class, family, and schizophrenia; we now suggest that a more fruitful approach would be in terms of the inadequacies of a conformist orientational system for dealing with stress.

There is fairly substantial evidence that the incidence of schizophrenia is especially great at the lowest class levels.[7] It is not evident from published research reports, however, precisely which lower-class conditions of life actually are relevant to schizophrenia. There is some indication (Rogler and Hollingshead, 1965) that the great stress to which lower-class people are subjected is directly implicated. But

---

[7]For comprehensive reviews of the research literature on class and schizophrenia, see Kohn, 1968; Mishler and Scotch, 1963; and Roman and Trice, 1967.

more than stress is involved, for as Langner and Michael (1963) discovered, no matter how high the level of stress that people experience, social class continues to be correlated with the probability of mental disturbance. One implication is that people of lower class position are less prepared to deal with the stresses they encounter.

We think that the *family* is relevant to schizophrenia because of its role in preparing children to cope with the stresses of adult life. Because lower-class families teach an orientational system that may be too gross and inflexible for critical circumstances that require subtlety and flexibility, they often fail to prepare children adequately to meet stress.

This formulation reduces the emphasis on the family as uniquely important for schizophrenia, and says instead that the family provides one institutional mechanism—perhaps, but not necessarily, the most important one—for teaching an orientational system that is conducive to schizophrenia. The crucial family processes are less a matter of role-allocation (domineering mothers, for example) than many past discussions have emphasized, and more a matter of how children are taught to perceive, to assess, and to deal with reality. [8] The orientational system that lower-class parents transmit to their children is not likely to provide a sufficient sense of the complexity of life or the analytic tools needed to cope with the dilemmas and problems men encounter. These deficiencies could be overcome by later educational and occupational experience; but often they are not, in part because people who have learned this orientational system are unlikely to want to overcome them, in larger part because circumstances probably would not be propitious even if they were.

Certainly there is a vast gap between the inadequacies of a conformist orientational system and the severe disabilities of schizophrenia. What makes the possibility of a connection seem worth taking seriously, nevertheless, is the pointed correspondence of the two phenomena. Schizophrenia is quintessentially a disorder of orientation—a severe defect in men's ability to accurately comprehend the world about them. If one looks at it clinically, it is a caricature of precisely the outstanding features of the conformist

---

[8]This is clearly consistent with the ideas of Wynne and his colleagues on cognitive processes in the families of schizophrenics, and with those of Bateson and Jackson on communication processes in such families. (Cf. Wynne, *et al.*, 1958; Ryckoff, *et al.*, 1959; Bateson, *et al.*, 1956; Mishler and Waxler, 1965.)

orientation—an over-simple and rigid conception of reality, fearfulness and distrust, and a lack of empathic understanding of other people's motives and feelings. One reason for the disproportionately high incidence of schizophrenia at lower social class levels may be that the disorder builds on an orientational system firmly grounded in the experiences of these social classes.

The more general implication of these speculations is that conformist values and orientation may be personally disastrous to men who are confronted with difficult circumstances that require an innovative response.

The Perpetuation of Inequality

A second implication of class differences in values and orientation is that they contribute to the perpetuation of inequality. Whether consciously or not, parents tend to impart to their children lessons derived from the conditions of life of their own social class—and thus help prepare their children for a similar class position. An obvious factor is the higher educational and occupational aspirations that parents of higher class position hold for their children. Less obvious but perhaps more important: Class differences in parental values and child-rearing practices influence the development of the capacities that children someday will need for coping with problems and with conditions of change.

The conformist values and orientation of lower- and working-class parents, with their emphases on externals and consequences, often are inappropriate for training children to deal with the problems of middle-class and professional life. Conformist values and orientation are inflexible—not in the sense that people cannot learn to obey new directives, but in the sense that conformity is inadequate for meeting new situations, solving new problems—in short, for dealing with change. Whatever the defects of the self-directed orientation of the middle and upper classes, it is well adapted to meeting the new and the problematic. At its best, it teaches children to develop their analytic and their empathic abilities. These are the essentials for handling responsibility, for initiating change rather than merely reacting to it. Without such skills, horizons are severely restricted.

The family, then, functions as a mechanism for perpetuating inequality. At lower levels of the stratification order, parents are likely to be ill-equipped and often will be ill-disposed to train their children in the skills needed at higher class levels. Other social institutions—notably, formal educational institutions—can counteract this influence, but they do so to only a small extent; as the Coleman study (1966) shows, the capacity of the schools to overcome the limitations of the home is not great.

The result is that family and occupation usually reinforce each other in molding values and orientation. The influences of the family have temporal priority and have commonly been viewed as predominant in importance. Our data argue otherwise, suggesting that where there is conflict between early family experience and later occupational conditions, the latter are likely to prevail. The more important point, though, is that early family and later occupational experiences seldom conflict. No matter how dramatic the exceptions, it is usual that families prepare their offspring for the world as they know it and that the conditions of life eventually faced by the offspring are not very different from those for which they have been prepared.

Political Implications

Our data touch only lightly on political issues, but political implications are clearly evident. Conformity, as we conceive and index it, includes a strong component of intolerance of nonconformity. This conception is based on Stouffer's demonstration, in *Communism, Conformity, and Civil Liberties* (1955), that generalized conformity necessarily entails an unwillingness to permit other people to deviate from paths of established belief; conformist beliefs are necessarily anti-civil-libertarian.

Stouffer's analysis focuses on intolerance of political dissent; our analysis, particularly as embodied in the index of authoritarian conservatism, is addressed to intolerance of any behavior at odds with the dictates of authority. A self-directed orientation includes (but is not confined to) a willingness to allow others to deviate, within some broad limits, from the prescribed; a conformist orientation includes an unwillingness to permit others to step out of narrowly defined limits of what is proper and acceptable. Thus, a conformist orientation implies not only intolerance of deviant political belief, but also intolerance of any beliefs thought to be threatening to the social order—religious beliefs, ethnic and racial identifications, even beliefs about proper dress and deportment.

The political implications of conformist values and orientation extend beyond issues of civil liberties. As Lipset (1959:485) points out, people less favorably situated in the class hierarchy tend to be illiberal about many noneconomic issues:

The poorer everywhere are more liberal or leftist on [economic] issues; they favor more welfare state measures, higher wages, graduated income taxes, support of trade-unions, and other measures opposed by those of higher class position. On the other hand, when liberalism is defined in non-economic terms—so as to support, for example, civil liberties for political dissidents, civil rights for ethnic and racial minorities, internationalist foreign policies, and liberal immigration legislation—the correlation is reversed.

Lipset cites an impressive array of evidence from several countries to support his empirical assertion that, on noneconomic issues, people of lower social class position tend to be illiberal. But he is unable to specify the determinants of this illiberalism, thus in effect concluding that *everything* about their conditions of life is relevant. Moreover, in choosing the intriguing term, "working-class authoritarianism," to describe these illiberal beliefs, he implies that the beliefs are an expression of authoritarian personality structure. That there are authoritarian components to the beliefs is indisputable, but to label the entire orientational system authoritarian*ism* is to explain its content in terms of the personality structures of those who endorse it.

Our data help explain working-class authoritarianism without requiring the psychodynamic assumptions of past interpretations.[9] We would contend that this illiberalism is an expression of conformist values and orientation—notably, intolerance (and perhaps fear) of nonconformity. Its explanation, we have come to think, lies not in an especially high incidence of authoritarian personality structure at lower levels of the class hierarchy, nor in "everything" about the conditions of life characteristic of these social classes. Rather, the explanation lies specifically in those social structural conditions that we have found to be most determinative of class differences in values and orientation: education and occupational self-direction.

The negative consequences of conformist values and orientation

---

[9]As Miller and Riessman (1961b) point out, psychological theories developed to explain the personality structure of middle-class authoritarians are probably not valid for explaining the authoritarian beliefs of the working class.

are of great importance, whatever their origins. Our understanding of these beliefs—and our ability as a society to change them—are increased by recognizing precisely where in the structure of society their sources lie.

APPENDIXES

Methods of the Washington Study

Washington, D.C.—the locus of the first study—has a large proportion of people employed by government, relatively little heavy industry, few recent immigrants, a white working class drawn heavily from rural areas, and an unusually large proportion of blacks, particularly at lower economic levels. In short, this city is far from typical of urban areas in the United States. A study based on a representative sample of Washington families would have given a distorted impression, for we wanted to generalize, not to Washington, but to middle- and working-class families everywhere. To select an appropriate sample required a two-step design—the selection of areas of the city that are representative of the types of neighborhoods in which middle- and working-class families live, then the random selection of middle- and working-class families living in those areas.

We wanted to secure two subsamples, one of approximately 175 working-class, and another of approximately 175 middle-class families, each having a child within a narrowly limited age range. We decided on fifth-grade children because we wanted the children to be old enough (approximately 10 or 11 years old) to have a developed capacity for verbal communication. We excluded black families because their inclusion would have required a larger sample than we could afford, if we were to have any basis for systematically examining the possibility that social class might have differing effects for white and black families. We decided, too, to exclude families from the top and bottom of the class hierarchy.

The actual sampling procedure started with the selection of Census tracts. Tracts with 20 percent or more black population were excluded. From the remaining tracts we then selected four that had a predominantly working-class population, four that had a predominantly middle-class population, and three that had sizeable proportions of both. Five criteria were used in selecting these tracts

(Table A-1). The most important was the proportion of men employed in manual occupations—the Census categories "operatives," "laborers," "craftsmen" and "foremen." For Washington (and this would certainly be different in cities with other occupational distributions) we arbitrarily set the divisions as follows: at least 55 percent of employed males in manual occupations as the criterion for working-class tracts, less than 25 percent so employed for middle-class tracts, and between 40 and 55 percent for "mixed" tracts.

TABLE A-1
Criteria for Selection of Census Tracts

Census Characteristics	Middle-Class Tracts	Mixed Tracts	Working-Class Tracts
Occupation: percent of employed males in census categories operatives, laborers, craftsmen and foremen	Less than 25%	40-55%	55% or more
Median income: rank of tract in a series proceeding from highest to lowest median income	Second or third quartile	Second or third quartile	Fourth quartile
Median rent of rented homes	More than $60/month	$50 to $60/month	$40 to $50/month
Median value of owner-occupied homes	More than $15,000	--	Less than $15,000
Median education of adults	More than 12.6 years	11.6 to 12.6 years	Less than 11.6 years

Median income was the second criterion, valuable primarily for distinguishing the high and low extremes. This criterion is not sufficiently sensitive to differentiate mixed from middle-class areas—there is little difference in family income in the two types of area because a high proportion of working-class wives in the mixed areas are wage-earners—but it does help in differentiating mixed from working-class tracts. We ranked all predominantly white census tracts in a series from highest to lowest median incomes. Those in the highest quartile were excluded (along with a few tracts in the second quartile that included small neighborhoods with a concentration of wealthy families). Those in the second and third quartiles were eligible as either middle-class or mixed tracts. Working-class tracts were restricted to the fourth quartile. Having stratified on occupation and income, we found that median rental, median value of owner-occupied homes, and median education of adults fell directly into line.

The criteria for middle-class and working-class tracts were met by four tracts each, all of which were included in the study. The criteria for mixed tracts were also met by four tracts, but we arbitrarily limited the sample to three of these. The 11 chosen tracts are not concentrated in any particular part of the city.

Then, from records made available by the public and parochial school systems, we compiled lists of all families in the selected tracts who had fifth-grade children. Using school records and the local city directory, we randomly selected from these lists 200 families in which the father had a white-collar occupation and another 200 in which he had a manual occupation. This procedure was used solely to secure approximately equal samples of middle- and working-class families; the final occupational classification of all families was based on the data later secured in the interviews.

In all 400 families, the mother was to be interviewed. Whenever it occurred that we selected a black family, a family where the child was not living with his mother, or a non-English speaking family, a substitute was selected, again randomly. In every fourth family we scheduled interviews with the father and the fifth-grade child, too. When a broken family fell into this subsample, a substitute was chosen from our overall sample, and the broken family was retained in the overall sample.

INTERVIEWERS

The core interviewing staff consisted of four people (Eleanor Carroll, Mary Freeman, Paul Hanlon, and Melvin Kohn), supplemented by three colleagues (Leila Deasy, Erwin Linn, and Harriet Murphy) who generously helped with the overwhelming number of night and weekend interviews. All of the principal interviewers worked with all types of families, in all three types of tracts.

The procedure was long and drawn out—we worked in the office most days and interviewed many nights for a full year, from March, 1956 to March, 1957. This procedure enabled the interviewers to double as a coding staff, resulting in greater interviewer sensitivity to how much information was needed in response to each question for reliable coding.

With this small a staff it is impossible to compare the effectiveness of particular interviewers. In terms of refusal rates and gross disparities in types of information secured from comparable groups of respondents, there seem to be no differences among the interviewers.

We believe we have been able to produce a uniformly high quality of interview data. Beyond that, all that can be said is that such data are always influenced by the particular relationships developed between interviewer and interviewee—and unfortunately we know all too little about how the interview relationship affects what finally appears in a statistical comparison.

FIELD WORK PROCEDURES

In families where only the mother was to be interviewed, initial contact was made by an interviewer knocking at the door. In each case we would visit the home, present a card identifying ourselves as employees of the U.S. Public Health Service, explain the purpose of the study, and give an honest estimate of how long the interview would take (approximately an hour and a half). The basic explanation was that we were attempting to interview parents in a cross section of families throughout the city of Washington in order to find out how normal families raise their children. When further explanation was necessary, we stated that we had not been able to secure this information from existing books and articles because they stressed the ways the authors thought people ought to raise their children and we were interested in how people actually did raise their children.

Wherever possible, we obtained the interview on the first contact. When this was not possible, we tried to set up an appointment for another time. We returned to the home as often as necessary, never dropping any respondent because we could not find her at home. Nor did we drop any respondent because she broke an appointment. We persisted to the point of an interview, a definite refusal, or despair—while at the same time trying not to hound any potential respondent.

The procedure for establishing contact with the families where we intended to interview mother, father, and child was different. Since we wanted the interviews to be independent, we had to arrange a time when both parents could see us. And, since each family required a man and a woman interviewer, scheduling our own time posed major problems. The general procedure was to send letters to five or six families early in the week and to follow up with telephone calls or personal visits late in the week, in order to schedule the next week's interviews. The letter explained the general purposes of the study; the telephone call or visit provided an opportunity for the respondent to ask us questions, and for us to gain an initial impression of the family.

On the evening of the interview, two of us visited the home together—a man to interview the father, a woman to interview the mother. In almost all cases, we were able to interview them in separate rooms, thus assuring that the interviews were independent. Even in those few instances where the physical facilities did not permit using different rooms, the interviews were conducted as separately and independently as possible.

The first interviewer to finish asked if he might interview the fifth-grade child. (Occasionally we asked permission beforehand, but this was not standard practice.) No parent refused permission, nor did any child. In fact, we often found it expedient to interview some of the other children, who felt neglected by our singling out the fifth-grader for special attention.

We do not have complete assurance that the interviews with the children were independent of parental influence. In a few cases, one or both parents sat in while we talked to the child; in several other cases, the child had overheard portions of the interview with one of his parents. Nevertheless, most interviews with children were essentially free of parental influence.

The interviews with the parents were based on identical schedules, the interview with the child on a modified and abridged version of that schedule.

NONRESPONDENTS: SAMPLE WHERE ONLY MOTHERS WERE TO BE INTERVIEWED

We secured the cooperation of 86 percent of the mothers we tried to interview. Rates of nonresponse do not vary appreciably by social class,[1] type of neighborhood, or type of school (Table A-2).

---

[1] The rates presented here are based on occupational data secured from school records and from the city directory. These were not entirely accurate, but we never got more accurate data about those families who did not cooperate. It seems more reasonable to use the same basis of classification for all families than to revise our classification for the interviewed families alone.

Something can be learned about other possible selective biases by examining the interviewers' characterizations of the nonrespondents and the reasons they gave for not granting an interview (Table A-3). The data on which this analysis is based are limited and one must be cautious about their accuracy. But in almost every case we have the appraisals of at least two interviewers, and they are highly consistent.

TABLE A-2
Distribution of 257 Respondents and 43 Nonrespondents by Status of Area,
Status of Family, and Type of School
(families where mother alone was to be interviewed)

	Working-Class Families		Middle-Class Families	
	Public School	Parochial School	Public School	Parochial School
Working-class areas				
Number of respondents	19	3	4	1
Number of nonrespondents	5	1	1	0
Total	24	4	5	1
Mixed areas				
Number of respondents	70	21	49	23
Number of nonrespondents	12	4	6	3
Total	82	25	55	26
Middle-class areas				
Number of respondents	7	4	46	10
Number of nonrespondents	4	0	7	0
Total	11	4	53	10

Middle- and working-class nonrespondents gave much the same reasons for not granting an interview. The mode of expression varied: Middle-class nonrespondents said that they did not have time for an interview; working-class nonrespondents told us more bluntly that they could not be bothered. But these would appear to be merely surface differences. A more meaningful class difference may be in the number of inveterate stallers. (These are the people who never said no, but for whom circumstances were never opportune.) It may be that these people—a working-class group—are cut of the same cloth as those middle-class people who told us they did not have time. We strongly suspect, however, that more than this is involved; they did not seem able to refuse directly, so they stalled indefinitely, hoping we'd eventually get tired. Those stallers whom we finally did

TABLE A-3
Reasons Given by Nonrespondents for Not Granting an Interview
and Interviewers' Characterizations of These People

Interviewers' Characterization	Principal Reason Given for Not Granting an Interview	Number of Cases	
		Middle Class	Working Class
Inconsiderate and seemingly hostile	Interview is an invasion of privacy	2	0
	Can't be bothered	2	3
	No time.................................	1	0
		5	3
Nervous or upset	Specified difficulties within the family (divorce, tension, etc.)	3	5
	Can't be bothered	0	1
		3	6
Considerate and seemingly reasonable	Husband objects to interview	1	1
	Adverse newpaper publicity	2	2
	No time.................................	0	1
		3	4
Inveterate staller	No reason given	1	5
Suspicious or seemingly uncomprehending	Husband objects to interview	0	2
	Adverse newspaper publicity	0	2
	Can't be bothered	0	2
	No time.................................	2	0
	No reason given	1	2
		3	8
(Inadequate data)	No time.................................	2	0
	Totals all classifications	17	26

interview (and by sheer persistence we got most) seemed, at the beginning of the interview, rather frightened of something that appeared to be totally out of line with their past experience.

Another predominantly working-class group seems quite similar to the stallers—those who were considered by the interviewers to be suspicious or uncomprehending. They struck the interviewers as nonverbal, probably little educated, and somewhat frightened. We were able to reassure some, but not all, of them.

Three other types of nonrespondents may be isolated from Table A-3, none of them preponderantly of one social class. (1) There are a few people who were frank enough to tell an interviewer that they were facing a difficult personal situation—an impending breakup of the marriage, for example—and were not willing to discuss it. (2)

Another half-dozen people refused an interview during a two-week period following an article in the *Washington Star* that criticized us for refusing to give them permission to publish the interview schedule. This incident appears to have increased the nonresponse rate by perhaps 2 percent but did not otherwise affect the study, however much it affected the interviewers' equanimity. (3) We undoubtedly encountered a few basically uncooperative people. This probably includes those we characterized as inconsiderate and seemingly hostile and perhaps some of the suspicious ones as well.

From additional sources of information, we were able to isolate one more type of nonrespondent. Because of the happenstances of sampling, we encountered several small clusters of families living close together and probably sharing a good deal of communication. In most cases, the first woman we approached granted an interview and told her neighbors that it was an interesting experience. Our way was paved. In a few instances, we were not so fortunate. The first woman refused, and the others followed suit. Usually we were able to break the pattern by finding one cooperative soul—and then were able to return to the others with far better probability of cooperation. Twice we failed.

Our conclusion is that the nonrespondents represent small clusters of people from several segments of the population. One cluster seems to be composed of a stratum, probably the lowest educational stratum, of the working class who are most easily threatened by the prospect of an interview. Underrepresentation of this group indicates a bias in our data, though even here the nonrespondents are but a small minority. The other groups occur in both social classes; these do not seem to affect the interpretations we can draw from our data in any very important way. For no distinguishable segment of our total sample does it appear that the nonrespondents were numerous. In sum: We do not have to face the problem of one or two sizeable biasing effects; instead, we have the less serious problem of the possibly additive effect of small numbers of nonrespondents in each of several population segments.

NONRESPONDENTS: SAMPLE WHERE MOTHER, FATHER, AND CHILD WERE TO BE INTERVIEWED

We secured the cooperation of 82 percent of the families where we attempted to interview mother, father, and child. This is almost as high as the rate of cooperation in the sample where only mothers were to be interviewed, even though there were some difficulties in scheduling interviews with families where the husband had an erratic work schedule or where he worked evenings on a second job. The patterns of nonresponse (as far as we can tell, from limited data) conformed to those of the larger sample.

Our analysis has attempted to account for the nonrespondents. A word should be said in explanation of why so many people did grant an interview. We were repeatedly surprised at how willing parents were to oblige us, often at considerable inconvenience and sometimes even at the cost of taking time from their jobs. We believe that part of the explanation lies in our asking so much from them, that it was difficult to view our request as incidental or inconsequential. Furthermore, the topic was of considerable interest to them; both mothers and fathers wanted to talk on and on about their families. Some wanted to know how they compared to other parents; others thought the interview would provide a good occasion for organizing their own thoughts and reflections (many more thought so after the interview had been completed); some wanted help, therapeutic or otherwise; and a good many regarded their cooperation as something of a social contribution.

PROCESSING OF DATA

Coding the data proceeded almost simultaneously with interviewing. The core interviewing staff (joined by Eleanor Wolff, who manned the office) doubled as coders.[2] Every tenth interview, randomly selected, was independently recoded. For each code where agreement between coders did not reach an absolute level of 90 percent, we analyzed the discrepancies and either combined categories to resolve these discrepancies or developed a new code and reclassified all respondents. In their final version, all but three codes represent at least 90 percent intercoder agreement on independent trials. These three, it turns out, are not of any great importance for

---

[2]Data analysis was done by these same people, joined later by Alexander Shakow, Bernard Finifter, Sylvia Marshall, Mary K. Foreshew, Elizabeth Howell, Jay Kenvin, and Jonathan Wallach.

the analyses discussed in this book. Even on these, intercoder agreement approximated 85 percent.

INTERVIEW SCHEDULE: FOR PARENTS

For those readers who would like to see the actual questions that were asked of the respondents, we include an abridged version of the interview schedule. Some irrelevant questions, space-consuming answer categories, and interviewer instructions have been deleted, but the questions are listed exactly as the interviewers were instructed to ask them. This form of the interview schedule was used for parents. A separate schedule, essentially an abridgment of this one with appropriate changes of personal pronoun, was used for interviewing the children.

1. Name of respondent:
2. Address:
3. Do you have any children? Would you tell me their names, beginning with the oldest? Their ages? Grades in school? Do they all live at home? [If "no" to the last, find out where they do live and why.]
4. What do you find most difficult about being a mother (father)?
5. What do you think are the most important *problems* in raising a child?
6. If you could be granted anything you wished for, what would you most want for your children?
7. What would you most want to protect them from?
8. a) What kinds of things do you most enjoy doing with the children?
   b) How often do you do this (these things)?
   c) Are there *other* things you do with them?
   d) What kinds of things does your husband (wife) most enjoy doing with the children?
   e) How often does he (she) do this (these things)?
   f) What *other* kinds of things does he (she) do with them?
   g) Can you think of anything that the whole family did together during the past month?
9. Would you say that you and your husband (wife) show a good deal of affection toward the children, or are you more reserved about showing affection to them?

If family has more than one child:
10. Would you say that you are closer to one of your children than to the others?
    If yes:
    a) Which child?
    b) Why?

11. How about your husband (wife)?
    If yes:
    a)   Which child?
    b)   Why?
12. Would you say that you are the type of person who keeps his troubles to himself, or the type who "talks them out"?
13. How about your husband (wife)?
14. Are you ever bothered by nervousness? (Would you say often, sometimes, or never?)
15. a)   When you get angry with someone, do you let yourself go, or do you try to hold in your feelings?
    b)   How about your husband (wife)?
16. When you and your husband (wife) *disagree,* do you try to keep the children from knowing about it?
17. Would you say that you and your husband (wife) *quarrel* often, occasionally, or rarely?
18. a)   When you do quarrel, do you get together and discuss it, or do you just let it ride?
    If discuss it:
    b)   Do you discuss it immediately, or do you wait awhile before you get around to discussing it?

From this point on, almost all of the questions will be about your ( )-year-old, _____ .

19. *General form of question*
    Can you tell me whether you or your husband (wife) is (stricter) toward (*child*)—or would you say that you are both equally (strict) or that neither is (strict)? [When respondent states that one parent is (stricter), ask if other is (strict) too.]
    a)   Stricter.
    b)   More sure of himself in the way he handles (*child*).
    c)   More likely to get upset at things (*child*) does.
    d)   More likely to give in when (*child*) demands something.
    e)   Gets angry with (*child*) more easily.
    f)   More warm and loving to (*child*).
    g)   More likely to restrict (*child's*) freedom. [Probe: limit his freedom to do things he wants to do.]
    h)   More anxious for (*child*) to get ahead.
    i)   Quicker to praise (*child*) for the things he does well.
    j)   More likely to lay down the law when (*child*) misbehaves.
    k)   More likely to dominate (*child*).
    l)   Are there any ways you'd rather act differently toward (*child*) from the way you do?
    m)   Are there any ways you'd rather your husband (wife) acted differently toward (*child*) from the way he (she) does?

20. a) Which of you makes most of the day-to-day decisions in the home? [Probe: like planning menus and arranging that household tasks get done.]

    b) How about the *major* decisions that affect the family? [Probe: like moving to a new place or making a major expenditure.]

    c) How about the decisions that *affect* (*child*) most directly? [Probe: like what he is and is not allowed to do.]

21. When you think of a boy (girl) of (*child's*) age, are there any things that you look for as *most* important or *most* desirable? [Check each that respondent mentions.]

22. [Hand card to respondent] Which three of the things listed on this card would you say are the *most important* in a boy (girl) of (*child's*) age? [Order will be scrambled.]

    a) That he is popular with other children.

    b) That he has good manners.

    c) That he is ambitious.

    d) That he is neat and clean.

    e) That he is liked by adults.

    f) That he acts in a serious way.

    g) That he is able to defend himself.

    h) That he has self-control.

    i) That he is affectionate.

    j) That he is happy.

    k) That he is able to play by himself.

    l) That he obeys his parents well.

    m) That he is honest.

    n) That he is dependable.

    o) That he is considerate of others.

    p) That he is curious about things.

    q) That he is a good student.

23. Compared to other boys (girls) of his (her) age, would you say that (*child*):

    a) is *very* popular with other children, *fairly* popular with other children, or *not particularly* popular with other children?

    b) has *very* good manners, . . .

    c) is *very* ambitious, . . .

    d) is *very* neat and clean, . . .

    e) is *very* well liked by adults, . . .

    f) acts in a *very* serious way, . . .

    g) is *very* well able to defend himself (herself), . . .

    h) has *very good* self-control, . . .

    i) is *very* affectionate, . . .

    j) is a *very* happy child, . . .

    k) is *very* able to play by himself (herself), . . .

l) obeys his (her) parents *very* well, . . .

m) is *very* honest, . . .

n) is *very* dependable, . . .

o) is *very* considerate of others, . . .

p) is *very* curious about things, . . .

[If respondent has mentioned other characteristics in response to question 21, add those.]

24. How well does (*child*) do in school? [Probe: What are his (her) grades like?]

25. Would you say you are satisfied with his (her) school work?

26. When (*child*) brings home a report card that pleases you, what do you do? [If more than one response, number in order of relative frequency.]

27. How about when he (she) brings home a report card that displeases you? [If more than one response, number in order of relative frequency.]

28. About how much time does (*child*) spend on homework?

29. How far would you *like* (*child*) to go in school?

30. a) How far do you think he (she) probably will go?

b) [If there is a discrepancy between answers to 29 and 30a, ask why the discrepancy.]

31. a) Is there any particular occupation or type of occupation you'd like to see him (her) go into when he's (she's) an adult?

If yes:

b) What?

c) Why?

32. a) Are there any occupations you would *not* like to see him (her) go into?

If yes:

b) What?

c) Why?

33. a) Do you feel it is very important that (*child*) not miss school unless he (she) is ill, or do you feel that it's all right if once in a while he (she) misses a day or so for other reasons?

b) Why do you feel this way?

34. a) Have you spoken to (*child's*) teacher any time this year?

If yes:

b) What did you talk about?

c) What did you think of the teacher?

d) How often have you spoken to him (her)? (When?)

If no or don't remember:

e) Do you have any idea of what the teacher is like, from what your child has told you?

35. Do you belong to the PTA or any organization like that?

If yes: How often do you attend meetings?

36. a) Does (*child*) ever play wildly?

If yes:

b) What does he (she) do when he (she) plays wildly?

c) What do you generally do when he (she) acts this way?

d) Do you ever find it necessary to do anything else?

If yes to (d):

e) What else do you do?

f) Under what circumstances?

g) What does your husband (wife) generally do when (*child*) plays wildly? [Check if the situation is hypothetical for spouse.]

If no or don't know:

h) What would you regard as "playing wildly"?

i) How would you *feel* if he (she) played wildly?

j) What do you think you would do if he (she) played wildly?

k) What do you think your husband (wife) would do if he (she) played wildly?

37. a) Does (*child*) ever fight with his (her) brothers or sisters? [Check if no siblings or none living at home.]

If yes:

b) What do you regard as "fighting"? Does he (she) fight with older brothers (sisters) or younger? [Note whether brothers and/or sisters.]

c) What do you generally do when he (she) acts this way?

d) Do you ever find it necessary to do anything else?

If yes to (d):

e) What else do you do?

f) Under what circumstances?

g) What does your husband (wife) generally do when (*child*) fights with his (her) brothers or sisters? [Check if the situation is hypothetical for spouse.]

If no or don't know:

h) What would you regard as "fighting"?

i) How would you *feel* if he (she) fought with his (her) brothers or sisters?

j) What do you think you would do if he (she) fought with his (her) brothers or sisters?

k) What do you think your husband (wife) would do if he (she) fought with his (her) brothers or sisters?

38. a) Does (*child*) ever fight with *other* children?

If yes:

b) What do you regard as "fighting"? Does he (she) fight with children who are older, younger, or the same age? [Note sex of children.]

c) What do you generally do when he (she) acts this way?

d) Do you ever find it necessary to do anything else?

If yes to (d):

e) What else do you do?

f) Under what circumstances?

g) What does your husband (wife) generally do when (*child*) fights with other children? [Check if the situation is hypothetical for spouse.]

If no or don't know:

h) What would you regard as "fighting"?

i) How would you *feel* if he (she) fought with other children?

j) What do you think you would do if he (she) fought with other children?

k) What do you think your husband (wife) would do if he (she) fought with other children?

39. a) Does (*child*) ever really lose his (her) temper?

If yes:

b) What does he (she) do when he (she) loses his temper?

c) What do you generally do when he (she) acts this way?

d) Do you ever find it necessary to do anything else?

If yes to (d):

e) What else do you do?

f) Under what circumstances?

g) What does your husband (wife) generally do when (*child*) loses his (her) temper? [Check if the situation is hypothetical for spouse.]

If no or don't know:

h) What would you regard as "really losing his temper"?

i) How would you *feel* if he (she) lost his (her) temper?

j) What do you think you would do if he (she) lost his (her) temper?

k) What do you think your husband (wife) would do if he (she) lost his (her) temper?

40. a) Does (*child*) ever *refuse* to do what you tell him (her) to do? [Stress "refuse."]

If yes:

b) What do you regard as a refusal to do what you tell him (her) to do?

c) What do you generally do when he (she) acts this way?

d) Do you ever find it necessary to do anything else?

If yes to (d):

e) What else do you do?

f) Under what circumstances?

g) What does your husband (wife) generally do when (*child*) refuses to do what he (she) tells him (her) to do? [Check if the situation is hypothetical for spouse.]

If no or don't know:

h) What would you regard as a refusal to do what you tell him (her) to do?

i) How would you feel if he (she) refused to do what you told him (her) to do?

j) What do you think you would do if he (she) refused to do what you told him (her) to do?

k) What do you think your husband (wife) would do if he (she) refused to do what he (she) told him (her) to do?

41. a)   Has (*child*) ever swiped anything from home or from other children?
     If yes:
    b)   What do you regard as "swiping"? What has he swiped? From whom? How often has he (she) done this?
    c)   What did you do when he (she) did this?
    d)   Have you ever found it necessary to do anything else?
         If yes to (d):
        e)   What else did you do?
        f)   Under what circumstances?
        g)   What has your husband (wife) done when (*child*) has swiped something? [Check if the situation is hypothetical for spouse.]
    If no or don't know:
    h)   What would you regard as "swiping"?
    i)   How would you *feel* if he (she) swiped something from home or from other children?
    j)   What do you think you would do if he (she) swiped something from home or from other children?
    k)   What do you think your husband (wife) would do if he (she) swiped something from home or from other children?

42. a)   Has (*child*) ever smoked cigarettes?
     If yes:
    b)   How often has he (she) done this? (When? Where?) How did you happen to find out?
    c)   What did you do when he (she) did this?
    d)   Have you ever found it necessary to do anything else?
         If yes to (d):
        e)   What else did you do?
        f)   Under what circumstances?
        g)   What has your husband (wife) done when (*child*) smoked? [Check if the situation is hypothetical for spouse.]
    If no or don't know:
    h)   How would you *feel* if he (she) smoked?
    i)   What do you think you would do if he (she) smoked?
    j)   What do you think your husband (wife) would do if he (she) smoked?

43. a)   Does (*child*) ever use language you don't want him (her) to use?
     If yes:
    b)   What kind of language does he (she) use?
    c)   What do you generally do when he (she) acts this way?
    d)   Do you ever find it necessary to do anything else?
         If yes to (d):
        e)   What else do you do?
        f)   Under what circumstances?
        g)   What does your husband (wife) generally do when (*child*) uses

language he (she) doesn't want him (her) to use? [Check if the situation is hypothetical for spouse.]

If no or don't know:

h) What kind of language would you *not* approve of his (her) using?

i) How would you *feel* if he (she) did use such language?

j) What do you think you would do if he (she) used such language?

k) What do you think your husband (wife) would do if he (she) used such language?

44. a) When was the last time you remember *physically* punishing (*child*)—spanking or hitting or swatting him (her)?

b) What was it for?

c) How did he (she) feel about it?

d) During the past six months, how often have you physically punished (*child*)?

45. a) What do you do when (*child*) does not behave *even after* you've tried to get him (her) to behave? [If more than one response, number in order of frequency.]

b) How often would you say you *threaten* to punish (*child*) but do not actually do so—fairly frequently, only occasionally, or rarely?

If ever:

c) When does this happen?

d) How does (*child*) react?

e) How about your husband (wife): How often would you say he (she) threatens to punish (*child*) but does not actually do so?

If ever:

f) When does this happen?

46. Are there any things (*child*) does that annoy you, even though you know he (she) doesn't mean to annoy you?

If yes:

a) What types of things?

b) What do you do then?

c) What does (*child*) do then?

47. a) Do you *ever* get just furious at (*child*)?

If yes:

b) How often does this happen?

c) What sorts of things make you furious?

d) What do you do when this happens?

e) How does the child react?

48. a) How about your husband (wife): Does he (she) ever get just furious at (*child*)?

If yes:

b) How often does this happen?

c) What sorts of things make him (her) furious?

d) What does he (she) do when this happens?

e) How does the child react?

49. When (*child*) does something that pleases you, what do you usually do? [If more than one response given, number them in descending order.]

50. What things that (*child*) does please you?

51. How about your husband (wife): What does he (she) usually do when (*child*) does something that pleases him (her)?

52. What things that (*child*) does please him (her)?

53. Would you say that you are closer to (*child*) than most mothers (fathers) are to children of his (her) age, about as close, or not quite as close?

54. How about your husband (wife)—would you say that he (she) is closer to (*child*) than most fathers (mothers) are to children of his (her) age, about as close, or not quite as close?

55. Which parent is (*child*) more likely to feel he can talk things over with?

56. To whom does (*child*) turn when he's (she's) troubled, or feels unhappy—or doesn't he (she) turn to anyone in particular?

57. To which parent would you say (*child*) feels closer?

58. Whom does (*child*) try to act like—if anyone? [Number responses in order of decreasing importance.]

59. What sorts of things are most likely to upset (*child*)?

60. What do you do when (*child*) is upset?

I'd like to ask a few concluding questions about your and your husband's (wife's) background and experiences—these are items we need to have for our statistical analysis.

61. What is your age?

62. Your occupation? [Get in sufficient detail for Census code of occupations.] [If in Government, ask for grade.]

If respondent works:

63. Where do you work? [In sufficient detail to classify as government; large industry, small industry, commercial, etc.]

64. How far did you go in school?

65. What is husband's (wife's) age?

66. His (her) occupation? [Get in sufficient detail for Census code of occupations.] [If in Government, ask for grade.]

If respondent's spouse works:

67. Where does he (she) work? [In sufficient detail to classify as government; large industry, small industry, commercial, etc.]

68. How far did he (she) go in school?

69. What has *your* father's usual occupation been?

70. Your husband's (wife's) father's usual occupation?

71. Were you born in the United States?

If yes: In what country were your parents born?

If no: In what country were you born?

72. How about your husband (wife)—was he (she) born in the United States?
    If yes: In what country were his (her) parents born?
    If no: In what country was he (she) born?

73. a) How long have you lived in this neighborhood?
    b) Have you or your husband (wife) ever lived on a farm?
    If yes: Which of you? When?

74. May I ask what is your religious background? [If respondent says he has no religious affiliation, explain that we merely want to know about his family's religious background—whether Catholic, Protestant, or Jewish—and this for statistical purposes only.]

75. Your husband's (wife's)?

76. a) If you were asked to use one of these four names for your social class, which would you say you belonged in: the middle class, lower class, working class or upper class?
    b) Why do you consider yourself to be _____ class?
    c) Which of these groups of people would you say you belong to: those who are going up in the world, those who have gone down somewhat, or those who are not really going up or down?

77. a) Can you estimate your family's yearly income?
    b) [If not obvious] Do you own or rent your home?
    c) How much rent do you pay per month? (Or: What is the approximate value of your home?)

78. [If respondent has not already answered this] What is your marital status: are you living with your husband (wife), separated, or divorced?

79. a) How long have you been married?
    b) Everything considered, would you say your marriage has been happier than those of most people you know, about as happy, or not quite as happy?

80. Have either you or your husband (wife) been married before?
    If yes: Which of you? When? Any children?

81. Have you (has your wife) ever worked outside the home since the birth of your first child?
    [*If yes*: Periods involved, time per week, type of work, arrangements made for care of children.]

82. Do you (does your wife) belong to any clubs or organizations, or engage in any other activities that take you (takes her) away from home during the day?
    If yes: Estimate of time per week. Types of activities. Arrangements for children.

83. About how often do you and your husband (wife) go out during the evenings or on weekends—without the children?
    If ever: What arrangements are made for the children when you go out?

84. About how frequently do you (does your wife) go out, leaving the children in your husband's (your) care?

85. Does your husband's (your) work ever take him (you) away from home for periods of more than two days? Does he work evenings more than once or twice a week?
   (*If yes:* Details)

86. Does anyone else live with the family—besides you, your husband (wife), and the children?
   If yes: Who are they? How well does (*child*) get along with them?

87. Have you read any magazine articles or books on child care during the past couple of years?
   If yes: Do you remember what they were? What were your reactions to them?

88. Have you talked with a doctor or other professional person about problems of child care during the past couple of years?
   (*If yes:* Details)

89. All things considered, what do you think are the major reasons why children get into trouble?

90. Are there any aspects of your family life that I have not asked about that would be important for an understanding of how families raise their children?

Interviewer

Was the respondent's spouse present during interview?

Were any of the children at home during the interview?

   If yes:
   1. Who?
   2. Were they present during the interview, or in another room, etc.?
      If present:
      3. How did respondent cope with them?
         a) To keep them from interfering with interview?
         b) To meet their demands or wants?
         c) When questions pertaining to them were asked?
   4. Any further impressions of the parent-child relationships not adequately covered in the interview schedule.

Methods of the Turin Study

Turin (Torino), the capital city of the Piedmont region of northwestern Italy, is located in the shadow of the Alps. The availability of hydroelectric power has helped make it the fourth largest city of Italy, with a population of over one million. It has long been a principal industrial center; currently, it produces 90 percent of the nation's automobiles and much of its output of metallurgical and textile products. Historically, it has been an important center of political ferment and activity. Much of the impetus for the reunification of Italy in the middle of the 19th century originated in this city; indeed Turin was the first capital of Italy. To this day it has a lively political climate, mirrored by many informal discussion groups in the city's *piazze* as well as by a broad spectrum of trade unions that reflect the principal political currents of the country.

PREPARATION OF THE INTERVIEW SCHEDULE

The Turin study, conducted by Leonard I. Pearlin during 1962-63, was designed to be comparable to the Washington study of 1956-57. Pearlin prepared a preliminary interview schedule before going to Italy, with emphasis on those questions designed to be comparable to the Washington study. There was also an effort to build in questions on occupation that would be comparable to those of the National study, but this could be done only approximately, for the planning of the National study was at an early stage.

When Pearlin arrived in Italy, his Italian collaborator (Pier Brunetti), a bilingual secretary (Ina Cabutti Velline), and a small group of trained interviewers translated the questions into Italian. Then, in the course of exploratory and pretest interviews, the research group modified the original questions and added others. Late in the pretesting, Kohn joined the group for an intensive evaluation of the retranslated (back into English) interview schedule, to be certain that the efforts to make the questions fully appropriate to Italian language and culture had not rendered them incomparable to the American version. In fact, every instance where interviewers thought a question too American turned out to indicate that a literal translation had lost something of the original connotation; making the questions more Italian was in fact to make them more comparable to those used in the Washington study.

SAMPLE SELECTION

As in the Washington study, interviews were conducted with approximately equal numbers of middle- and working-class parents of fifth-grade children. This was accomplished by overselecting schools whose records showed that they had a heavy representation of pupils from middle-class families. There was also a deliberate underselection of schools serving migrants from southern Italy. Once the schools were selected, the choice of families was randomly made from the rosters of fifth-grade pupils. The final sample deliberately does not reflect the class distribution of Turin, but the sample from each social class is reasonably representative of families of that social class who are native to Turin or long-term residents of that city.

FIELD WORK PROCEDURES

Letters were sent in advance of the interview to the parents chosen for the sample, informing them of the nature and purpose of the interviews and of the joint sponsorship of the study by the U.S. National Institute of Mental Health and the *Fondazione Adriano Olivetti* of Turin.

In almost all cases, interviews with mothers and with fathers were conducted independently. Usually, a pair of interviewers visited the home together, each interviewing one parent, with the interviews conducted in separate rooms. Where this was not possible, every effort was made to keep the interviews independent, by asking the parents not to discuss them until both had been interviewed.

There were a dozen interviewers, all of them women, nearly all of them bilingual. Most of them had had interviewing experience on a research project conducted in Turin the preceding year. They were nevertheless given additional training for this study.

Approximately 85 percent of the families contacted participated in the study; interviews were completed with 341 fathers and 520 mothers, including 314 husband-wife pairs. It has not been possible to do a systematic analysis of the nonrespondents.

PROCESSING OF DATA

The interviews were translated into English by Ina Cabutti Velline and Franca Brunetti and were then coded by Thelma Gardner, Eleanor Carroll, and Erma Jean Surman.

Instead of an analysis of coding reliability, there was complete verification of the coding of qualitative information and systematic spot-checking of precoded information.

INDEX OF SOCIAL CLASS

In this study, as in cross-national studies generally, the critical methodological problem is to devise indices that measure the same thing in all countries being compared. For the present analysis, it is especially important that the index of social class be as equivalent[1] as possible for the United States and Italy.

There is considerable evidence that all industrialized societies have essentially similar class systems;[2] our observations of this industrialized area of Italy attest to the comparability of its class system to that of the United States. Comparability of class systems does not necessarily insure the equivalence of indices, however; the problem is to find objective characteristics that indicate essentially the same class position in both countries. Characteristics relevant to class position in one society may be irrelevant in the other and, more problematic, characteristics equally relevant in both countries need not indicate equivalent positions in both. Education, for example, is a valid index of social class in both Italy and the United States, but any given level of education implies higher status in Italy than in the United States. To use such a characteristic as an index of class in cross-national comparisons would require the use of a weighted correction whose validation would be a sizeable task.

Occupational position is the one characteristic that indicates closest equivalence of class position in the two countries. In

---

[1]We have adopted the term "equivalence" from Almond and Verba, 1963: 57-72.

[2]For documentation of this assertion, see the references listed in the discussion of the adequacy of the Hollingshead Index, in Chapter 1.

particular, professionals, managers, proprietors, and white-collar workers have higher class positions in both countries than do foremen or skilled, semiskilled, and unskilled workers. The location of an individual's occupation within this ranking, therefore, provides a basis for determining class position in both societies.

Our sampling procedures in both Washington and Turin were designed to minimize the number of families from the upper and lower extremes of the social class distribution. Since we have largely excluded the upper-class extreme, our sample of professionals, managers, proprietors, and white-collar workers comprises a reasonably representative sample of the middle class. Our exclusion of the lower extreme means that our sample of foremen and skilled, semiskilled, and unskilled workers comprises a reasonably representative sample of the working class. Some intraclass variation is obscured by using only these two broad social class categories, but what is lost in precision is gained in increased cross-national comparability.

INTERVIEW SCHEDULES

Since this book utilizes only a small portion of the data from the Turin study, we present only the relevant questions. These are given both in Italian, as they were asked, and in an approximate English translation. The questions about parental values were asked both of mothers and of fathers; those about occupation were asked only of fathers.

Italian Questions	English Questions
1. Su questo foglio sono elencate diverse caratteristiche personali. Tenendo presente X, quali ritiene siano le più importanti per un bambino della sua età? Tra esse, quali considera prima, seconda, terza in importanza?	1. A number of characteristics are listed below. Parents differ in the things they think are desirable or important on this list. Thinking mainly of your fifth-grade child, which do you personally feel are important? Of the things you say are important, which one do you consider *most* important? Second most important? Third most important?
a. Che sia simpatico agli altri bambini	a. That he is popular with other children.
b. Che sia ben educato	b. That he has good manners.

c. Che sia ambizioso di riuscire
d. Che si tenga pulito ed abbia buona presenza
e. Che sia benvoluto dagli adulti
f. Che si comporti in modo serio
g. Che sappia difendersi

h. Che sia capace di controllarsi
i. Che sia affettuoso
j. Che sia felice
k. Che sappia giocare da solo

l. Che obbedisca ai suoi genitori

m. Che sia onesto
n. Che si possa contare su la sua parola
o. Che abbia considerazione per gli altri
p. Che abbia uno spirito indagatore
q. Che sia un buon scolaro

2. Ci sono altre importanti qualità non indicate nella lista che Le abbiamo presentato che Lei trova desiderabili per X?

Ora vorremmo chiederLe del Suo lavoro.
3. In che cosa consiste il Suo lavoro?
4. Lavora Ella per altri o in proprio?
Se lavora per altri:
5. Quanti dipendenti lavorano nell'azienda?
6. In che sezione o reparto lavora Lei?
7. Quante persone vi lavorano?
8. Che qualifica (posizione, titolo) ha il direttore della Sua sezione o reparto?
   a. Ha con lui contatti quotidiani?

c. That he is ambitious.
d. That he is neat and clean.
e. That he is liked by adults.
f. That he acts in a serious way.
g. That he is able to defend himself.
h. That he has self-control.
i. That he is affectionate.
j. That he is happy.
k. That he is able to play by himself.
l. That he obeys his parents well.

m. That he is honest.
n. That he is dependable.
o. That he is considerate of others.
p. That he is curious about things.
q. That he is a good student.

2. Are there other important qualities not found in the list that we have given you that you think desirable for X? (your fifth-grade child)?

Now we should like to ask about your own occupation.
3. What does your work consist of?
4. Do you work for others or self?
If not self-employed:
5. How many people work in your company?
6. In which section do you work?
7. How many people work there?
8. What is the title of the department head?
   a. Do you have everyday contact with him?

b. Chi è il responsabile dopo di lui?

c. Ha con lui contatti quotidiani?

[Continuare finché si arriva alla posizione del superiore diretto e dell'intervistato]

9. Tra le persone in autorità chi dirige più direttamente il Suo lavoro?

10. Quanto controllo il Suo superiore diretto (persona indicata alla domanda 9) esercita sul Suo lavoro?

11. Accade sovente che Ella comunichi a questa persona le Sue idee su come svolgere il lavoro?

12. Come sono i Suoi rapporti con questa persona?

13. Quando il Suo superiore vuole ottenere qualcosa da Lei, come fa a comunicarLe quello che vuole?

14. Accade spesso che Ella nel Suo lavoro faccia delle cose che non farebbe se dispendesse da Lei?

15. Ha Ella molta influenza sul modo in cui viene svolto il lavoro?

16. E' d'accordo sulle seguenti affermazioni?

a. Nel mio ambiente di lavoro non ha importanza quello che uno sa, ma sono le raccomandazioni che contano.

b. Sento di avere molto potere di decisione nelle cose che hanno veramente importanza nel mio lavoro.

c. Nel mio lavoro sento di essere padrone del mio futuro.

17. Le presento adesso una lista di qualità personali. In base alla Sua esperienza quali di queste sono necessarie per svolgere bene il Suo lavoro?

b. Who is responsible after him?

c. Do you have everyday contact with him?

[Continue these questions until reaching the supervisor directly above respondent]

9. Which of these authorities has most responsibility for the direction of your work?

10. How much control does your direct supervisor (the person indicated in question 9) exercise over your work?

11. How often do you talk to this person concerning your ideas about the work?

12. How do you get along with this person?

13. When your supervisor wants you to do something, how does he let you know what he wants?

14. Do you do things in your work that you wouldn't do if it were up to you?

15. Do you have much influence on the way things go at your work?

16. Are you in agreement with the following statements?

a. In my place of work it is not important what one knows; it is who one knows that matters.

b. I feel that I have the power to make decisions about the things that have true importance to my work.

c. In my work, I feel that I am master of my future.

17. Here is a list of personal qualities. Based on your experience, which qualities are necessary for you to do well at your work?

h

a. stretta obbedienza ai superiori
b. capire se stesso
c. intelligenza
d. non fare né più né meno di quello che è richiesto
e. essere simpatico
f. perserveranza nel lavoro
g. essere ambizioso di migliorare la propria posizione
h. sapere lavorare con gli altri
i. saper evitare le grane
j. essere capace di fare sacrifici oggi per ottenere risultati domani
k. rispetto dei regolamenti
l. ardita immaginazione
m. fiducia in sé
n. essere molto onesto
o. avere un genuino interesse in ciò che si fa
p. essere capace di sopportare gli affronti
q. avere senso di responsabilità

a. Strict obedience to superiors
b. Understanding oneself
c. Intelligence
d. Doing neither more nor less than is required
e. Being likeable
f. Perseverance in work
g. Being ambitious to improve one's position
h. Knowing how to work with others
i. Knowing how to avoid trouble
j. Being able to sacrifice today for tomorrow's results
k. Respect for rules
l. Bold imagination
m. Trust in oneself
n. To be very honest
o. To have genuine interest in one's work
p. To be able to bear affronts
q. To have a sense of responsibility

18. Ci sono altre qualità, qui sopra elencate, che Ella ritiene importanti per svolgere bene il Suo lavoro?

19. In quasi tutte le occupazioni è neccessario lavorare con *cose* (come attrezzi, strumenti, macchine, ecc.), con *persone* (riunioni, contrattazioni, assistenza, ecc.) e con *idee* (programmare − calcolare − scrivere, ecc.) ma le varie occupazioni richiedono in proporzione diversa ognuno di questi tre tipi di attività. Considerando ora una Sua tipica giornata di lavoro, in quale proporzione il

18. Are there some other qualities that you feel are important in doing a good job that are not listed above?

19. In almost all occupations, it is necessary to work with things (such as tools, instruments, machines, etc.), with people (conferences, negotiations, seeing customers, etc.), and with ideas (planning, computing, writing, etc.), but various occupations differ in the extent to which they require these three types of activities. Considering now your typical day's work, what propor-

Suo tempo viene dedicato alle seguenti: cose, persone, idee?

20. Quale di questi tre aspetti del lavoro è più importante nella Sua occupazione?

Vorremmo ora terminare ponendoLe alcune altre domande che ci serviranno per la nostra analisi statistica.

21. Qual'è la Sua età?
22. Che studi ha compiuto?

tions of your time are given to the following: things, people, ideas?

20. Which of these three is most important in your work?

I should like to ask a few concluding questions about your background and experiences. These items we need to have for our statistical analysis.

21. What is your age?
22. How far did you go in school?

Methods of the National Study

The National study gave us the opportunity to make many methodological and substantive improvements on the Washington and Turin studies. By including families with children of a wide range of ages, we could systematically examine the impact of children's age upon the relationship of social class to parental values. We could trace the relationships of class not only with parental values, but also with values and orientation in general. We could refine the indices employed in the prior analyses and, with the aid of a sufficiently large sample and the technology of computers, bring more variables into play simultaneously—thus strengthening the analysis. Finally, we could do all this with a sample representative of the nation as a whole, encompassing a broader class distribution than had been used in the earlier studies and including all major ethnic, religious, racial, and regional segments of the society.

DIMENSIONS OF OCCUPATION

The single most important decision in designing this study was to focus on *dimensions* of occupation rather than on particular named occupations, each one an immensely complicated cluster of dimensions. Most previous studies (other than those using occupation solely as an index of social class) had been limited to descriptions of a single occupation or at most to comparisons of two or three discrete occupations. Cottrell's (1940) study of railroaders, for example, pointed out a multitude of ways in which the job conditions of the men who operate trains differ from those of men in many other occupations—including the unpredictability of working hours, geographical mobility, precision of timing, "outsider" status in the home community, and unusual recruitment and promotion practices. Since all these job conditions are tied together in one occupational package, it is not possible to disentangle the social psychological effects of each. Similarly, Blauner's (1964) comparative study of blue-collar workers in four industries, chosen to represent four technological levels—printing (craft), textile (machine), automobile manufacture (assembly line), and chemicals (continuous process-automated)—showed that systematic differences in work conditions are associated with the stage of technological development of the particular industry. But these differences, too, come in packages; printing differs from automobile manufacture, for example, not only in the skill levels of the workers, but also in the pace of the work, the closeness of supervision, the freedom of physical movement, and a multitude of other conditions.

If we were to trace the effects of occupational conditions on values and orientation, we would somehow have to separate occupational conditions from one another. To do this required two things—that we have a sufficiently large sample to enable us to disentangle the intercorrelated dimensions of occupation and that we have reasonably good indices of as many of the important occupational dimensions as possible.

We wanted to measure the facets of occupation that had proved to be important in our earlier work. To be certain that we did not overlook other relevant aspects of occupation, we searched a variety of disparate sources. A number of sociological studies of work, occupation, industry, and bureaucracy proved valuable in alerting us to potentially important dimensions of occupation. (Particularly useful were the two studies just referred to—Cottrell, 1940; and Blauner, 1964—and Waller, 1932; Mills, 1953; Foote, 1953; Chinoy, 1955; Blau, 1955; Lipset, *et al.,* 1956; Becker and Carper, 1956; Hughes, 1958; Edwards, 1959; Morris and Murphy, 1959; Whyte, 1961; and Pearlin, 1962.) Even more useful were our own and our colleagues' past occupational experiences; novels and plays; and the *Dictionary of Occupational Titles* (U.S. Department of Labor, 1949), whose thumbnail sketches of occupations sensitized us to many important distinctions. Most useful of all were the semistructured pretest interviews held with a large number of respondents.

The final battery of occupational dimensions and the indices developed to measure them are given in Chapters 9 and 10.

SAMPLE

We had considered using a sample that was stratified along three or four major dimensions of occupation—in particular, size of the firm or organization in which men are employed; whether the occupation deals principally with things, with data, or with people; ownership or nonownership; and occupational status. Selection of the sample could have been accomplished at reasonable cost by employing a census-type inquiry that asked only the questions crucial for stratification and used any knowledgeable informant. From this census, respondents could have been selected for the survey proper. The advantage of this procedure would have been the assurance that we would get a sufficient number of men in critical categories—men in higher status jobs who work primarily with things, for example, and men in lower status jobs who work at complex data tasks.

When we specified the requirements for stratifying the sample, however, we found that a representative sample of all men employed in civilian occupations would provide a sufficient number of men in each critical category. A representative sample is less expensive and poses fewer problems for generalizing to a larger population. So we decided on a representative sample, and chose 3,000 as the smallest number of men that would make feasible the major lines of analysis we intended.

In our original conception, the study was to be limited to urban occupations, but we found that with minor modification the inquiry was applicable to rural occupations, too. Because the experiences of unemployment might overshadow the experiences of past employment (cf. Bakke, 1940), we excluded men not currently employed. We also excluded men in the military, since the problems both of sampling and of inquiry seemed too formidable to make their inclusion worthwhile. And we excluded women, reluctantly, because of possible differences between men and women in the meaning of job and occupation; to investigate this question would have extended the inquiry unduly. We did not exclude anyone on grounds of age, race, language (a few men were interviewed in languages other than English), or any other basis. We are defining *men* to be males, 16 years of age or older, and *employed* to mean working at least 25 hours a week.

The one remaining sampling problem was that Census data suggested that only half of the men included in such a sample could be expected to be fathers with children of an appropriate age living at home. It would have been possible to limit the study to such men, but this would have introduced an unknown degree of bias to all other aspects of the inquiry. So we decided to include all men employed in civilian occupations, even though half of the sample would be irrelevant for analyses of parental values and parent-child relationships.

In interviewing the fathers, we wanted to direct the questions about values and parent-child relationships to one specific child, so chosen as to insure an even distribution of ages and an unbiased selection. The mechanism for doing this was to require the interviewer to list all children aged 3 through 15 who were living at home, and then to focus on the child specified by a chart that we supplied. The chart (Figure C-1) was essentially a random-sampling device for assuring an even distribution of birthranks (and therefore ages) within families of each possible size. The key to its effectiveness is that we had randomly assigned each respondent to one of six categories and had also randomized the selection of birthranks among the six categories—a complicated scheme, but it made possible a systematic investigation of the effects of children's age on fathers' values.

FIGURE C-1
Sampling Instructions to Secure an Even Distribution of Children

Sampling Table
(Circle Appropriate Number)

If Number of Children Listed
in Box B Is . . .

And Your Assignment Sheet Contained the Letter . . .	Two	Three	Four	Five	Six	Seven	Eight or More
A, then ask questions about child on line	2	3	1	5	1	7	2
B, then ask questions about child on line	1	2	2	4	2	6	1
C, then ask questions about child on line	2	1	3	3	3	5	6
D, then ask questions about child on line	2	3	4	2	4	4	8
E, then ask questions about child on line	1	2	4	1	5	2	3
F, then ask questions about child on line	1	1	2	1	6	1	7

DEVELOPMENT OF THE INTERVIEW SCHEDULE
AND ADMINISTRATION OF THE SURVEY

If ever investigators had the opportunity for unhurried planning, we did. We spent many months drawing up and refining lists of dimensions; reading all sorts of relevant, tangential, and barely relevant materials; doing informal, unstructured interviews; and preparing long lists of questions to try out on respondents. The intent was to begin with a comprehensive, even if horrendously long, interview schedule and then to pare it down ruthlessly.

The early rounds of unstructured and, later, pretest interviews were conducted by Eleanor Carroll, Judith Fiorello, Elizabeth Howell, Melvin Kohn, Carmi Schooler, and Erma Jean Surman. The final pretests were conducted by the National Opinion Research Center (NORC), under the field direction of Paul Sheatsley and Eve Weinberg. NORC conducted 100 interviews—6 in each of 10 widely separated places, with an emphasis on small towns and rural areas, 20 in Chicago, and 20 in New York City—with an emphasis in these cities on less educated respondents. (The intent in concentrating on small town, rural, and less educated respondents was to subject the interview schedule to the most demanding tests.) We received detailed reports on each interview and met with the Chicago and New York interviewers to discuss the schedule question by question. The information provided by the interviewers, together with preliminary statistical analyses of the interviews, provided the basis for one final revision of the schedule. The batteries of items designed to measure the several aspects of self-conception and social orientation were tested for their scale characteristics, other items for their clarity of meaning and distributional characteristics. The schedule was shortened once again, and then it was ready for use in the survey proper.

An area probability sample was specially drawn by Seymour Sudman.[1] The survey was carried out by the field staff of NORC (under the direction of Paul Sheatsley, Eve Weinberg, and Marilyn Haskell) during the spring and summer of 1964. The completed interview schedules were then turned over to us for processing.

---

[1]For a description of the area probability sampling methods used by the National Opinion Research Center, see Sudman and Feldman, 1965.

NONRESPONDENTS

Overall, 76 percent of the men included in the sample gave reasonably complete interviews. Considering that it is always more difficult to get employed men than most other people to cooperate in a survey, and that the interviewers were asking them to participate in an especially long interview (the median interview took two and a half hours), we think this rate is acceptable. But from the point of view of generalizing to the population at large, we find the other 24 percent worrisome. We must examine their characteristics.

First, a general classification of the reasons for the losses (Table C-1): Two thirds of the nonrespondents simply refused to be interviewed; most of the others were not available for one reason or another—in some cases because of illness or other incapacitation, in others because the interviewer could not find them at home at a time convenient for an interview. In only a minute proportion of cases was an interview broken off, once begun.

TABLE C-1
Types of Nonresponse

	Number	Proportion of Original Sample
Completed interviews....................	3101	.76
Incomplete or lost interviews:		
Refusals	650	.16
Breakoff	46	.01
Temporarily unavailable (ill, hospitalized, etc.)	97	.02
Never at home, on repeated visits	118	.03
Interviewer made contact, but respondent not at home on subsequent visits	41	.01
Other (or inadequate data)	52	.01
Total.....................	4105	1.00

The .16, .01, .02, .03, .01, .01 proportions are bracketed together to total .24.

Further analysis shows that the interviewers considered only 15 percent of the nonrespondents to be hostile or suspicious; in the overwhelming majority of cases, the interviewers concluded that the men were simply insufficiently interested to participate in so long an interview. We seem to have asked more than they were willing to contribute.

Loss of respondents assumes particular importance if it occurs disproportionately in delimited segments of the population. For our research, it is especially important that nonrespondents not be concentrated in a particular social class. A complete analysis of this issue is not possible here, for we lack data on the social class position of many of the nonrespondents. One important source of information, however, is available to us: Most medium-sized cities have city directories that contain tolerably accurate occupational data. For those cities, it is possible to determine whether or not the nonrespondents differ in occupational level from the men who granted interviews.

We find little difference overall (Table C-2). The nonresponse rate for small business owners is somewhat higher than that for other men, but even this difference is probably an artifact of city directories having more complete coverage of these men. We conclude that, for cities where data are available, nonresponse rates do not seem to vary appreciably by occupational level. Furthermore, for those cases where data on occupational level are available, there is no relationship between the occupational levels of nonrespondents and their reasons for not granting an interview. Nor is there any relationship between nonrespondents' occupational levels and the interviewers' characterizations of their apparent attitudes. Rates and types of nonresponse do not seem to be appreciably related to social class.

There is, however, one social fact that did seem to make a notable difference in the rate of nonresponse—the size of the community in which men live. These rates are directly proportional to size of

TABLE C-2
Rates of Nonresponse by Occupation Level
(for cities having city directories)

Hollingshead Occupational Rating	Original Sample Size	Number of Non- respondents	Rate of Non- response
Higher executives, professionals, etc.	68	12	.18
Business managers in large concerns, proprietors of medium-size businesses, etc. .	60	9	.15
Small business owners, semiprofessionals, etc.	196	61	.31
Clerical and sales workers, technicians, owners of little businesses, etc.	136	18	.13
Skilled workers	231	56	.24
Semiskilled workers	198	38	.19
Unskilled workers	77	9	.12
Total for these cities	966	203	.21

community (Table C-3). Nothing in the data explains this phenomenon. The simple fact is that the larger the community, the more difficult it is to get employed men to grant long interviews.

TABLE C-3
Rates of Nonresponse, by Size of Community

	Original Sample Size	Number of Non-respondents	Rate of Nonresponse
Metropolitan areas of 2 million population or more	1055	354	.34
Other metropolitan areas	1672	418	.25
Nonmetropolitan counties containing a city of at least 10,000 people	599	115	.19
Nonmetropolitan counties with no city of at least 10,000 people	771	109	.14
(Not classifiable)	8	8	
Total	4105	1004	

These analyses suggest that our final sample is reasonably representative of the population to which we intend to generalize, except insofar as it underrepresents larger cities and overrepresents smaller communities. Furthermore, comparisons between the social characteristics of our respondents and those of the population of employed m~'es—as reported by the U.S. Census—substantiate the representativeness of the sample. This representativeness will be apparent from examining the marginal distributions in all the relevant tables in this book. It is apparent, too, in a peculiarly reassuring phenomenon: A representative sample of 3,100 men should contain a handful of respondents of just about every statistically unusual sort; it does. We have, for example, a few men whose favorite sport is to jump from airplanes and a few who play whist, a few millionaires, a few members of each of the smaller churches and sects, about the right number of people of every ethnic group that makes up the country—in short, just about what you would expect of a large sample of employed men.

PROCESSING OF DATA

We had already prepared a coding manual for the analysis of pretest interviews, because only by classifying answers into appropriate categories could we be certain that questions yielded the information that they were designed to elicit. With minor revision, the coding manual has proved usable for processing the final interview data.

The coding operation has been the closely coordinated effort of a small group of people—principally Margaret Renfors, Mimi Silberman, Carrie Schoenbach, Julie Forrest, Frances Prestianni, Garrett Bagley, and Evelyn Wiszinckas, under the direction of Elizabeth Howell. We think we have gained in accuracy enough to repay the effort of more than two years of painstaking work that went into the coding.

We employed three tests of coding reliability. First, the coding of 400 randomly selected interviews was appraised by the coding supervisor. She agreed with the original coder's classification of each question *at least* 95 percent of the time. Second was a blind experiment based on a random sample of 50 interviews. Five people independently coded all items on which there was any possibility that knowledge of how another person had coded the material might affect one's judgment. A majority of the five agreed, absolutely, at least 90 percent of the time, on all but two of the classifications made. Since this level of agreement was reached under the special circumstances of everyone knowing that this was a reliability study, we employed a third test. This test compared the consensus of the five coders with the original classification that had been made under altogether routine conditions. Except for two classifications, which we shall treat cautiously, there was at least 80 percent absolute agreement on each.

Subsequently, a detailed check was done of all possible inconsistencies[2] in respondents' answers—for example, self-employed men telling us about their supervisors. These were individually checked against the original interviews and corrected. Then we searched out "implausibilities"—things that might be true, but were unlikely to happen often, for example, men being married to considerably older women, or men whose first full-time job started at an improbably early age. These too were checked against the original interviews. Only then was data-analysis begun.

INTERVIEW SCHEDULE

The actual interview schedule follows. No questions have been

---

[2]This programming was done by Curtis Huntington.

deleted or abridged, but answer categories and detailed instructions have been omitted.

1. Would you please tell me exactly what your job is called?
2. For whom do you work?
3. Do you have any other jobs?
   If yes:
   a.   What are they?
   b.   For whom do you work?
   c.   How many hours a week do you work on (each)?
4. Is the place for which you work a profit-making firm, a nonprofit organization, or a governmental agency?
   If profit-making or self-employed:
   a.   Are you an owner?
5. *If employee:*
   a.   How long have you worked for this employer?
   b.   How long have you held your present position?
   If owner:
   c.   How long have you had this business?
   d.   Are there any other owners?
         If yes:
         (1)   What is your percentage interest in the business?
   If self-employed professional:
   e.   How long have you had this practice?
If profit-making firm, self-employed, or nonprofit organization (Q. 4):
6. What does the firm (organization) do?
If governmental agency:
7. Is that the U.S. government, a state government, or a local government?
   If state government:
   a.   Which state?
   If local government:
   b.   Which?
8. What department of the government do you work for?
9. *Altogether,* about how many people work for the *entire* (firm), (organization), (department or agency)?
   If 10 or more but less than 500 employees:
   a.   Is this a firm (organization, department) where everyone is supervised directly by the same man, where there is one level of supervision between the people at the bottom and the top, or where there are two or more levels of supervision between the people at the bottom and the top?

One thing we'd like to be able to pin down particularly accurately is how much of your working time is spent reading and writing, how much working with your hands, and how much dealing with people. We realize, of course, that you can be doing two or even all three of these at the same time.

10. First—reading or writing. Here we should like to include any type of written materials—letters, files, memos, books, or blueprints. About how many hours a week do you spend reading, writing, dictating, or dealing with any kind of written materials on your job?
If any time at all:
   a. What do you do?
   b. What are they about?

11. Second—working with your hands, using tools, using or repairing machines. We should like to include everything that involves working with your hands—operating a lathe or a dentist's drill, moving furniture, playing the piano. About how many hours a week do you spend working with your hands on your job?
If any time at all:
   a. What do you do? (*Probe:* What operations do you perform?)
   b. What materials do you work on?
   c. What tools or equipment do you use?
   d. What do you do to set up and maintain your equipment?

12. Third—dealing with people. Here we do *not* mean to include passing the time of day, but only conversations necessary for the job; for example, talking to your boss, teaching, supervising, selling, advising clients. About how many hours a week does your job require you to spend dealing with people?
If any time at all:
   a. What kinds of things do you do—do you teach students, supervise subordinates, receive instructions from the boss, sell to customers, advise clients, discuss the work with co-workers, or what? [Be sure to ascertain *what* he does and to *whom*.]
   If more than one such activity:
   (1) At which one of these do you spend the most time?

13. a. Which of these three—working with written materials, working with your hands, or dealing with people—is the most important for doing your job?
   b. What's the second most important?
   If two of equal importance:
   (1) Which ones?

14. a. Of all the persons above you in the (firm, organization, department), who has the most control over what you actually do on the job?
   b. Is he the man immediately above you, the man above him, someone higher still, or someone in another chain of command?

15. How closely does he supervise you—does he decide what you do and how you do it; does he decide what you do but let *you* decide how you do it;

do you have some freedom in deciding both what you do and how you do it; or are you your own boss so long as you stay within the general policies of the firm (organization, department)?

16. When he wants you to do something, does he usually just tell you to do it, does he usually discuss it with you, or is it about half and half? (*If respondent says that he knows what to do, so boss doesn't have to tell him, check box and ask:* How about when something unusual comes up?)

17. How free do you feel to disagree with him—completely free, largely but not completely, moderately, not particularly, or not at all free?

18. Are there any employees of the (firm, organization, department) who are under you, either because they are directly under you or because they are under people you supervise?

19. Altogether, how many employees are under you?

20. How many of these are directly under you, with nobody in between?

21. How important is it for doing your job well that you get on well personally with the people under you—is it absolutely necessary, is it very important, fairly important, or not particularly important?

22. Do you work together with other people on the same task as a team, or do you work independently of other people? *If both:*
    a.   How much of the time do you work with other people? *If both, or work with others:*
    b.   With whom do you work—your supervisor, subordinates, co-workers, people in other occupations, or whom?
    c.   How many people are on this work team?

23. All things considered, whose opinion of your work is most important for such things as . . . (*For employees:* keeping your job, getting a raise, and getting ahead?) (*For self-employed:* the success of your business or practice?) (*If he says "my own," check box, and ask:* Who else's opinion matters?)

24. How good a position (is he, are they) in for judging your work—an excellent position, good, fair, or (does he, do they) have little or no basis for judging your work?

Ask everyone except self-employed:

25. Are there any people who are in competition with you for your job, for advancement, for sales, or for anything else of importance? (For what?) *If yes:*
    a.   Who are they?
    b.   How much competition is there?

Ask everyone:

26. Aside from working overtime, are you expected to begin and end your day's work at approximately the same time every day? *If no or don't know:*

a.   Why is that? Is it because you work different shifts, because you work only when work is available, or because you're free to decide for yourself what hours you work?

If different shifts:

b.   On what schedule do you work?

Everybody except shift workers:

c.   What hours of the day or night do you (most often) work?

d.   What days of the week?

27. Do you ever work overtime or outside of your usual hours, either paid or unpaid?

If work overtime:

a.   How many times in an average month do you do this?

b.   On a day that you do, how many extra hours do you put in?

28. Is the speed at which you work controlled mostly by you, your boss, your work group, the speed of machinery with which you work, or what?

29. How often do you have to work under pressure of time?

If ever work under pressure:

a.   When you're working under time pressure, does this involve working longer hours, heavier physical work, faster physical movements, or faster thinking?

30. Are you required to sit, stand, or walk for long stretches of time in your work, or can you switch when you want to?

If required or depends:

a.   Does this bother you a great deal, somewhat, or not at all?

31. How dirty do you get on the job—very dirty, fairly dirty, a little, or not at all?

32. What type of clothing do you usually wear on the job—a uniform, a suit, a jacket and tie but not necessarily a suit, an apron or lab coat, a sport shirt and slacks, work clothes, or what?

33. How much of the time do you work out of doors?

34. How much of the time do you work in a room by yourself? (*For those who work outdoors:* alone, with no one nearby?)

If less than full time alone:

a.   How much of the time do you work in the presence of five or more people?

35. Does your work involve doing the same thing in the same way repeatedly, the same kind of thing in a number of different ways, or a number of different kinds of things?

If different kinds of things:

a.   When you begin your day's work, can you predict what kinds of things are going to happen on the job that day, or is it a job in which you can't tell what may come up?

36. What it takes to do a complete job varies a great deal from occupation to

occupation. To a worker on an assembly line a complete job may be to tighten two or three bolts; to an auto mechanic a complete job is to repair a car; to a coal miner, a complete job may be to load 18 tons.

  a.   What do you ordinarily think of as a complete job in your occupation? (*Probe:* What do you have to do in order to feel that you've finished a piece of work? *Second probe:* Do you ever feel that you've finished? At what point?)

  b.   How long does it take you to do a complete job? (*If it varies:* What is the range of variation?)

37. Consider all the things you have to think about on your job. Of everything you did during the past week or so, what did you have to think hardest about to figure out? (*Probe:* What was the most difficult thing to figure out?)

38. How often are you held responsible for things that are really outside of your control?

  If sometimes or frequently:

  a.   For what sorts of things outside of your control are you held responsible?

39. a.   If you were to make a wrong decision on the job, or do something wrong, what is the worst thing that could happen to you?

  b.   Aside from what might happen to you, what is the worst thing that could happen?

40. I'm going to show you a list of things that people may have to do on different jobs.

  a.   Would you tell me which three of these things are most necessary for doing your job well?

  b.   Which one of these three is most necessary of all?

  c.   All of these may be necessary for doing your job well, but would you tell me which three are least important?

  d.   And which one of these three is least important of all?

  1)   Make a good impression on others.
  2)   Have a good memory.
  3)   Think quickly.
  4)   Organize things systematically.
  5)   Think up new ways of doing things.
  6)   Plan ahead.
  7)   Handle people well.
  8)   Obey the rules.
  9)   Do heavy work.
  10) Stick to a job until it's finished.
  11) Work accurately.
  12) Communicate clearly.
  13) Do what you're told.
  14) Move quickly.

41. How are you paid on this job—by piecework, hourly wages, a salary, overtime, profits, fees, tips, commissions, bonuses, housing, food, or other benefits, or what?

If overtime pay:

a.   How much do you get in overtime pay, in the average week?

(If can't say):

(1)   What is the least and what is the most you get in overtime pay?

If any income from fees, tips, or commissions:

b.   How big is the usual (fee, tip, commission)?

(If can't say):

(1)   What is the smallest and what is the largest?

If any income in the form of housing, food, or other benefits:

c.   What sort of things do you get (in lieu of salary or wages)?

d.   About how much would these cost, if you had to pay for them?

42. Is there any variation in your earnings from week to week, month to month, or season to season, while working on this job?

If other basis:

a.   What basis?

If variation or other basis:

b.   What is the least and what is the most you make from this job—before taxes?

c.   How much did you make from this job last year—before taxes?

If no variation or don't know:

d.   All in all, how much do you make from this job—before taxes?

(If can't say):

(1)   How much did you make from this job last year—before taxes?

43. What is your family's total income—before taxes—including what you make from this job, any other income you have, and any income that other members of your immediate family bring in?

(If respondent says total income varies, ask for last year's income.)

Ask Qs. 44-47 of all except self-employed.

If self-employed, skip to Q. 48.

44. Do you have any job protection—like seniority rights, contract guarantees, union support, Civil Service, or any other form of job protection?

45. Is there a formal grievance procedure that you can use if you feel you are treated unfairly?

46. As things look now, how likely is it that you could be laid off from your job in the next year or so because of a cutback in the number of people your (firm, organization, department) employs—is it very likely, fairly likely, not very likely, or not possible?

47. Does your job provide for your being paid while sick?

Ask self-employed only:

48. How much competition is there in your field—a great deal, a fair amount, some but not much, very little, or none?

49. How great is the risk of failure in your field—very great, fairly great, some risk but not much, very little risk, or no risk?

50. What do you see as the advantages of being in business for yourself instead of working for someone else?

51. What are the disadvantages?

Ask everyone:

52. Does your job involve any traveling that requires you to be away from home overnight or longer?

    If travels overnight or longer:

    a. How many trips do you take in the course of a year?

    b. How long are you gone, on the average?

    c. All in all, do you consider the traveling you do a good or a bad feature of your job?

53. I'd like to find out how important a number of things are to you in judging jobs in general—not just your job but any job. For instance, how much difference does the pay make in how you rate a job—is pay very important, fairly important, or not particularly important?

    (*Then ask:* How important are the fringe benefits? . . . etc., *going through entire list.*)

54. Now I'd like to find out how satisfied you are in your own job with those things you consider very important or fairly important. Would you say you are very satisfied, fairly satisfied, somewhat dissatisfied, or very dissatisfied with . . .?

    a. The pay?

    b. Fringe benefits?

    c. How interesting the work is?

    d. The supervisor?

    e. Your co-workers?

    f. How clean the work is?

    g. The hours you work?

    h. How tiring the work is?

    i. How highly people regard the job?

    j. Job security?

    k. The amount of freedom you have?

    l. The chance to help people?

    m. Not being under too much pressure?

    n. The chance to get ahead?

    o. The chance to use your abilities?

55. All things considered, how satisfied are you with the job as a whole?

56. All things considered, what about the job do you like best? (*If earnings, check box and ask:* What's next best?)

57. What about the job do you like least? (*If earnings, check box and ask:* After that, what do you like least?)

Ask everyone except self-employed:

58. How do you feel about your (firm, organization, department)—are you proud of working there, embarrassed, or neither?

Ask everyone:

59. Did you have to have any sort of license, pass a formal examination, or go through any formal probationary or apprenticeship experience to get or to keep your job?
    If yes:
    a.   What was that?

60. We've been talking about your present job. Now I'd like to get a rundown on your past jobs. Would you tell me all the full-time jobs you've ever held for six months or more, and the dates you started and ended each one. Let's start with the job you held just before this one. (*Probe for full job title and approximate dates job started and ended. Then go on to the job before that, etc.*)

61. *If any of the jobs listed in Q. 60 seem to be in same occupation as present job, ask:* All in all, how long have you been a (*respondent's occupation*)?

62. Were any of your earlier jobs stepping-stones to your present job?
    If yes:
    a.   Which ones?

63. Did you like any of your other jobs better than your present job?
    If yes:
    a.   Which ones?
    b.   Why did you leave (each)?

Ask everyone:

64. Have you been unemployed or out of work for at least a month at any time during the past 10 years?
    If yes:
    a.   When? (Any other times?)
    b.   Why were you out of work (each time)?
    c.   For how long (each time)?

65. Did you serve in the armed forces at any time?
    If yes:
    a.   What branch of the service were you in?
    b.   When?
    c.   What was your highest rank?
    d.   What did you do?

66. Compared to the people who started out in your line of work at about the same time you did, would you say you have done much better than most, better than most, about average, or less well than most?

67. What do you expect in the future—by the time you retire, will you have done much better than most people in your line of work, better than most, about average, or less well than most?

68. Ten years from now do you expect your income from your occupation to be about the same as it is now, higher, or lower?
    If income will go up or down:
    a.   How much (higher, lower)?
69. Is yours a field where there can be a sudden and dramatic change in your income, reputation, or position?
    If yes:
    a.   Is the change likely to be for the better or for the worse?
    b.   How often does this happen to people in your field?
    c.   When it does happen, is it usually because of some achievement, because of a good or bad break, poor performance, or for some other reason?
70. How likely is it that sooner or later—but before you want to retire—you may not be able to keep up with the work in your present job?
    If at all likely:
    a.   Why might it possibly happen?
    b.   What would most likely happen in that event—would you remain on the job not functioning as well, would you be given another job, dropped (*Self-employed:* fail), or what?
71. Some people are so attached to their occupation that they cannot imagine wanting to do anything else, while others would be only too glad to change to some other occupation. How about you?
    If would change:
    a.   What occupation would you prefer?
72. If the income were the same, would you prefer to be in business for yourself, or work for somebody else?
73. If you were to inherit a million dollars, would you continue doing the work you do now, shift to something else, or retire?
    If shift to another occupation:
    a.   Which one?
74. Do you think it is a real accomplishment to be a good (*respondent's occupation*)?
75. How much good do you think your work does for mankind—a great deal, some, a little, it doesn't help but doesn't hurt, or does it hurt?
76. A few years ago, in another survey, people were asked to rate the general prestige of a number of occupations. This card shows the order in which a selected group of 17 occupations were rated. Where on the list would you place your occupation?
77. Where do you think most people today would place your occupation?

Occupations

1) Physician
2) College professor
3) Lawyer
4) Dentist
5) Airline pilot
6) Public school teacher

7) Electrician	8) Policeman
9) Carpenter	10) Plumber
11) Garage mechanic	12) Milk routeman
13) Filling station attendant	14) Janitor
15) Clothes presser in a laundry	16) Garbage collector

17) Shoe shiner

78. When you were a boy of 12 or so, what occupation did your parents want you to go into?

Ask all except self-employed:

79. Do you belong to a union?

If yes:

a. Which union do you belong to?
   (1) Local No.
   (2) Name of union
   (3) Is that part of the AFL-CIO?

b. Did you have to belong to the union in order to get or keep your job?

c. Do you attend meetings, serve on committees, serve as an officer or steward, or engage in any union social or recreational activities?
   If social or recreational activities:
   (1) How often?

d. How important do you feel the union is to you—very important, somewhat important, or not important at all?

If not union member:

e. Is there a union where you work, that you could join if you wanted to?
   If no:
   (1) Would you join, if there were a union?

Ask everyone:

80. Aside from unions, do you belong to any organizations or associations that are primarily for people in your line of work?

If yes:

a. Which ones?

b. Do you attend meetings, serve on committees, serve as an officer, or engage in any of their social or recreational activities?

81. Do you belong to any other organizations?

If yes:

a. Which?

b. About how many hours a month do you spend on (its, their) activities?

c. Did you join (it, any of them) because of, or in connection with, your occupation?

Now I'd like to ask some questions about your background and experiences.

82. How old are you?
83. What was the highest grade you completed in school?
    If some grade school:
    a.   What was the highest grade you completed?
    If some high school/college/graduate work:
    b.   How many years of (high school/college/graduate work) did you complete?
    If advanced degree/beyond:
    c.   Which degree?
    If beyond degree:
    d.   How many years of graduate work beyond the degree?
84. *If some college or more:*
    a.   What college did you go to (as an undergraduate)?
    If more than two years of college:
    b.   What did you major in (as an undergraduate)?
    If went to graduate or professional school:
    c.   What field were you in, in graduate or professional school?
85. In what country were you born?
    If born outside of continental United States:
    86. How old were you when you came to this country?
87. In what state did you live longest, up to the age of 16?
88. Up to the age of 16, did you live mostly on a farm, in a village or small town, or in a city or its suburbs?
    If city or suburbs:
    a.   How large was the city at that time—would you say 50,000 or less, up to half a million, or even larger?
    b.   Did you live mostly in the city itself or in the suburbs?
    c.   Before you were 16, did you ever live on a farm or in a village or small town for two years or more?
         If yes:
         (1)   At what ages did you live there?
         (2)   Was this on a farm, or in a village or small town?
89. Did you have any brothers or sisters—including step-brothers or step-sisters—who grew up with you?
    If yes:
    a.   How many older sisters did you have?
    b.   How many younger sisters did you have?
    c.   How many older brothers did you have?
    d.   And how many younger brothers did you have?
         If had any brothers:
         (1)   What is, or was, the main occupation of each of your brothers, starting with the oldest?

90. Were you living with both your father and mother until you were 16 years old?
If no:
a.   What happened?
b.   How old were you at that time?
c.   With whom did you live between that time and the time you were 16?
d.   (*If lived with stepfather or other substitute father*): What was his occupation?

91. What was your father's occupation when you were about 16? (*If father was dead or not around:* What had his occupation been?)

92. What was the highest grade your father completed in school?

93. In what country was he born?

94. Did your mother have a full-time job at any time after you were born? (*If mother was dead or not around, ask about mother-substitute.*)
If yes:
a.   How old were you when she went to work?
b.   How long did she work?
c.   What sort of work did she do?

95. In what country was she born?

96. How old was your mother when you were born?

97. What was your father's father's usual occupation?

98. In what country was he born?

99. In what country was his wife born?

100. What was your mother's father's usual occupation?

101. In what country was he born?

102. In what country was his wife born?

103. Besides American, which nationality in your background has had the greatest influence on you?

104. How great an influence would you say your (*nationality*) background has had on you—a great influence, a moderate influence, some but not much, or none at all?

105. If you were asked to use one of these names for your social class, which would you say you belonged in—upper class, upper-middle, middle, working, or lower class?

106. What is your religious background?
If Protestant:
a.   What denomination?

107. About how often would you say you attend church (synagogue)?

108. Who lives in the household with you?

109. Are you presently married, single and never married, separated, divorced, or widowed?

110. How old is your wife?
111. What was the highest grade she completed in school?
112. Does she have a job?
    If yes:
    a.   What does she do?
113. Besides American, which nationality in her background has had the greatest influence on her?
114. What is her religious background?
    If Protestant:
    a.   What denomination?
115. How long have you been married to her?
116. Everything considered, would you say your marriage is much happier than most, somewhat happier than most, just about average, or less happy than most?
117. a.   How many children have you and your wife had—including those now living at home, those who are no longer living at home, and any who may have died?
    b.   Do you have any other children living in your household—children of previous marriages, foster children or adopted children? (*If yes:* How many?)
118. a.   I'm interested first in any children you have who are 16 years of age or older. What is the age, sex, and occupation of each one? Let's start with the oldest.
        Then ask: What is the highest grade (each) completed in school?
    b.   Now, any children you have between the ages of 3 and 16. What is the age, sex, and grade in school of (oldest, next oldest, etc.)?
    c.   And now, any children you have who are under the age of 3. (What is the age and sex of each?)
    d.   Have you ever had any children who have died?
        Then ask: In what year did (each) die?
    e.   Which of your children are now living with you in this household?
    f.   Would you tell me which of the children you told me about are children of previous marriages, foster children, or adopted children?
119. Have any of your children left school before you wanted them to?
    If yes:
    a.   Which ones?
    b.   Why did (each) do it?
120. *Consider only those children between the ages of 3 and 16 who are living in household. If there are no such children, skip to Q. 135. If there is only one such child, ask Qs. 121-134 about this child. If there is more than one such child, use sampling table to select the appropriate one, and check designated child.*
121. *Explain to respondent:* From here on, I'm going to ask specifically about your (   )-year-old. What is (his, her) name?

Ask only if currently married:
122. Would you say that you or your wife is stricter toward (child), or would you say that you are both equally strict, or that neither is strict? (*Repeat for each of the following.*)
   a)   Stricter.
   b)   More warm and loving.
   c)   More likely to restrict (child's) freedom.
   d)   Quicker to praise (him, her) for the things (he, she) does well.
   e)   More likely to lay down the law when (he, she) misbehaves.
   f)   More likely to dominate (him, her).
123. When (child) does something that pleases you, what do you usually do?
Ask only if child 13 or less:
124. How often during the past week did you hug or kiss (child)?
Ask everyone:
125. How often during the past week did you scold (child) or show (him, her) you were angry at (him, her)?
Ask only if currently married:
126. With which parent is (child) more likely to feel (he, she) can talk things over?
127. To whom does (child) turn when troubled or unhappy?
128. a.   Which three qualities listed on this card would you say are the most desirable for a (boy, girl) of (child's) age to have?
   b.   Which one of these three is the most desirable of all?
   c.   All of these may be desirable, but could you tell me which three you consider least important?
   d.   And which one of these three is least important of all?
      1)   that he has good manners.
      2)   that he tries hard to succeed.
      3)   that he is honest.
      4)   that he is neat and clean.
      5)   that he has good sense and sound judgment.
      6)   that he has self-control.
      7)   that he acts like a boy (she acts like a girl) should.
      8)   that he gets along well with other children.
      9)   that he obeys his parents well.
      10) that he is responsible.
      11) that he is considerate of others.
      12) that he is interested in how and why things happen.
      13) that he is a good student.
129. a.   How far would you like (child) to go in school?
   b.   How far do you think (he, she) probably will go in school?
130. a.   What type of occupation would you like (him, her) to go into?
   b.   And what type of occupation do you think (he, she) will probably go into?

131. Does (child) ever play wildly?
    If yes:
    a.   What does (he, she) do when (he, she) plays wildly?
    b.   What do you generally do when (he, she) acts this way?
    c.   Do you ever find it necessary to do anything else? (*If yes:* What else do you do?)

If child has one or more brothers or sisters:

132. Does (child) ever fight with (his, her) brothers or sisters?
    If yes:
    a.   What does (he, she) do when (he, she) fights with (him, her, them)?
    b.   What do you generally do when (he, she) acts this way?
    c.   Do you ever find it necessary to do anything else? (*If yes:* What else do you do?)

133. Does (child) ever really lose (his, her) temper?
    If yes:
    a.   What does (he, she) do when (he, she) loses his temper?
    b.   What do you generally do when (he, she) loses his temper?
    c.   Do you ever find it necessary to do anything else? (*If yes:* What else do you do?)

134. Does (child) ever refuse to do what you tell (him, her) to do?
    If yes:
    a.   What does (he, she) do?
    b.   What do you generally do when (he, she) refuses to do what you tell him to do?
    c.   Do you ever find it necessary to do anything else? (*If yes:* What else do you do?)

Ask only if any children under 13:

135. About how often does your wife go out, leaving the child(ren) in your care?

Ask only if any children under 17:

136. How much time do you spend talking or playing with your child(ren) in the course of a week?

Ask only if currently married:

137. About how much time do you spend just sitting down and talking with your wife? (We'd like to know how many hours per week, including the weekend.)

Ask only if not presently married:

138. In an average month, how often do you go out on dates?

Ask everyone:

139. In an average day, how many hours do you spend watching television?

140. About how many hours of sleep do you get in an average night?

141. a.   During an average month, how many times have you visited or been visited by relatives?
    b.   Which relatives do you see regularly?

142. a.   During an average month, how many times do you get together with friends in the evening or on the weekend?

If currently married:

b.   Do you mostly get together with your friends alone or do you and your wife go out together?

143. During the average week, how much time do you spend working around the house, gardening, or fixing things?

144. During the last six months, how often have you gone to a museum, concert, or play?

145. Do you read any magazines regularly?

If yes:

a.   Which ones?

146. a.   During the last six months, how many books have you read in your spare time?

b.   What type of books do you read most?

c.   What book did you most enjoy reading?

147. During the last year, how many baseball, basketball, football, or other games have you gone out to see?

148. Do you play any sports, like baseball, bowling, fishing, or golf?

If yes:

a.   Which?

b.   About how many times a month do you play during the season?

149. Do you have any interests or hobbies at which you spend much time—like music, or cards, or collecting things?

If yes:

a.   Which?

b.   How many hours a month do you spend at them?

Now I'd like to present some problems to you.

150. Suppose you wanted to open a hamburger stand and there were two locations available. What questions would you consider, in deciding which of the two locations offers a better business opportunity? (*Probe:* Anything else?) (*If adds to answer, probe again*: Anything else?)

151. We know that there are people who commit a crime but are never caught by the police. Do you think that such people are usually punished anyway?

If yes:

a.   In what way?

If depends:

b.   On what?

152. A company manufactures both missiles and washing machines. Engineer A develops a brilliant idea for missile construction, but the government cancels the contract. Engineer B designs an ordinary washing machine. Suddenly there is an increased demand for washing machines and the company makes big profits. To whom should the company give a larger

bonus—the engineer who designed the missile or the engineer who designed the washing machine?

153. a.   What are all the arguments you can think of for and against allowing cigarette commercials on TV? First, can you think of arguments *for* allowing cigarette commercials on TV?

   b.   And can you think of arguments *against* allowing cigarette commercials on TV?

154. Do you think cigarette commercials should be allowed on TV?

I am now going to read a number of statements dealing with your beliefs and feelings. Would you tell me whether you agree strongly, agree somewhat, neither agree nor disagree, disagree somewhat, or disagree strongly with each of these statements? (Q. 155-185)

155. When you get right down to it, no one cares much what happens to you.

156. There are things I can do that might influence national policy.

157. If something works, it doesn't matter whether it's right or wrong.

158. Young people should not be allowed to read books that are likely to confuse them.

159. In this complicated world, the only way to know what to do is to rely on leaders and experts.

160. I become uneasy when things are not neat and orderly.

161. I feel useless at times.

162. People who question the old and accepted ways of doing things usually just end up causing trouble.

163. There are two kinds of people in the world: the weak and the strong.

164. I generally have confidence that when I make plans I will be able to carry them out.

165. Prison is too good for sex criminals. They should be publicly whipped or worse.

166. I take a positive attitude toward myself.

167. It's all right to get around the law as long as you don't actually break it.

168. I wish I could be as happy as others seem to be.

169. The most important thing to teach children is absolute obedience to their parents.

170. I wish I could have more respect for myself.

171. Any good leader should be strict with people under him in order to gain their respect.

172. It's wrong to do things differently from the way our forefathers did.

173. Once I've made up my mind, I seldom change it.

174. I feel that I'm a person of worth, at least on an equal plane with others.

175. Human nature is really cooperative.

176. I am able to do most things as well as other people can.

177. You should obey your superiors whether or not you think they're right.

178. It's all right to do anything you want as long as you stay out of trouble.

179. At times I think I am no good at all.
180. There are very few things about which I'm absolutely certain.
181. On the whole, I think I am quite a happy person.
182. One should always show respect to those in authority.
183. It generally works out best to keep on doing things the way they have been done before.
184. If you don't watch out, people will take advantage of you.
185. No decent man can respect a woman who has had sex relations before marriage.
186. When you get angry at a friend, are you generally more likely to let him know you're angry or to keep your feelings to yourself?
187. How about when a friend gets angry at you—are you generally more likely to feel upset with yourself or angry at him?
188. When you meet someone and find you like him, do you generally show it right away, keep your feelings to yourself until you see how he feels, or not show your feelings?
189. To what extent would you say you are to blame for the problems you have—would you say that you are mostly to blame, partly to blame, or hardly at all to blame?
190. Are you the sort of person who takes life as it comes or are you working toward some definite goal?
191. Do you think that most people can be trusted?
192. Are you generally one of the first people to try out something new or do you wait until you see how it's worked out for other people?
193. Do you believe that it's all right to do whatever the law allows, or are there some things that are wrong even if they are legal?
194. Do you feel that most of the things that happen to you are the result of your own decisions or of things over which you have no control?
195. Here are a number of statements that someone might make in reviewing his life.
    a. When you are 70, which three of these would you most like to be able to say about yourself?
    b. Of these three, which one would you most like to be able to say about yourself?
    c. All of these may be important, but which three are least important to you?
    d. Which one is least important of all?
        1) I have had many pleasurable experiences.
        2) I have been loved.
        3) I have had respect and recognition.
        4) I have gained truth and understanding.
        5) I have appreciated the beautiful things in life.
        6) I have done something for the benefit of others.

      7)   I have gained great wealth.

      8)   I have lived a moral life.

I am now going to read a series of questions asking you how often you do or feel something. Would you tell me for each of these whether it happens always, frequently, sometimes, rarely, or never.

196. How often do you have trouble in getting to sleep or staying asleep?

197. How often are you bothered by nervousness?

198. How often are you troubled by your hands sweating so that they feel damp and clammy?

199. How often are you troubled with severe headaches?

200. How often are you bothered by having an upset stomach?

201. According to your general impression, how often do your ideas and opinions about important matters differ from those of your relatives?

202. How often do your ideas and opinions differ from those of your friends?

203. How about from those of other people with your religious background?

204. Those of most people in the country?

205. How often do you feel that there isn't much purpose to being alive?

206. How often do you find that you can't get rid of some thought or idea that keeps running through your mind?

207. How frequently do you find yourself anxious and worrying about something?

208. How often do you find yourself following little rules you've made up, like always getting dressed in the same order or not stepping on the cracks in sidewalks?

209. How often do you feel that you can't tell what other people are likely to do, at times when it matters?

210. When things go wrong for you, how often would you say it is your own fault?

211. How often do you find yourself counting unimportant things, such as the number of cars passing by?

212. How often do you feel that you're really enjoying yourself?

213. How often do you feel bored with everything?

214. How often do you feel powerless to get what you want out of life?

215. How often do you feel so restless that you cannot sit still?

216. How often do you feel that the world just isn't very understandable?

217. How often do you feel downcast and dejected?

218. How often do you feel that you are about to go to pieces?

219. How often do you feel guilty for having done something wrong?

220. How often do you feel uneasy about something without knowing why?

221. a.   Would you tell me which three characteristics listed on this card are most important to you in judging yourself as a person? The question is not which characteristics you have, but which three you consider most important.

b.   Which one characteristic is the most important of all?

c.   Which three do you consider least important?

d.   Which one is least important of all?

1)   Interested in how and why things happen.

2)   Able to get along well with people.

3)   Responsible.

4)   Self-reliant.

5)   Good sense and sound judgment.

6)   Helpful to others.

7)   Able to face facts squarely.

8)   Able to do well under pressure.

9)   Truthful.

10)   Able to do many things well.

11)   Respectable.

12)   Successful.

222. *Hand respondent booklet.*

This booklet contains a series of colored designs. The page after each colored design contains a simpler and smaller black and white design. You are to find the smaller black and white design in the larger colored design. When you have found it, trace it out with this pencil. (*Hand respondent pencil.*) If you forget what the smaller design looks like, you may turn the page to look at it.

Now open the booklet. On the first page you will see three designs. The first is an example of a larger colored design. The second is a simple black and white design. The third shows the simple design traced out on the larger colored one. Let's try one for practice. Turn the page. This is the larger design. You can look at it for 15 seconds. (*Wait 15 seconds.*) Now turn the page. This is the smaller design which is contained in he larger design you just saw. You will have 10 seconds to look at it. (*Wait 10 seconds.*) Now turn back to the larger design. You will have 90 seconds to find the smaller design in the larger one. Tell me as soon as you have found it. Then trace it. That's good. Now we will begin. Turn to the next colored design.

223. *Hand respondent drawing card, No. 2 pencil with eraser, and ask:*

Would you please draw a picture of a man—not just the head but the whole figure. Please do the best you can. We realize that not everybody is an artist. (*If respondent draws a stick figure, ask:* Could you please draw a fuller figure?)

INTERVIEWER REMARKS

1. Time interview ended.

2. Total length of interview.

3. Was anyone else present during any part of the interview?

   If yes:

   a.   Who?

4. In general, what was the respondent's attitude toward the interview?
5. Rate the respondent's use of grammar.
6. Rate respondent's behavior during the interview.
7. Rate respondent's alertness and estimated intelligence.
8. Type of dwelling.
9. Condition of furnishing.
10. Respondent's apparent race.
11. Books in evidence in living room or elsewhere.
12. Did respondent smoke at any time during your visit?

Indices of Self-Conception and Social Orientation

Our intent was to measure those aspects of men's orientations to self and to society that might be most meaningfully related to social class or to occupational experience. Some 14 analytically separable, but not necessarily empirically independent, aspects of orientation were included. These were: authoritarianism; obeisance to authority; trustfulness; four distinct components of alienation—power, conceptions of morality, idea-conformity, and purposefulness; dogmatism; receptiveness to innovation; self-esteem; anxiety; attribution of responsibility; happiness/depression; and compulsiveness.

Where an adequate index existed, we used it, modifying or adding questions in order to elicit the connotations needed. The index of authoritarianism, for example, is based on Srole's (1956) shorter version of the body of questions developed for *The Authoritarian Personality* (Adorno, *et al.,* 1950); and the indices of trustfulness, self-esteem, and anxiety are adapted from those developed by Rosenberg (1957, 1962a). In other cases, we used the conceptual analyses of previous investigators as the basis for developing new indices. Thus, the index of obeisance to authority—intended to indicate a decided willingness to defer to constituted authority, but without the implications of rigidity built into the concept of authoritarianism—is based on the ideas of Pearlin (1962); the indices of alienation owe much to Seeman's analysis (1959). Most of the other indices are based on questions that we developed *de novo* or adapted from the Minnesota Multiphasic Personality Inventory (Hathaway and McKinley, 1940, 1942; McKinley and Hathaway, 1940, 1942, 1944; McKinley, *et al.,* 1948) and its innumerable modifications.

We initially developed a sizeable battery of questions to index each concept. During pretests of the interview schedule, these batteries were pared down to 4 or 5 questions each, the final step being tests of unidimensionality on a selected set of 100 men. (The

TABLE D-1
Rotated Factor Loadings, Self-Conception and Social Orientation

	1	2	3	4	5	6	7	8	9	10	11	12
Q.155	-.282	-.040	.070	-.070	-.003	-.309	.188	-.356	.008	.058	-.161	.059
Q.156	.012	.033	.197	-.012	-.109	.160	.205	-.017	-.053	-.052	.622	.092
Q.157	-.190	.036	-.043	.039	-.045	-.569	.097	-.134	-.018	.048	-.024	.170
Q.158	-.581	-.026	.041	.079	.021	.145	-.058	.006	-.051	.001	-.243	.011
Q.159	-.519	.025	.010	.037	-.099	-.133	.121	.097	.011	-.014	-.041	-.104
Q.160	-.246	-.015	.230	.039	-.061	.136	.216	.119	-.344	-.014	-.178	.311
Q.161	-.036	-.310	-.119	-.025	.074	.038	.540	.053	-.122	-.016	-.155	.045
Q.162	-.548	-.036	-.042	.030	-.050	-.108	.199	.051	-.015	-.031	-.042	.110
Q.163	-.580	-.010	.105	.039	-.075	-.071	.126	.002	.087	.180	-.056	-.041
Q.164	-.113	.111	.596	.014	.095	.048	-.113	-.045	-.040	-.050	-.007	.061
Q.165	-.505	-.052	-.108	.037	-.049	-.113	-.055	-.038	.096	.069	.083	.030
Q.166	-.053	.072	.619	-.053	.066	.032	-.159	-.020	-.066	-.040	.053	.056
Q.167	-.129	-.044	.054	.052	-.058	-.536	.189	.021	.020	.344	.018	.066
Q.168	-.309	-.132	-.011	.005	-.083	-.058	.532	-.138	-.071	.018	.133	-.063
Q.169	-.605	.016	.072	.061	-.141	-.156	.115	.219	-.047	.157	-.068	-.042
Q.170	-.264	-.132	-.098	-.017	.025	-.121	.615	-.028	-.092	.069	.166	-.052
Q.171	-.447	-.004	.118	.007	-.071	-.061	.206	.183	.022	.149	.105	-.084
Q.172	-.434	-.032	-.096	.044	-.053	-.356	.064	-.036	-.051	-.078	.288	-.133
Q.173	-.365	.038	.378	.004	.063	-.211	.043	-.123	-.077	-.034	-.067	-.047
Q.174	.135	.033	.605	-.094	-.016	.045	-.016	.292	-.044	.124	-.045	.057
Q.175	-.064	.056	.356	.102	-.009	-.096	.073	.202	.132	-.423	.156	-.034
Q.176	.127	-.059	.599	-.000	-.069	-.068	.011	.179	.127	.031	.128	.095
Q.177	-.224	-.066	.011	.046	-.063	-.248	.118	.438	.030	-.227	-.128	-.017
Q.178	-.224	-.072	.029	.009	-.076	-.655	.100	.129	.051	.094	.003	-.072
Q.179	-.041	-.312	-.213	-.015	.154	-.094	.548	-.030	.032	-.026	-.066	-.052
Q.180	-.064	-.042	-.017	.018	.017	-.089	.427	.004	.034	.166	.235	-.197
Q.181	.029	.232	.330	-.003	.152	-.013	-.221	.483	-.023	.017	.087	-.077
Q.182	-.229	-.016	.151	.038	-.047	-.000	.039	.610	-.051	-.068	-.077	.021
Q.183	-.325	.029	.058	.060	-.077	-.269	.148	.136	-.099	-.124	.119	-.330
Q.184	-.297	-.084	.117	-.004	-.056	-.102	.264	.208	-.008	.476	-.191	.015
Q.185	-.511	.006	-.097	.065	-.026	-.085	-.075	-.068	-.016	-.049	.200	-.117
Q.189	.115	-.003	.030	-.009	.682	.091	.120	.057	.004	.022	-.056	.039
Q.190	-.115	.035	-.145	.032	-.052	-.153	.153	-.028	.165	.018	-.283	-.434
Q.191	.165	.105	.013	-.030	.077	.171	-.042	.124	-.094	-.617	-.075	.066
Q.192	.100	-.020	.148	-.099	.045	-.100	-.088	-.033	.075	-.044	.007	.613
Q.193	-.054	.051	-.010	.046	.019	-.506	-.085	.061	-.050	-.063	-.096	-.108
Q.194	.212	.072	.044	.037	.603	-.080	-.082	-.066	-.028	-.112	.055	.064
Q.201	.006	-.117	.013	-.677	.065	.021	.042	.050	.085	.072	.005	.152
Q.202	.004	-.083	.029	-.744	-.005	.040	.055	-.005	-.002	.048	-.040	.080
Q.203	.154	-.089	.029	-.699	-.016	-.029	-.027	-.061	-.114	-.084	.024	-.041
Q.204	.119	-.071	.009	-.669	.042	.080	-.051	-.043	-.072	-.014	.021	-.060
Q.205	.050	-.396	-.013	-.055	-.096	-.159	.264	-.286	.009	-.140	-.190	-.134
Q.206	.042	-.555	-.004	-.124	.046	.040	.027	.020	-.150	.013	.037	.180
Q.207	-.028	-.620	-.024	-.081	.046	.091	.032	.058	-.074	.017	.037	.188
Q.208	-.002	-.196	.050	-.020	.020	-.038	.046	-.004	-.724	-.032	.011	.021
Q.209	-.012	-.179	.032	-.270	.007	.097	.020	.006	-.431	.309	.001	-.134
Q.210	.063	-.095	.048	-.104	.721	.105	.038	.029	.062	-.022	-.072	-.011
Q.211	.097	-.276	-.058	-.016	-.059	-.081	.060	.061	-.562	-.071	.089	-.016
Q.212	-.014	.305	.071	-.051	.237	-.081	-.206	.359	-.088	.067	.090	.041
Q.213	.025	-.550	-.053	-.036	-.144	-.088	.173	-.071	-.030	.097	-.139	-.078
Q.214	-.016	-.501	-.057	-.071	-.105	-.068	.207	-.048	-.055	.079	-.153	-.143
Q.215	.015	-.581	-.002	-.054	.079	-.056	-.035	.077	-.067	.073	-.052	.158
Q.216	-.109	-.452	.079	-.121	-.068	-.021	.037	-.173	-.080	.236	-.004	-.313

TABLE D-1 (Continued)

	1	2	3	4	5	6	7	8	9	10	11	12
Q.217	.016	-.649	-.021	-.038	-.048	-.005	.169	-.133	.019	.022	.000	-.179
Q.218	-.053	-.654	.006	.025	-.052	-.012	.097	-.080	-.059	-.066	.001	-.040
Q.219	.022	-.476	-.106	-.081	.216	.116	.076	.218	-.062	.019	.215	.072
Q.220	-.125	-.585	-.095	-.043	.133	.049	-.038	.011	-.143	.027	.204	-.035

Note: The questions are identified (in the left-hand column) by the numbers assigned to them in Appendix C. The "agree-disagree" type questions have been coded on a 0-to-4 scale (0 = strongly agree, 4 = strongly disagree); the "how often?" type questions have similarly been coded on a 0-to-4 scale (0 = always, 4 = never).
We identify the factors as representing:
1. Authoritarian conservatism (authoritarian/nonauthoritarian)
2. Anxiety (anxious/collected)
3. Self-confidence (diffident/self-confident)
4. Idea-conformity (independent/conforming)
5. Attribution of responsibility (fatalistic/accountable)
6. Criteria of morality (amoral/moral)
7. Self-deprecation (self-endorsing/self-deprecating)
8. Generalized disenchantment (?) (disenchanted/contented)
9. Compulsiveness (compulsive/noncompulsive)
10. Trustfulness (trustful/distrustful)
11.   ?
12. Stance toward change (resistant/receptive)

model of unidimensionality employed at this stage was that of the Guttman Scale. Essentially, the model holds that, insofar as a set of answers to manifestly similar questions can be arrayed in an order such that knowing *how many* questions an individual answers affirmatively tells us exactly *which* questions he answers affirmatively, these questions measure a single dimension. Cf. Guttman, 1944, 1950a, b; Suchman, 1950.) All 14 indices met the usual criteria for unidimensional scales.[1] When the data for the final representative sample of 3,100 men were collected, we confirmed the unidimensionality of each index.

The Guttman scaling technique served well for developing a parsimonious set of indices. But there are reasons for not using these scales as the final indices. Useful as the technique is for eliminating questions that do not fall along a single dimension, it provides no

---

[1]There is no conceptually adequate rationale for judging whether or not a set of data that approximates, but does not exactly fit, Guttman's model can be considered unidimensional. But gradually research workers have come to agree on *ad hoc* criteria that have seemed to be sufficiently rigorous. These criteria require that there be few departures from the model of perfect unidimensionality and that departures not be concentrated in one or a few error patterns. The principal criteria are Guttman's (1950b: 117) test of Reproducibility, Menzel's (1953) test of Scalability, and the several tests of error-concentration proposed by Ford (1950).

definitive evidence that the retained questions all do fall along that dimension.[2] Moreover, the set of scales might be redundant—it might even give us 14 measures of the same thing. To overcome these limitations, we subjected the entire battery of 57 questions, of which the scales were constituted, to a factor analysis.[3]

This analysis yielded 12 independent factors, several of them better representations of our concepts than the original scales. (Table D-1 gives the factor loadings of each of the 57 items on each of the factors.) Most of the original scales appear as factors—either essentially unchanged or strengthened by the addition of related items. Self-esteem is divided into self-confidence and self-deprecation—which is clearer than a single index of self-esteem. Obeisance to authority, dogmatism, and happiness/depression prove to be too closely related to other, empirically more powerful, dimensions and are lost. Only two of the four components of alienation—criteria of morality and idea-conformity—emerge as independent factors; we thus lose the opportunity to deal with alienation as a totality. In view of the conceptual ambiguities of alienation, that loss may not be great. Taken altogether, the factor analysis confirms (and strengthens) the principal indices on which we shall rely, while eliminating redundancy.

Nine of the twelve factors are directly pertinent to the purposes of this book and are used as indices.[4] Four of these measure social

---

[2]The crux of the problem is that any set of questions having an appropriate marginal distribution necessarily approximates the model of unidimensionality tolerably well—regardless of the content of the questions. To be appropriate for Guttman scaling, a set of questions must be graduated in degree of extremeness—so that one question is answered positively by relatively few people, the next by more, and each succeeding one by even more. This being the case, the joint probabilities of correct answer patterns are high, by chance alone, unless one uses a large number of questions—too large a number for practical purposes. (Cf. Sagi, 1959; Schuessler, 1961; Chilton, 1966; Schooler, 1968.)

Chilton (1966) has developed a test to determine whether or not a given body of data is significantly more unidimensional than the chance probability for a set of data having its marginal distribution. But since chance probabilities are high, this test will hardly satisfy a research worker.

[3]This was an orthogonal principal component factor analysis, rotated to simple structure through the varimax procedure, based on the computer program presented by Clyde, et al., 1966.

In turning to factor analysis, we lose the advantage that Guttman scaling treats the items as ordinal scales, while factor analysis treats them as interval scales. This does not seem too high a price to pay for the gains.

[4]We used the same procedure as that used for previous factor scores (see Chapter 4), but, because one third of the respondents failed to give an unambiguous answer to one or another of the 57 questions, it was necessary to estimate scores for men who gave incomplete data.   (*Footnote continues.*)

orientation (authoritarian conservatism, criteria of morality, trustfulness, and stance toward change); the others index self-conception (idea-conformity, attribution of responsibility, anxiety, self-confidence, and self-deprecation). Had we based the indices on separate factor analyses of the questions that deal with social orientation and those that deal with self-conception, they would be virtually the same.

The principal conclusions from the analyses based on these indices (in Chapters 5, 8, and 10) are equally well supported by similar analyses based on the original Guttman scales.

The logic of our procedure was to transform the metric from that on which the incomplete scores had been computed to that on which the scores *would have been* computed had the data been complete. Concretely, we tested to be certain that questions accounting for at least half the variance of the particular factor had been answered. If so, we then calculated partial factor scores for those items answered, and weighted the total score in proportion to this ratio: (*a*) the total of the squared loadings for all questions, divided by (*b*) the total of the squared loadings for those questions answered.

There are two indications that this procedure was satisfactory: The standard deviations of the factor scores for those people who gave incomplete data are nearly equal to those for the people who answered all questions; the correlations of items to factor scores, *after* this procedure was followed, are nearly identical to the original loadings of the items on the factors.

Using these procedures, we computed factor scores for 3035 of the 3101 respondents.

Classifications of the Complexity of Work

The classifications of the complexity of men's work with data, with people, and with things are based on those of the *Dictionary of Occupational Titles* (3rd edition, 1965, Vol. 2: 649-650).[1] The classification of the overall complexity of the job is new.

COMPLEXITY OF WORK WITH DATA

Data are defined as information, knowledge, and conceptions, related to data, people, or things, obtained by observation, investigation, interpretation, visualization, mental creation. Written data take the form of numbers, words, symbols; other data are ideas, concepts, oral verbalization.

1. *Synthesizing:* Integrating analyses of data to discover facts and/or develop knowledge, concepts, or interpretations. Conceiving new approaches to problems, including their restatement; discovering new facts and relationships; inventing new devices; creating original works of art; or reinterpreting existing information and ideas.

2. *Coordinating:* Determining time, place, and sequence of

---

[1]Aside from elaborating on the *Dictionary's* code for the complexity of work with data (by adding a category for "reading instructions"), we have adopted its classificatory system virtually intact. There are some differences, however, in how we use the system, principally in that: (1) We assess supervision more attentively (the *Dictionary* sometimes classifies supervisors on the basis of what their subordinates do). (2) We have greater flexibility in our ratings of multiple job-functions, whereas the *Dictionary* sometimes has to limit its rating to one function. (3) Our judgments of the degree of complexity in men's work with data are more stringent than some of those used in the *Dictionary*. (4) We assign a rating to things in many instances where the *Dictionary* describes dealings with things but evaluates them as "nonsignificant." (5) We emphasize a relationship to people in the case of consultants and teachers, where the *Dictionary* sometimes rates them solely on the basis of the substance of their consultation or teaching. These differences are minor; they result from the difference between our research purposes and the employment counseling purposes for which the *Dictionary* is designed.

Although the third edition of the *Dictionary* appeared long after our survey was undertaken, our plans were based on it—thanks to the foreknowledge and advice provided by Sidney Fine, the originator of this very important classificatory system.

operations or action to be taken on the basis of analysis of data; executing determinations and/or reporting on events. Deciding whether emerging performance and/or problems call for new goals, policies, or procedures.

3. *Analyzing:* Examining and evaluating data. Presenting alternative actions in relation to the evaluation is frequently involved. Examples are: evaluating items for purchase; exploring modifications and adaptations of existing designs and testing them; carrying out feasibility studies of revised inputs, including developing new tests or extending range of old ones.

4. *Compiling:* Gathering, collating, or classifying information about data, people, or things. Reporting and/or carrying out a prescribed action in relation to the information is frequently involved. Applying routine standard tests to determine conformance to specifications. Reporting and/or carrying out prescribed actions to attain specifications called for by tests may also be involved. Examples are routine testing, checkout, and troubleshooting of circuits, mechanical units, and subsystems; drafting plans and blueprints from sketches; fabrication from blueprints; and scheduling events within known conditions. Does not involve fundamental changes of input and output.

5. *Computing:* Performing arithmetic operations and reporting on and/or carrying out a prescribed action in relation to them. Does not include counting.

6. *Copying:* Transcribing, entering, or posting data.

7. *Comparing:* Judging the readily observable functional, structural, or compositional characteristics (whether similar to or divergent from obvious standards) of data, people, or things.

8. *Reading Instructions:* Following written instructions, generally of a simple and highly specific nature.

9. *No Significant Relationship.*

COMPLEXITY OF WORK WITH THINGS

Things are defined as inanimate objects as distinguished from human beings; substances or materials; machines, tools, equipment; products. A thing is tangible and has shape, form, and other physical characteristics.

1. *Setting Up:* Adjusting machines or equipment by replacing or altering tools, jigs, fixtures, and attachments to prepare them to perform their functions, change their performance, or restore their

proper functioning if they break down. Workers who set up one or a number of machines for other workers or who set up and personally operate a variety of machines are included here.

2. *Precision Working:* Using body members and/or tools or work aids to work, move, guide, or place objects or materials in situations where ultimate responsibility for the attainment of standards occurs and selection of appropriate tools, objects, or materials, and the adjustment of the tool to the task require exercise of considerable judgment.

3. *Operating-Controlling:* Starting, stopping, controlling, and adjusting the progress of machines or equipment designed to fabricate and/or process objects or materials. Operating machines involves setting up the machine and adjusting the machine or material as the work progresses. Controlling equipment involves observing gauges, dials, etc., and turning valves and other devices to control such factors as temperature, pressure, flow of liquids, speed of pumps, and reactions of materials. Several variables are involved and adjustment is more frequent than in tending.

4. *Driving-Operating:* Starting, stopping, and controlling the actions of machines or equipment for which a course must be steered, or which must be guided, in order to fabricate, process, and/or move things or people. Involves such activities as observing gauges and dials; estimating distances and determining speed and direction of other objects; turning cranks and wheels; pushing clutches or brakes; and pushing or pulling gear lifts or levers. Includes such machines as cranes, conveyor systems, tractors, furnace charging machines, paving machines, and hoisting machines. Excludes manually powered machines such as handtrucks and dollies, and power assisted machines such as electric wheelbarrows and handtrucks.

5. *Manipulating:* Using body members, tools, or special devices to work, move, guide, or place objects or materials. Involves some latitude for judgment with regard to precision attained and selecting appropriate tool, object, or material, although this is readily manifest.

6. *Tending:* Starting, stopping, and observing the functioning of machines and equipment. Involves adjusting materials or controls of the machine, such as changing guides, adjusting timers and temperature gauges, turning valves to allow flow of materials, and flipping switches in response to lights. Little judgment is involved in making these adjustments.

7. *Feeding-Offbearing:* Inserting, throwing, dumping, or placing

materials in or removing them from machines or equipment which are automatic or tended or operated by other workers. Repetitive, short duration work actions are usually paced by the machine. The standards depend on the existence of appropriate controls in the machine.

8. *Handling:* Using body members, hand tools, and/or special devices to work, move, or carry objects or materials. Involves little or no latitude for judgment with regard to attainment of standards or in selecting appropriate tool, object, or material. Examples include situations that involve a small number of special tools obvious as to purpose, such as a broom, a special purpose end wrench, a grass shears, go/no-go gauges. Dimensional precision can vary from rough to fine, being built into the structure of the task(s).

9. *No Significant Relationship.*

COMPLEXITY OF WORK WITH PEOPLE

People are defined as human beings; also animals dealt with on an individual basis as if they were human.

1. *Mentoring:* Dealing with individuals in terms of their total personality in order to advise, counsel, and/or guide them with regard to problems that may be resolved by legal, scientific, clinical, spiritual, and/or other professional principles.

2. *Negotiating:* Exchanging ideas, information, and opinions with others to formulate policies and programs and/or arrive jointly at decisions, conclusions, or solutions.

3. *Instructing:* Teaching subject matter to others, or training others (including animals) through explanation, demonstration, and supervised practice; or making recommendations on the basis of technical disciplines.

4. *Supervising:* Determining or interpreting work procedures for a group of workers, assigning specific duties to them, maintaining harmonious relations among them, and promoting efficiency.

5. *Diverting:* Amusing others.

Persuading: Influencing others in favor of a product, service, or point of view.

6. *Speaking-Signaling:* Talking with and/or signaling people to convey or exchange information. Includes giving assignments and/or directions to helpers or assistants.

7. *Serving:* Attending to the needs or requests of people or animals or the expressed or implicit wishes of people. Immediate response is involved.

Receiving Instructions-Helping: Attending to the work assignment instructions or orders of supervisors. (No immediate response required unless clarification of instruction or order is needed.) Helping applies to "non-learning" helpers.

8. *No Significant Relationship.*

OVERALL COMPLEXITY OF THE JOB

1. Not at all complex. Altogether routine and takes no thought— individual can daydream and still perform his work satisfactorily.

2. Minimal thought. A certain degree of attention is required; for example, to keep from getting hands caught in machinery, to be certain to pick up the right pieces, to remember where something was put. But no planning, scheduling, calculating, or prolonged thought is required.

3. Simple measurements, scheduling of activities, or rudimentary planning may be required, but most or all considerations are readily apparent and predictable and not very many considerations are needed for any decision.

4. Problem-solving, involving relatively simple remedies for unforeseen circumstances and/or the application of some practical or technical knowledge (not theoretical, but the type known to an experienced practitioner of the trade) to an atypical situation. Does *not* extend to very complex problems requiring much originality, theoretical knowledge, or foresight.

5. Problem-solving, involving the necessity of dealing with people or other relatively unpredictable or obstinate things—animals, for example, or fairly complex machines—where a moderate degree of empathy, insight, or ingenuity is needed to effect small to moderate changes in outcome. Routine selling and auto repairing would fit here.

6. Complex problem-solving, requiring a substantial but not an exceptional degree of insight, originality, or thought. This may involve many variables, but the relationships among the variables will not be extremely complex.

7. The setting up of a complex system of analysis and/or synthesis in which little is fixed beforehand, many variables are involved, their relationships are complex, and outcomes are hard to predict.

BIBLIOGRAPHY

BIBLIOGRAPHY

Aberle, David F. and Kasper D. Naegele
1952   Middle-class fathers' occupational role and attitudes toward children. *American Journal of Orthopsychiatry* 22 (April): 366-378.

Adorno, T.W., Else Frenkel-Brunswik, Daniel J. Levinson, and R. Nevitt Sanford
1950   *The Authoritarian Personality.* New York: Harper.

Almond, Gabriel A. and Sidney Verba
1963   *The Civic Culture: Political Attitudes and Democracy in Five Nations.* Princeton, New Jersey: Princeton University Press.

Anderson, John E.
1936   *The Young Child in the Home: A Survey of Three Thousand American Families.* New York: Appleton-Century.

Antonovsky, Aaron
1967   Social class, life expectancy and overall mortality. *Milbank Memorial Fund Quarterly* 45 (April): 31-73.
1968   Social class and the major cardiovascular diseases. *Journal of Chronic Diseases* 21 (May): 65-106.

Argyle, Michael
1958   *Religious Behavior.* London: Routledge and Kegan Paul, Inc.

Asch, Solomon E.
1952   *Social Psychology.* New York: Prentice Hall.

Bakke, Edward W.
1940   *The Unemployed Worker: A Study of the Task of Making a Living without a Job.* New Haven: Yale University Press.

Baldwin, Alfred L., Joan Kalhorn, and Fay Huffman Breese
1945   Patterns of parent behavior. *Psychological Monographs* 58: 1-75.

Barber, Bernard
1957   *Social Stratification: A Comparative Analysis of Structure and Process.* New York: Harcourt, Brace and Company, Inc.
1968   Social stratification. Pp. 288-296 in David L. Sills (Ed.), *International Encyclopedia of the Social Sciences,* Vol. 15. New York: Macmillan Company and Free Press.

Bateson, Gregory, Don D. Jackson, Jay Haley, and John Weakland
    1956   Toward a theory of schizophrenia. *Behavioral Science* 1 (October):
            251-264.

Bayley, Nancy and Earl S. Schaefer
    1960   Relationships between socioeconomic variables and the behavior of
            mothers toward young children. *The Journal of Genetic Psychology*
            96 (March): 61-77.

Becker, Howard S. and James W. Carper
    1956   The development of identification with an occupation. *American
            Journal of Sociology* 61 (January): 289-298.

Berelson, Bernard R., Paul F. Lazarsfeld, and William N. McPhee
    1954   *Voting: A Study of Opinion Formation in a Presidential Campaign.*
            Chicago: University of Chicago Press.

Berelson, Bernard and Gary A. Steiner
    1964   *Human Behavior: An Inventory of Scientific Findings.* New York:
            Harcourt, Brace and World, Inc.

Blalock, Hubert M. Jr.
    1960   *Social Statistics.* New York: McGraw-Hill.
    1964   *Causal Inferences in Nonexperimental Research.* Chapel Hill: Univer-
            sity of North Carolina Press.
    1967   Status inconsistency, social mobility, status integration and structural
            effects. *American Sociological Review* 32 (October): 790-801.

Blau, Peter M.
    1955   *The Dynamics of Bureaucracy: A Study of Interpersonal Relations in
            Two Government Agencies.* Chicago: University of Chicago Press.
    1960   Structural effects. *American Sociological Review* 25 (April):
            178-193.

Blau, Peter M. and Otis Dudley Duncan
    1967   *The American Occupational Structure.* New York: John Wiley.

Blauner, Robert
    1964   *Alienation and Freedom: The Factory Worker and His Industry.*
            Chicago: University of Chicago Press.
    1966   Work satisfaction and industrial trends in modern society. Pp.
            473-487 in Reinhard Bendix and Seymour Martin Lipset (Eds.),
            Class, Status, and Power. Glencoe, Illinois: Free Press. Second
            edition.

Boek, Walter E., Edwin D. Lawson, Alfred Yankauer, and Marvin B. Sussman
    1957   *Social Class, Maternal Health, and Child Care.* Albany: New York
            State Department of Health.

Bonjean, Charles M., Richard J. Hill, and S. Dale McLemore
1967   *Sociological Measurement: An Inventory of Scales and Indices.* San Francisco: Chandler.

Breer, Paul E. and Edwin A. Locke
1965   *Task Experience as a Source of Attitudes.* Homewood, Illinois: The Dorsey Press.

Bronfenbrenner, Urie
1958   Socialization and social class through time and space. Pp. 400-425 in Eleanor E. Maccoby, *et al.* (Eds.), *Readings in Social Psychology.* New York: Holt, Rinehart and Winston.
1960   Freudian theories of identification and their derivatives. *Child Development* 31 (March): 15-40.
1961a The changing American child—A speculative analysis. *Journal of Social Issues* 17: 6-18.
1961b Some familial antecedents of responsibility and leadership in adolescents. Pp. 239-271 in Luigi Petrullo and Bernard M. Bass (Eds.), *Leadership and Interpersonal Behavior.* New York: Holt, Rinehart and Winston.

Bronson, Wanda C., Edith S. Katten, and Norman Livson
1959   Patterns of authority and affection in two generations. *Journal of Abnormal and Social Psychology* 58 (March): 143-152.

Campbell, Angus, Philip E. Converse, Warren E. Miller, and Donald E. Stokes
1960   *The American Voter.* New York: John Wiley.

Caudill, William and Harry A. Scarr
1962   Japanese value orientations and culture change. *Ethnology* 1 (January): 53-91.

Chilton, Roland J.
1966   Computer generated data and the statistical significance of scalogram. *Sociometry* 29 (June): 175-181.

Chinoy, Ely
1955   *Automobile Workers and the American Dream.* Garden City, New York: Doubleday.

Christie, Richard
1954   Authoritarianism re-examined. Pp. 123-196 in Richard Christie and Marie Jahoda (Eds.), *Studies in the Scope and Method of "The Authoritarian Personality."* Glencoe, Illinois: The Free Press.

Clyde, Dean J., Elliot M. Cramer, and Richard J. Sherin
1966   *Multivariate Statistical Programs.* Coral Gables, Florida: Biometry Laboratory of the University of Miami.

Cochran, William G.
1954   Some methods for strengthening the common χ^2 tests. *Biometrics* 10 (December): 417-451.

Cohen, Jacob
1965   Some statistical issues in psychological research. Pp. 95-121 in B. B. Wolman (Ed.), *Handbook of Clinical Psychology.* New York: McGraw-Hill.

1968   Multiple regression as a general data-analytic system. *Psychological Bulletin* 70 (December): 426-443.

Coleman, James S., Ernest Q. Campbell, Carol J. Hobson, James Mc Partland, Alexander M. Mood, Frederick D. Weinfeld, and Robert L. York
1966   *Equality of Educational Opportunity.* Washington, D.C.: U.S. Government Printing Office.

Cooley, William W. and Paul R. Lohnes
1962   *Multivariate Procedures for the Behavioral Sciences.* New York: John Wiley.

Costner, Herbert L.
1965   Criteria for measures of association. *American Sociological Review* 30 (June): 341-353.

Cottrell, W. Fred
1940   *The Railroader.* Stanford, California: Stanford University Press.

Dahrendorf, Ralf
1959   *Class and Class Conflict in Industrial Society.* Stanford, California: Stanford University Press.

Davis, Allison and Robert J. Havighurst
1946   Social class and color differences in child-rearing. *American Sociological Review* 11 (December): 698-710.

Demerath, Nicholas J.
1965   *Social Class in American Protestantism.* Chicago: Rand McNally and Company.

Duncan, Otis Dudley
1961a   A socioeconomic index for all occupations. Pp. 109-138 in Albert J. Reiss, *et al.* (Eds.), *Occupations and Social Status.* New York: Free Press of Glencoe.

1961b   Properties and characteristics of the socioeconomic index. Pp. 139-161 in Albert J. Reiss, *et al.* (Eds.), *Occupations and Social Status.* New York: Free Press of Glencoe.

Durkheim, Emile
1954   *The Elementary Forms of the Religious Life.* Glencoe, Illinois: Free Press.

Duvall, Evelyn M.
1946   Conceptions of parenthood. *American Journal of Sociology* 52 (November): 193-203.

Edwards, Alba M.
1938   *A Social-Economic Grouping of the Gainful Workers of the United States.* Washington, D.C.: U.S. Government Printing Office.

Edwards, G. Franklin
1959   *The Negro Professional Class.* Glencoe, Illinois: Free Press.

Elder, Glen H. Jr.
1962   Structural variations in the child rearing relationship. *Sociometry* 25 (September): 241-262.

Fieller, E. C.
1944   A fundamental formula in the statistics of biological assay, and some applications. *Quarterly Journal of Pharmacy and Pharmacology* 17 (April-June): 117-123.

Foote, Nelson N.
1953   The professionalization of labor in Detroit. *American Journal of Sociology* 58 (January): 371-380.

Ford, Robert N.
1950   A rapid scoring procedure for scaling attitude questions. *Public Opinion Quarterly* 14 (Fall): 507-532.

Furstenberg, Frank F. Jr.
1966   Industrialization and the American family: A look backward. *American Sociological Review* 31 (June): 326-337.

Geiger, H. Jack and Norman A. Scotch
1963   The epidemiology of essential hypertension. I. Biologic mechanisms and descriptive epidemiology. *Journal of Chronic Diseases* 16 (November): 1151-1182.

Gerth, H. H. and C. Wright Mills (Eds.)
1946   *From Max Weber: Essays in Sociology.* New York: Oxford University Press.

Goffman, Irwin W.
1957   Status consistency and preference for change in power distribution. *American Sociological Review* 22 (June): 275-281.

Gusfield, Joseph R. and Michael Schwartz
1963   The meanings of occupational prestige: Reconsideration of the NORC scale. *American Sociological Review* 28 (April): 265-271.

Guttman, Louis
  1944   A basis for scaling qualitative data. *American Sociological Review* 9 (April): 139-150.
  1950a   The basis for scalogram analysis. Pp. 60-90 in Samuel A. Stouffer, *et al.* (Eds.), *Measurement and Prediction.* Princeton, New Jersey: Princeton University Press.
  1950b   The scalogram board technique for scale analysis. Pp. 91-121 in Samuel A. Stouffer, *et al.* (Eds.), *Measurement and Prediction.* Princeton, New Jersey: Princeton University Press.

Haller, Archibold O. and David M. Lewis
  1966   The hypothesis of intersocietal similarity in occupational prestige hierarchies. *American Journal of Sociology* 72 (September): 210-216.

Hathaway, S. R. and J. C. McKinley
  1940   A multiphasic personality schedule (Minnesota): I. Construction of the schedule. *Journal of Psychology* 10 (October): 249-254.
  1942   A multiphasic personality schedule (Minnesota): III. The measurement of symptomatic depression. *Journal of Psychology* 14 (July): 73-84.

Hatt, Paul K.
  1950   Occupation and social stratification. *American Journal of Sociology* 55 (May): 533-543.

Havighurst, Robert J. and Allison Davis
  1955   A comparison of the Chicago and Harvard studies of social class differences in child-rearing. *American Sociological Review* 20 (August): 438-442.

Himmelweit, Hilde
  1957   Social class differences in parent-child relations in England. Pp. 161-170 in Nels Anderson (Ed.), *Studies of the Family,* Vol. II. Göttingen: Vandenhoeck and Ruprecht.

Hodge, Robert W., Paul M. Siegel, and Peter H. Rossi
  1964   Occupational prestige in the United States: 1925-1963. *American Journal of Sociology* 70 (November): 286-302.

Hodge, Robert W., Donald J. Treiman, and Peter H. Rossi
  1966   A comparative study of occupational prestige. Pp. 309-321 in Reinhard Bendix and Seymour Martin Lipset (Eds.), *Class, Status, and Power.* New York: Free Press.

Hodge, Robert W. and Paul M. Siegel
  1966   The classification of occupations: Some problems of sociological interpretation. Chicago: National Opinion Research Center, mimeograph.

Hodges, Harold M. Jr.
  1964   *Social Stratification; Class in America.* Cambridge: Schenkman.

Hollingshead, August B. and Fredrick C. Redlich
1958   *Social Class and Mental Illness: A Community Study.* New York: Wiley.

Hughes, Everett Cherrington
1958   *Men and Their Work.* Glencoe, Illinois: Free Press.

Hyman, Herbert H.
1953   The value systems of different classes: A social psychological contribution to the analysis of stratification. Pp. 426-442 in Reinhard Bendix and Seymour Martin Lipset (Eds.), *Class, Status, and Power.* Glencoe, Illinois: Free Press.

Hyman, Herbert H. and Paul B. Sheatsley
1954   The authoritarian personality: A methodological critique. Pp. 50-122 in Richard Christie and Marie Jahoda (Eds.), *Studies in the Scope and Method of "The Authoritarian Personality."* Glencoe, Illinois: Free Press.

Inkeles, Alex
1960   Industrial man: The relation of status to experience, perception, and value. *American Journal of Sociology* 66 (July): 1-31.
1966   The modernization of man. Pp. 138-150 in Myron Weiner (Ed.), *Modernization.* New York: Basic Books.

Inkeles, Alex and Peter H. Rossi
1956   National comparisons of occupational prestige. *American Journal of Sociology* 61 (January): 329-339.

Jahoda, Marie
1959   Conformity and independence: A psychological analysis. *Human Relations* 12: 99-120.

Johnsen, Kathryn P. and Gerald R. Leslie
1965   Methodological notes on research in childrearing and social class. *Merrill-Palmer Quarterly of Behavior and Development* 11 (October): 345-358.

Kahl, Joseph A.
1957   *The American Class Structure.* New York: Holt, Rinehart and Winston.

Kahl, Joseph A. and James A. Davis
1955   A comparison of indexes of socio-economic status. *American Sociological Review* 20 (June): 317-325.

Kasl, Stanislav V.
1967   Status inconsistency: Some conceptual and methodological considerations. Pp. 377-390 in John P. Robinson, *et al.* (Eds.), *Measures of Occupational Attitudes and Occupational Characteristics.* University of Michigan Survey Research Center, mimeographed.

Kinsey, Alfred C., Wardell B. Pomeroy, and Clyde E. Martin
1948   *Sexual Behavior in the Human Male.* Philadelphia: Saunders.

Kinsey, Alfred C., Wardell B. Pomeroy, Clyde E. Martin, and Paul H. Gebhard
1953   *Sexual Behavior in the Human Female.* Philadelphia: Saunders.

Kirscht, John P. and Ronald C. Dillehay
1967   *Dimensions of Authoritarianism: A Review of Research and Theory.*
Lexington: University of Kentucky Press.

Klatskin, Ethelyn Henry
1952   Shifts in child care practices in three social classes under an infant
care program of flexible methodology. *American Journal of Ortho-*
psychiatry 22 (January): 52-61.

Kluckhohn, Florence R. and Fred L. Strodtbeck
1961   *Variations in Value Orientations.* Evanston, Illinois: Row, Peterson.

Kohn, Melvin L.
1968   Social class and schizophrenia: A critical review. Pp. 155-173 in
David Rosenthal and Seymour S. Kety (Eds.), *The Transmission of*
Schizophrenia. Oxford: Pergamon Press, Ltd.

Kohn, Melvin L. and Robin M. Williams, Jr.
1956   Situational patterning in intergroup relations. *American Sociological*
Review 21 (April): 164-174.

Labovitz, Sanford
1967   Some observations on measurement and statistics. *Social Forces* 46
(December): 151-160.

Langner, Thomas S. and Stanley T. Michael
1963   *Life Stress and Mental Health.* New York: The Free Press of Glencoe.

LaPiere, Richard T.
1934   Attitudes vs. actions. *Social Forces* 13 (December): 230-237.

Lazarsfeld, Paul F., Bernard Berelson, and Hazel Gaudet
1948   *The People's Choice: How the Voter Makes Up His Mind in a*
Presidential Campaign. New York: Columbia University Press.

Lenski, Gerhard E.
1954   Status crystalization: A non-vertical dimension of social status.
American Sociological Review 19 (August): 405-413.
1961   *The Religious Factor: A Sociological Study of Religion's Impact on*
Politics, Economics and Family Life. Garden City, New York:
Doubleday.

Leshan, Lawrence L.
1952   Time orientation and social class. *The Journal of Abnormal and*
Social Psychology 47 (July): 589-592.

Lipset, Seymour Martin
1959   Democracy and working-class authoritarianism. *American Sociological Review* 24 (August): 482-501.
1960   *Political Man: The Social Bases of Politics.* New York: Doubleday.
1961   A changing American character? Pp. 136-171 in Seymour Martin Lipset and Leo Lowenthal (Eds.), *Culture and Social Character: The Work of David Riesman Reviewed.* New York: Free Press of Glencoe.
1963   *The First New Nation: The United States in Historical and Comparative Perspective.* New York: Basic Books.

Lipset, Seymour Martin, Martin A. Trow, and James S. Coleman
1956   *Union Democracy: The Internal Politics of the International Typographical Union.* Glencoe, Illinois: Free Press.

Lipsitz, Lewis
1965   Working-class authoritarianism: A re-evaluation. *American Sociological Review* 30 (February): 103-109.

Littman, Richard A., Robert C. A. Moore, and John Pierce-Jones
1957   Social class differences in child rearing: A third community for comparison with Chicago and Newton. *American Sociological Review* 22 (December): 694-704.

Lohman, Joseph D. and Dietrich C. Reitzes
1952   Note on race relations in mass society. *American Journal of Sociology* 58 (November): 240-246.

Lynd, Robert S. and Helen Merrell Lynd
1929   *Middletown: A Study in Contemporary American Culture.* New York: Harcourt, Brace and Company.

Maccoby, Eleanor E. and Patricia K. Gibbs
1954   Methods of child-rearing in two social classes. Pp. 380-396 in W. E. Martin and C. B. Stendler (Eds.), *Readings in Child Development.* New York: Harcourt, Brace.

Mannheim, Karl
1936   *Ideology and Utopia.* New York: Harcourt, Brace.
1941   *Man and Society in an Age of Reconstruction.* New York: Harcourt, Brace.

Marx, Karl
1906   *Capital: A Critique of Political Economy.* New York: Modern Library.
1964   *The Eighteenth Brumaire of Louis Bonaparte.* New York: International.

Marx, Karl and Friedrich Engels
1932   *The German Ideology.* New York: International.

Maxwell, A. E.
1961   *Analyzing Qualitative Data.* New York: John Wiley.

McClelland, D.C., A. Rindlisbacher, and R. deCharms
1955   Religious and other sources of parental attitudes toward independence training. Pp. 389-397 in D.C. McClelland (Ed.), *Studies in Motivation.* New York: Appleton-Century-Crofts, Inc.

McKinley, Donald Gilbert
1964   *Social Class and Family Life.* New York: Free Press of Glencoe.

McKinley, J. C. and S. R. Hathaway
1940   A multiphasic personality schedule (Minnesota): II. A differential study of hypochondriasis. *Journal of Psychology* 10 (October): 255-268.
1942   A multiphasic personality schedule (Minnesota): IV. Psychasthenia. *Journal of Applied Psychology* 26 (October): 614-624.
1944   The Minnesota multiphasic personality inventory: V. Hysteria, hypomania, and psychopathic deviate. *Journal of Applied Psychology* 28 (April): 153-174.

McKinley, J. C., S. R. Hathaway, and P. E. Meehl
1948   The Minnesota multiphasic personality inventory: VI. The K scale. *Journal of Consulting Psychology* 12 (January-February): 20-31.

Menzel, Herbert
1953   A new coefficient for scalogram analysis. *Public Opinion Quarterly* 17 (Summer): 268-280.

Merton, Robert K.
1949   The sociology of knowledge. Pp. 217-245 in Robert K. Merton, *Social Theory and Social Structure.* Glencoe, Illinois: The Free Press.
1952   Bureaucratic structure and personality. Pp. 361-371 in Robert K. Merton, *et al.* (Eds.), *Reader in Bureaucracy.* Glencoe, Illinois: The Free Press.

Miller, Daniel R. and Guy E. Swanson
1958   *The Changing American Parent: A Study in the Detroit Area.* New York: Wiley.
1960   *Inner Conflict and Defense.* New York: Holt.

Miller, S. M. and Frank Riessman
1961a   The working class subculture: A new view. *Social Problems* 9 (Summer): 86-97.
1961b   Working class authoritarianism: A critique of Lipset. *British Journal of Sociology* 12 (September): 263-276.

Mills, C. Wright
1953 *White Collar: The American Middle Classes.* New York: Oxford University Press.

Mishler, Elliot G. and Norman A. Scotch
1963 Sociocultural factors in the epidemiology of schizophrenia: A review. *Psychiatry* 26 (November): 315-351.

Mishler, Elliot G. and Nancy E. Waxler
1965 Family interaction processes and schizophrenia: A review of current theories. *Merrill-Palmer Quarterly of Behavior and Development 11* (October): 269-315.

Mitchell, Howard E.
1950 Social class and race as factors affecting the role of the family in Thematic Apperception Test stories. *American Psychologist* 5 (July): 299-300.

Morris, Richard T. and Raymond J. Murphy
1959 The situs dimension in occupational structure. *American Sociological Review* 24 (April): 231-239.

North, C. C. and P. K. Hatt
1953 Jobs and occupations: A popular evaluation. Pp. 411-426 in Reinhard Bendix and Seymour M. Lipset (Eds.), *Class, Status, and Power.* Glencoe, Illinois: Free Press.

Oeser, O. A. and S. B. Hammond (Eds.)
1954 *Social Structure and Personality in a City.* New York: Macmillan.

Parker, Seymour and Robert J. Kleiner
1966 *Mental Illness in the Urban Negro Community.* New York: Free Press.

Parsons, Talcott and Robert F. Bales
1955 *Family, Socialization and Interaction Process.* Glencoe, Illinois: Free Press.

Pearlin, Leonard I.
1962 Alienation from work: A study of nursing personnel. *American Sociological Review* 27 (June): 314-326.

Perrow, Charles
1967 A framework for the comparative analysis of organizations. *American Sociological Review* 32 (April): 194-208.

Peters, Charles C. and Walter R. Van Voorhis
1940 *Statistical Procedures and Their Mathematical Bases.* New York: McGraw-Hill.

Piaget, Jean
N.D. *The Moral Judgment of the Child.* Glencoe, Illinois: Free Press.

Pope, Liston
1948   Religion and the class structure. *Annals of the American Academy of Political and Social Science* 256 (March): 84-91.

Porter, Arthur R. Jr.
1954   *Job Property Rights.* New York: King's Crown Press.

Reiss, Albert J., Otis Dudley Duncan, Paul K. Hatt, and Cecil C. North
1961   *Occupations and Social Status.* New York: Free Press of Glencoe.

Rheinstein, Max (Ed.)
1954   *Max Weber on Law in Economy and Society.* Cambridge, Massachusetts: Harvard University Press.

Riesman, David, Reuel Denney, and Nathan Glazer
1950   *The Lonely Crowd: A Study of the Changing American Character.* New Haven: Yale University Press.

Rogler, Lloyd H. and August B. Hollingshead
1965   *Trapped: Families and Schizophrenia.* New York: John Wiley.

Roman, Paul M. and Harrison M. Trice
1967   *Schizophrenia and the Poor.* Ithaca: New York State School of Industrial and Labor Relations.

Rosenberg, Morris
1957   *Occupations and Values.* Glencoe, Illinois: Free Press.
1962a   The association between self-esteem and anxiety. *Journal of Psychiatric Research* 1 (September): 135-152.
1962b   Test factor standardization as a method of interpretation. *Social Forces* 41 (October): 53-61.
1965   *Society and the Adolescent Self-Image.* Princeton, New Jersey: Princeton University Press.
1968   *The Logic of Survey Analysis.* New York: Basic Books.

Ryckoff, Irving, Juliana Day, and Lyman C. Wynne
1959   Maintenance of stereotyped roles in the families of schizophrenics. *A.M.A. Archives of Psychiatry* 1 (July): 93-98.

Ryder, Robert G.
1965   Scoring orthogonally rotated factors. *Psychological Reports* 16 (June): 701-704.

Sagi, Phillip C.
1959   A statistical test for the significance of a coefficient of reproducibility. *Psychometrica* 24 (March): 19-27.

Schaefer, Earl S.
1959   A circumplex model for maternal behavior. *The Journal of Abnormal and Social Psychology* 59 (September): 226-235.

Schneider, Louis and Sverre Lysgaard
1953   The deferred gratification pattern: A preliminary study. *American Sociological Review* 18 (April): 142-149.

Schooler, Carmi
1968   A note of extreme caution on the use of Guttman scales. *American Journal of Sociology* 74 (November): 296-301.

Schuessler, Karl F.
1961   A note on the statistical significance of scalogram. *Sociometry* 24 (September): 312-318.

Scotch, Norman A. and H. Jack Geiger
1963   The epidemiology of essential hypertension. II. Psychologic and sociocultural factors in etiology. *Journal of Chronic Diseases* 16 (November): 1183-1213.

Sears, Robert R., Eleanor E. Maccoby, and Harry Levin
1957   *Patterns of Child Rearing.* Evanston, Illinois: Row, Peterson and Company.

Seeman, Melvin
1959   On the meaning of alienation. *American Sociological Review* 24 (December): 783-791.

Spinley, B. M.
1953   *The Deprived and the Privileged: Personality Development in English Society.* London: Routledge and Kegan Paul.

Srole, Leo
1956   Social integration and certain corollaries: An exploratory study. *American Sociological Review* 21 (December): 709-716.

Stouffer, Samuel A.
1955   *Communism, Conformity, and Civil Liberties: A Cross-Section of the Nation Speaks Its Mind.* New York: Doubleday.

Strodtbeck, Fred L.
1958   Family interaction, values, and achievement. Pp. 135-194 in David C. McClelland, *et al.* (Eds.), *Talent and Society.* New York: Van Nostrand.

Suchman, Edward A.
1950   The utility of scalogram analysis. Pp. 122-171 in Samuel A. Stouffer, *et al.* (Eds.), *Measurement and Prediction.* Princeton, New Jersey: Princeton University Press.

Sudman, Seymour and Jacob J. Feldman
1965   Sample design and field procedures. Pp. 482-485 of Appendix 1 in John W. C. Johnstone and Ramon J. Rivera (Eds.), *Volunteers for*

Learning: A Study of the Educational Pursuits of American Adults.
Chicago: Aldine.

Sukhatme, Pandurang V.
1954   *Sampling Theory of Surveys with Applications.* Ames, Iowa: Iowa
State College Press.

Svalastoga, Kaare
1959   *Prestige, Class and Mobility.* Copenhagen: Glydendal.

Tawney, R. H.
1926   *Religion and the Rise of Capitalism: A Historical Study.* New York:
Harcourt, Brace.

Thomas, R. Murray
1962   Reinspecting a structural position on occupational prestige. *American
Journal of Sociology* 67 (March): 561-565.

Thomas, W. I. and Dorothy S. Thomas
1928   *The Child in America.* New York: Knopf.

Tiryakian, Edward A.
1958   The prestige evaluation of occupations in an underdeveloped
country: The Philippines. *American Journal of Sociology* 63
(January): 390-399.

U.S. Department of Labor
1949   *Dictionary of Occupational Titles.* Washington, D.C.: U.S. Government Printing Office. Second ed.
1965   *Dictionary of Occupational Titles.* Washington, D.C.: U.S. Government Printing Office. Third ed.

Valen, Henry and Daniel Katz
1964   *Political Parties in Norway: A Community Study.* Oslo:
Universitetsforlaget.

Veblen, Thorstein
1957   *The Higher Learning in America.* New York: Sagamore Press.

Walker, Charles R.
1957   *Toward the Automatic Factory: A Case Study of Men and Machines.*
New Haven: Yale University Press.

Walker, Charles R. and Robert H. Guest
1952   *The Man on the Assembly Line.* Cambridge, Massachusetts: Harvard
University Press.

Waller, Willard
1932   *The Sociology of Teaching.* New York: Russell and Russell.

Weber, Max
1930   *The Protestant Ethic and the Spirit of Capitalism.* New York: Charles Scribner's Sons.

White, Martha Sturm
1957   Social class, child-rearing practices, and child behavior. *American Sociological Review* 22 (December): 704-712.

Whyte, William Foote
1961   *Men at Work.* Homewood, Illinois: The Dorsey Press.

Williams, Robin M. Jr.
1960   *American Society: A Sociological Interpretation.* New York: Alfred A. Knopf. Second ed.
1964   *Strangers Next Door: Ethnic Relations in American Communities.* Englewood Cliffs, New Jersey: Prentice-Hall, Inc.
1968   The concept of values. Pp. 283-287 in David L. Sills (Ed.), *International Encyclopedia of the Social Sciences,* Vol. 16. New York: Macmillan Company and Free Press.

Witkin, H. A., R. B. Dyk, H. F. Faterson, D. R. Goodenough, and S. A. Karp
1962   *Psychological Differentiation: Studies of Development.* New York: John Wiley.

Wynne, Lyman C., Irving M. Ryckoff, Juliana Day, and Stanley I. Hirsch
1958   Pseudo-mutuality in the family relations of schizophrenics. *Psychiatry* 22 (May): 205-220.

Yinger, J. Milton
1957   *Religion, Society, and the Individual.* New York: Macmillan.

Index

295